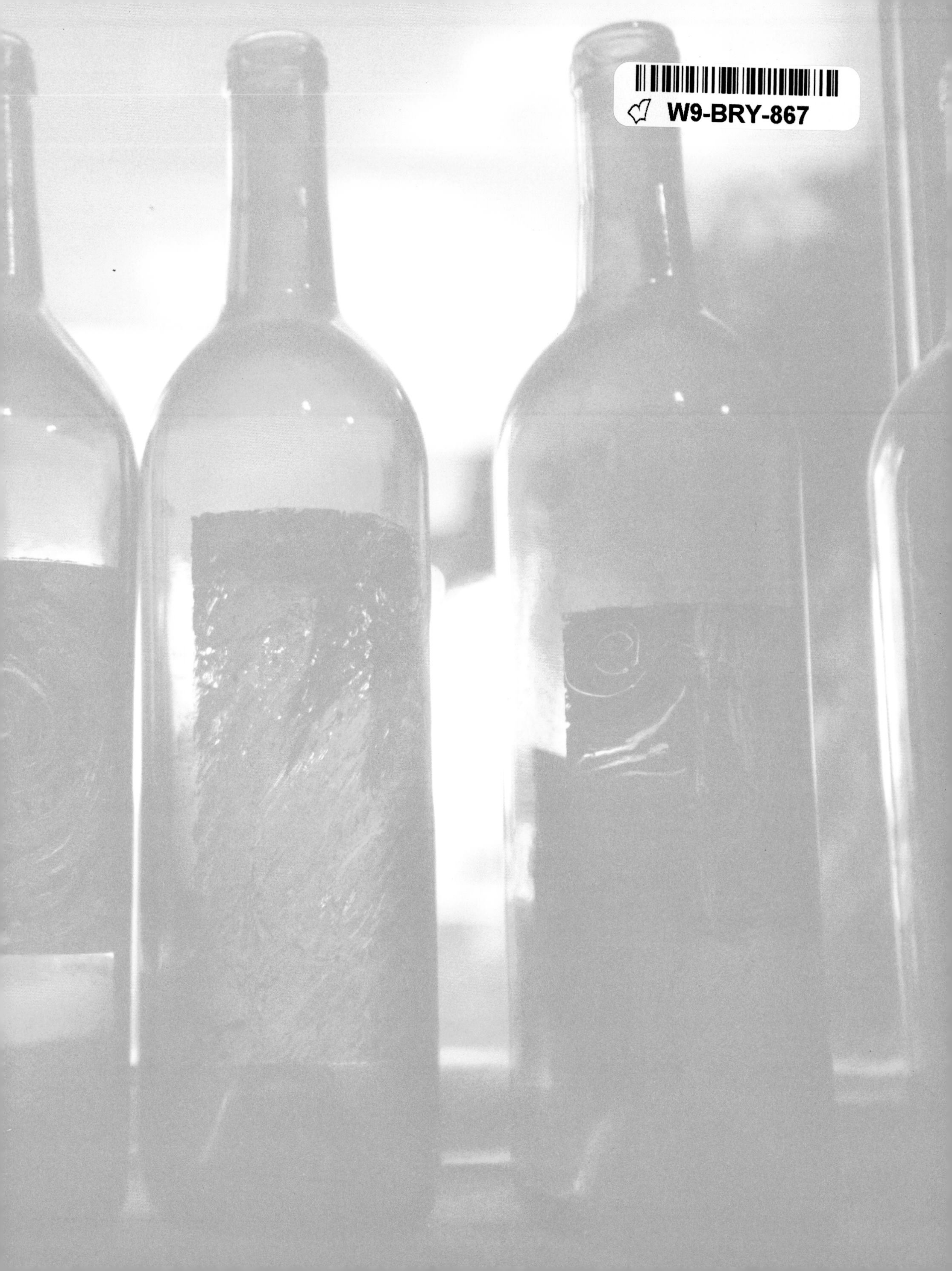

Pacific Northwest Wining and Dining

Pacific Northwest Wining and Dining

The People, Places, Food, and Drink of Washington, Oregon, Idaho, and British Columbia

Braiden Rex-Johnson   PHOTOGRAPHY BY Jackie Johnston

BICENTENNIAL
1807
WILEY
2007
BICENTENNIAL

John Wiley & Sons, Inc.

John Wiley & Sons, Inc.
This book is printed on acid-free paper. ⊗

For general information on our other products and services or for technical support, please contact our Customer Care Department within the United States at (800) 762-2974, outside the United States at (317) 572-3993 or fax (317) 572-4002.

Wiley also publishes its books in a variety of electronic formats. Some content that appears in print may not be available in electronic books. For more information about Wiley products, visit our web site at www.wiley.com.

Design by Vertigo Design, NYC www.vertigodesignnyc.com

Library of Congress Cataloging-in-Publication Data:

Rex-Johnson, Braiden, 1956-
Pacific Northwest wining and dining : the people, places, food, and drink of Washington, Oregon, Idaho, and British Columbia / Braiden Rex-Johnson ; photography by Jackie Johnston.
     p. cm.
  ISBN: 978-0-471-74685-0 (cloth)
  1. Restaurants--Northwest, Pacific--Guidebooks. 2. Cookery, American--Pacific
Northwest style. 3. Wineries--Northwest, Pacific--Guidebooks. I. Title.
  TX907.3.N96R49 2007
  641.59795--dc22
                                                    2006102197

Printed in China

10 9 8 7 6 5 4 3 2 1

Permissions

Duck Breasts with Lemon-Roasted Olives (page 12) reprinted with permission from
Savory Flavors with Wood: Plank-Roasted Foods from Your Oven, copyright 2004 by Nature's Cuisine.

Grilled Asparagus with Prosciutto, Parmigiano-Reggiano, and Balsamic Vinaigrette (page 198) reprinted with permission from
Lumière Light: Recipes from the Tasting Bar, by Rob Feenie and Marnie Coldham, copyright 2003 by Douglas & McIntyre.

Cover photo: Mission Hill Family Estate, Westbank, British Columbia
Visitors enjoy views of Lake Okanagan along with their meals at the Terrace restaurant at Mission Hill Family Estate.

To Spencer Johnson, the best gour-man in the world—friend, lover, curious eater and drinker, and travel partner

Workers at Preston Premium Wines in Pasco, Washington,
start harvesting before dawn.

Contents

Acknowledgments

A book of this size and scope is never, can never, be the work of one person alone. Many people, places, and factors had to come together during the two-year journey of research, writing, photographing, and recipe testing.

Early on, I relied on the advice of leading food and wine professionals (many of them long-time friends) to help me scout out the Northwest's best wine regions and, within those regions, the most talented winemakers, chefs, restaurants, and specialty-food sources that might serve as sources for the recipes.

My thanks to my Oregon contacts—Joan Cirillo, Linda Kaplan, Sue Horstmann, Lisa Donoughe, Lota LaMontagne, and Debra Wakefield—for their expert counsel and, in many cases, for providing food and lodging for the research trips I made to this part of the Northwest.

In Washington, similar thanks go to Krista McCorkle, Mike Davis, Mike Hogue (for the private plane ride over the Yakima Valley), Bill den Hoed (for his lively commentary during the plane ride!), Barb Glover, Lori Randall, Jen Doak, Katie Sims, Chris Upchurch, Theodora van den Beld, Robin Pollard, and Regan O'Leary.

I could never have researched Idaho wines as thoroughly without the help of Bob Corbell and Ricki Richards. Thanks for driving us all over the Snake River Valley and exposing us to 84 Idaho wines!

British Columbia may be the most "giving" of the regions, and I want to extend special thanks to the people I met there for "getting it" when it comes to generosity in providing for a writer's special needs. My heartiest thanks go to Blair Baldwin, Monica Dickenson, and Michael and Rosemary Botner.

On a more personal note, I want to thank Andy Perdue, founder and editor of *Wine Press Northwest* magazine, for giving me my first shot at being a wine writer with a food writer's perspective.

Lisa Ekus, literary agent extraordinaire, has been one of the lights of my life since July 7, 2004, when she not only agreed to become my agent, but also encouraged and nurtured the idea for this book from proposal through contract and into fruition. With her eagle eye for detail, Jane Falla helped mold the proposal into final, saleable shape. Thanks, Jane and Lisa!

A huge round of thanks goes to Justin Schwartz, my editor at John Wiley, whose way with words, keen appreciation for photography, and enthusiasm for the Northwest are impressive and much appreciated. Gypsy Lovett and David Greenberg reign supreme in publicity and promotions. Thanks to all, as well as to publisher Natalie Chapman, for taking a chance and believing in this book.

Jackie Johnston, photographer of *Pacific Northwest Wining and Dining,* not only has a divine artistic sensibility, but also a lovely working manner and amazing technological skills. She also helped us navigate our way around the far corners of the Northwest. Special thanks, Jackie, for leading us out of that ever-spiraling canyon in the Columbia Gorge!

Rhonda May, the publisher and editor of *CityFood* magazine, was a delightful travel companion in the Okanagan and a levelheaded sounding board once we returned to our respective homes.

Norene Gilletz, a Toronto-based cookbook author, took the Canadian recipes in the book and converted all the measurements, which saved this math-challenged writer hours of angst and heartache.

Best buddy Lorelle "Sis" Del Matto tested a baker's dozen of the meat recipes when I (not much of a meat-eater) could not face the prospect of pork tenderloin and roasted pheasant. Then, she stepped in to test 10 additional pastry and pasta recipes. I couldn't have done all this testing and tweaking without your support and guidance, Sis. You put the "pro" in "food professional"!

Girlfriends Mina Williams, Diane Morgan, and Martha Marino were there when I needed a shoulder to cry on, or just a savvy food professional to bounce ideas off of.

Workouts at the Washington Athletic Club provided exercise for both mind and body; various physicians (Drs. Ellen Wilber, Kavita Bansil, David Omdal, and Kitty Brown) helped me stay in tip-top shape. Doug Ethridge (our upstairs neighbor and computer expert) kept my Macs and my printer, as well as my Internet connection, up and running. His wife and my good buddy, "Miss" Sue Ethridge, taught me the ins and outs of Word for Mac.

My father, Eugene Rex, and brother Brad and his family were always there for me and for each other. Father-in-law Colon Johnson provided a good dash of 94-year-old Texan wisdom, until he finally passed on June 6, 2006.

The vendors at the Pike Place Market, especially Pure Food Fish, Sosio's Produce, Don & Joe's Meats, the Pike Place Market Creamery, DeLaurenti Specialty Food & Wine, and Beecher's Handmade Cheese, answered my many questions about ingredients, special-ordered items whenever I asked, and came through for me at a moment's notice. Thanks to all; your amazing products and attention to detail make me look good on a daily basis.

During the research and writing of this book, two important passages took place. On August 13, 2005, my beloved mother, Julia Looper Rex, died after a brave and lengthy battle with heart disease. We miss her sunny outlook and sweet Southern spirit.

And on August 10, 2004, our beloved feline of 15 years, Beauregard (Bo-Bo) Johnson, went to kitty heaven. During the writing of my prior books, he used to sit on my desk, his head resting against the computer, purring away. Many were the late nights I wished he'd been here "helping" me through my latest writing project.

Husband Spencer Johnson, who travels the globe for his architectural projects, almost always managed to drop his own work long enough to accompany me on "my" work travel. In addition to being a savvy traveler, he is the sweetest man in the world to put up with all my "nonsense." I owe him everything.

Finally, to all the winemakers, chefs, restaurateurs, hospitality professionals, and others involved in the burgeoning Northwest food-and-wine scene, *I thank you* for sharing your recipes, cooking hints, and wisdom, and for being visionaries and luminaries in the best food-and-wine-producing region of the world. I hope I have done you proud.

Preface

The idea for *Pacific Northwest Wining and Dining* did not come in a flurry, willy-nilly, all of a piece, as with some of my other books. Instead, it built from a slow simmer to a rolling boil over the course of the 17 years my husband, Spencer, and I have lived in the Pacific Northwest.

I began my career as a food writer, specializing in farmers' markets and Northwest seafood. I continually swore to anyone who would listen that because there was so much to learn about food, I would never branch out into wine, tea, or cheese. I considered them related but distinctly separate fields.

But as my husband and I began to live, understand, and appreciate the Northwest lifestyle, we learned that all these things—the produce that comes from the fields in a seasonal way; the Copper River salmon that run only during the late spring and summer; the grapes that ripen in the warm sun, just waiting for the perfect time for autumn harvesting; artisan cheeses made from contented cows raised on family farms—are inextricably linked. One without the other produces an incomplete meal, an unsatisfied palate.

Over the years, during visits to the wine-producing regions in Washington, Oregon, and British Columbia (and more recently, Idaho), we watched their steady growth and the rise in sophistication in both the varieties produced and the wineries themselves. While many of the regions still maintain a homey, folksy feel, there is an underlying current of commerce, a sense of business savvy that was (perhaps) missing in the earlier days.

The consolidation of many of the pioneering wineries under large corporate umbrellas (such as Constellation and Vincor) and the appreciation in land prices of prime grape-growing acreage have shown the world that Northwest wineries and vineyards are hot properties. Those in the know realize that Northwest wines are poised to take on the world!

I credit an article I wrote for *Seattle Homes & Lifestyles* (where I served as food editor from 2002 to 2006) for sparking the idea for this book. "Vineyard Cooking" told the story of Kay Simon and Clay Mackey, longtime winemakers in the Yakima Valley who own Chinook Wines. Kay just happens to be a great cook, and Clay mans the grill. Thanks to Kay's inspired recipes, I realized that many people involved in the wine industry also love to eat well. I began to explore further, and my hunch was confirmed.

Once the idea for this book gelled in my mind, the proposal written and the book sold, I started researching in earnest. During two-plus years of research, Spencer and I put thousands of miles on "D2," our trusty Land Rover, as we searched out the best winemaker-cooks, chefs and restaurants, bed-and-breakfast inns, and other atmospheric places in the Northwest that combine good food and good wine.

Research was a moving target, since almost weekly a new winery or destination restaurant opened, or another wine region or appellation was named. Nevertheless, I'll forever cherish sweet memories of Spencer and me bopping down the highway, the local oldies station blaring Smokey Robinson and the Miracles or George Harrison's "My Sweet Lord," as we searched out another enticing lead.

Along the very pleasurable way, we met a plethora of talented and creative winemakers and chefs who champion our local wines as much as our local bounty of food. Indeed, to many of them (and to me), wine is food!

The result of our two-year odyssey is the book you hold in your hands. Within its pages, you'll find 88 recipes from the region's leading winemakers, wine-grape growers, chefs, and other luminaries in the Northwest food-and-wine scene. The recipes are interspersed with eleven profiles of some of the favorite people and places we discovered along the way. They include small, family-owned wineries; artisan cheese makers; a family whose entire restaurant revolves around wild mushrooms; innovators in the Okanagan wine industry; and a winemaker who also crafts exquisite balsamic vinegar!

They say one picture is worth 1,000 words, and Jackie Johnston's lush photos, interwoven between the recipes and profiles, often speak louder than my recipe headnotes and narrative. These graphic images brilliantly complete this portrait of—my love song, if you will—the ultimate in Northwest cuisine and wine.

I've tested, retested, and simplified the recipes (as necessary) in my own home kitchen in downtown Seattle—just a tomato's toss from the venerable Pike Place Market—so they will easily translate to yours.

I purposefully kept the wine variety descriptions that appear on pages xiv–xvii simple (no cork-dork or wine-geek speak within these pages), so that the food-and-wine pairing concepts suggested by the winemakers and me will be easily accessible to both the novice and the more sophisticated oenophile and cook. Rest assured that you don't have to visit Yakima (Washington), Dayton (Oregon), or Kelowna (British Columbia) to experience those regions' world-class wines. Just drinking their products will begin your education in and appreciation for Northwest wines.

With *Pacific Northwest Wining and Dining* in hand, you have only to open a bottle of good Northwest wine, crank up the stove, and settle in for a whirlwind tour of the United States' and Canada's most exciting new wine-and-food regions.

Braiden Rex-Johnson
APRIL 2007

What Is Northwest Cuisine?

On the Northwest edge of the United States and Canada, a quiet revolution is taking place. Chefs, winemakers, and grape-growers in the states of Washington, Oregon, and Idaho, plus the province of British Columbia, are embracing organic produce from the region's farmers and farmers' markets, flapping-fresh fish from local sustainable fisheries and Alaska, and award-winning wines from more than 900 Northwest wineries to create a signature style of cooking: Northwest Cuisine.

Northwest Cuisine isn't evolving only in the city centers of Seattle, Portland, and Vancouver, but in small towns with rich culinary heritages—Walla Walla, Washington; McMinnville, Oregon; Salt Spring Island, British Columbia—as savvy chefs, winning winemakers, and artisan cheese makers and chocolatiers move to atmospheric towns to preserve their quality of life and offer new options to local townspeople and savvy tourists.

The Northwest's enticing indigenous ingredients—morels and chanterelles, clams and mussels, crab, salmon, lamb, berries, apples, pears, lettuces, and greens—help define the region's cuisine. There's a profound connection between Northwest Cuisine and the varied terrain that inspires it. But the starting point is always fresh ingredients—the natural bounty of the Northwest. It is a very seasonal cuisine, a cuisine solidly grounded in the local provender.

The thriving wine scene, with the emergence of more than a dozen strong varietals, including Chardonnay, Pinot Gris, Pinot Noir, Merlot, and Syrah, adds a whole new array of aromas and flavors for chefs to experiment with and consumers to enjoy.

The influence of Northwest Native Americans in modern-day Northwest Cuisine cannot be overemphasized. Native Americans' favorite way to cook salmon was to place an opened, cleaned fish between two tree branches fastened with small lateral twigs to hold the fish spread open before the fire. They also liked to plank their salmon on driftwood or sandwich it between alder wood, which was then laid over a bed of glowing embers. Clams, mussels, oysters, and barnacles were cooked in a similar fashion (they were never eaten raw), then strung on buckskin or cedar bark for winter storage.

Successive waves of immigrants to the Northwest left their mark, beginning with settlers from Europe around the turn of the 20th century. These settlers brought with them a European sensibility and traditions, including such foods as *lefse, lutefisk,* and pickled herring. Italian immigrants introduced Seattleites to *broccoli di rape* (broccoli rabe), arugula, and radicchio. Pesto became popular!

During this same time period, Sephardic Jews began emigrating from the eastern Mediterranean (mainly Turkey). They established successful seafood and produce stands in the Pike Place Market and introduced "exotic" new foodways to the Northwest.

Early Asian immigrants to the region were predominantly Chinese railroad workers who brought over their cuisine and Americanized it in dishes like chow mein and egg foo yung. Next came the Japanese, with their pristine culinary traditions based on seafood and vegetables. Filipinos added to the mix with their *adobo* and *pancit bihon.*

Among the more recent Asian immigrants have been the Vietnamese, with their ever-popular *pho* (beef noodle soup). The Cambodians and Laotians, many of them talented flower and vegetable farmers, introduced our region to Asian produce such as edible pea vines, bok choy, and *gai lan* (Chinese broccoli). The Koreans brought *bulgogi* (barbecue), hot-pot soups, and kimchee to the local dinner plate.

More recently, the Latino influence has introduced a spicy beat to the Northwest scene. We see a plethora of sweet and hot peppers and Mexican herbs such as epazote coming to local farmers' markets. It is a nod to their determination and strong work ethic that some of the most successful farmers at local farmers' markets started out as day laborers.

Throw all these elements into the stew pot, and my definition of Northwest cuisine cooks up as follows: It begins with the freshest local ingredients foraged or grown in season. These are prepared using traditional cooking techniques, many attributed to Native Americans—smoking, grilling, broiling, and steaming. A mixture of European cuisines (Scandinavian, Mediterranean), often spiced with Pacific Rim flare (Chinese, Japanese, Thai, Vietnamese, Mexican), gives Northwest Cuisine its enticing top notes. Here you'll discover hints of ginger, lemongrass, and Thai chili peppers; the pungent goodness of smoking over cedar planks; or the simple flavors of a just-baked huckleberry crisp. These luscious foods are complemented, their simple flavors enhanced, by the products of our emerging wine industry—the sweet perfume of an Oregon Pinot Noir or an intoxicating British Columbia ice wine. All of this cooks up into a distinct sense of place, a Northwest Cuisine that feeds mind, body, heart, and soul.

The wine and food scene in the Pacific Northwest is constantly changing. All information included herein was current and correct as of April 2007, but may have changed since the book was published.

Characteristic Wine Varietal Descriptors

A variety, or varietal, is the type of grape from which a wine is made, such as Chardonnay, Cabernet Sauvignon, or Syrah. According to American law, a varietal wine must contain at least 75 percent of the grape variety printed on the label. This differs from many wines in Europe, which take their names from the town, district, or vineyard in which the grapes are grown.

In British Columbia, wines bearing the Vintners Quality Alliance (VQA) symbol must be made entirely from grapes grown in specific provinces and regions in Canada, be produced to a set of production standards, and pass a sensory evaluation procedure. Participation in the VQA program is voluntary. Labeling regulations determine if a wine is to be labeled as a single varietal, dual varietal, or blend; labeling is vintage dated and includes sugar content and sweetness descriptors. Labeling regulations also control the use of geographic indicators.

In VQA single-varietal wines, not less than 85 percent of the wine must be made from the named individual grape variety. In dual-varietal wines, not less than 95 percent of the wine must be made from the two varieties named, with the second variety not less than 15 percent of the total. In triple-varietal wines, not less than 95 percent of the wine must be made from the three varieties named, with the second not being less than 15 percent and the third not being less than 10 percent of the total.

Wine aficionados are mainly concerned with grapes from the *Vitis vinifera* family, classic wine grapes that are centuries old and whose figurative roots can be traced to Europe. Non-vinifera grapes include the North American varietals Concord and Niagara, and are usually planted in colder growing areas. Wines made from non-vinifera grapes and crosses of European and non-vinifera grapes (known as hybrids) are considered inferior to wines made exclusively from vinifera grapes.

One of the most difficult parts of wine appreciation for the novice and even many knowledgeable wine aficionados is distinguishing the aromas and flavors inherent in each variety, or varietal, of wine. Chardonnay, the chameleon of wines, sometimes has oaky/vanilla flavors; other times it is crisp and fruit forward. Pinot Noir can vary from a bright burst of strawberry and cherry aromas and flavors to a dusty, mushroomy, forest-floor type of experience.

Yet even with such vast differences, each variety of wine commands its own distinct and unique characteristics (known as "markers" to wine professionals). The list below includes markers for each of the major (and a few minor) varietals associated with the Northwest wine-growing regions. Keep your eye on these "minor" varietals—many are up and coming and may end up being tomorrow's shining stars!

Major Northwest white varietals include Chardonnay, Gewürztraminer, Pinot Blanc, Pinot Gris, Riesling, Sauvignon Blanc, Semillon, and Viognier. Chenin Blanc, while once widely planted, has since become a more minor player in the Northwest wine scene.

Major red varietals include Cabernet Franc, Cabernet Sauvignon, Merlot, Pinot Noir, and Syrah. Minor varieties include Gamay Noir, Lemberger, and Zinfandel. Rosé, sparkling, and dessert wines (such as late-harvest wines and port) are also included in the list below.

Each recipe in *Pacific Northwest Wining and Dining* is paired with one of the 15 major, or one of the minor, Northwest wine varietals. I hope these brief, easy-to-understand varietal descriptors will make your wine-drinking experiences more understandable and more enjoyable. For part of the beauty and wonder of drinking wine is that no two bottles can ever be the same, because our moods, senses, and the people we consume them with are constantly changing. Sharing a bottle of wine is a unique experience each and every time.

Distinguishing Aromas and Textures in Wine

Pacific Northwest White Wines

Chardonnay
COLOR: Light to medium straw. Golden tones in older or oak-aged wines.
AROMAS/FLAVORS: Almond, apple/green apple, banana, butter, caramel/caramelized, citrus fruit, coconut, honey, nutty, pineapple, tropical fruit, vanilla
TEXTURE: Crisp, creamy, lively/fresh, round, supple, generous

Chenin Blanc
COLOR: Pale to medium straw. Sometimes displays glints of green.
AROMAS/FLAVORS: Apple, apricot, earth, herbaceous
TEXTURE: Refreshing, round

Gewürztraminer
COLOR: Pale to medium straw. Sometimes displays a pleasing rosy glow.
AROMAS/FLAVORS: Apricot, cinnamon, clove, floral, honey, lychee, perfume-y, roses/rose petals/rose water, peach, spicy, tropical fruit
TEXTURE: Lush

Pinot Blanc
COLOR: Light straw
AROMAS/FLAVORS: Apple/green apple, citrus fruit, melon, pear, sweet pea
TEXTURE: Delicate, light body; balanced/refreshing acidity

Pinot Gris
COLOR: Light straw. Sometimes displays a copper hue.
AROMAS/FLAVORS: Apple/green apple, citrus fruit, honeysuckle, pear, vanilla
TEXTURE: Lively, mouth coating

Riesling
COLOR: Pale to medium straw
AROMAS/FLAVORS: Apricot, citrus fruit, floral, kerosene, mineral, nectarine, passion fruit, petrol
TEXTURE: Light to medium

Sauvignon (Fumé) Blanc (Sauvignon Blanc/Semillon Blends)
COLOR: Pale to medium straw. Sometimes includes hints of gold or green.
AROMAS/FLAVORS: Asparagus, cat pee/litter box, citrus fruit, gooseberry, fresh-cut grass, grapefruit, green bean, herbal, melon
TEXTURE: Bracing, crisp, refreshing, supple; lighter in body than Chardonnay

Semillon

COLOR: Light to medium straw. Sometimes displays a hint of green.

AROMAS/FLAVORS: Citrus, fig, flinty, grassy, herbaceous, honey, pear, vanilla

TEXTURE: Sharp

Viognier

COLOR: Medium straw. Sometimes displays hints of gold.

AROMAS/FLAVORS: Apricot, citrus fruit, floral, honey, orange blossom/peel, peach, musk

TEXTURE: Lush

Rosé

COLOR: Pale to medium pink

AROMAS/FLAVORS: Cherry, dill, dried herbs, strawberry

TEXTURE: Lively/fresh, mellow

Pacific Northwest Red Wines

Cabernet Franc

COLOR: Deep ruby to purple

AROMAS/FLAVORS: Black currant, dusty, musk, pencil shavings, spice

TEXTURE: Lighter bodied than Cabernet Sauvignon

Cabernet Sauvignon

COLOR: Rich ruby garnet when young. Older wines tend toward brick colors with additional aging.

AROMAS/FLAVORS: Bell pepper, berry, black currant, black or green olive, cedar, cherry, chocolate, cigar box, earthy, eucalyptus, herbs, leather, mint, pepper, tobacco, vanilla, violets

TEXTURE: Austere, chewy, firm, fresh, medium to full body

Gamay Noir

COLOR: Deep pink

AROMAS/FLAVORS: Berry, cherry

TEXTURE: Light with low tannins

Lemberger

COLOR: Deep pink

AROMAS/FLAVORS: Berry, cherry, spice, strawberry

TEXTURE: Light to medium, refreshing

Merlot

COLOR: Deep ruby, sometimes almost purple

AROMAS/FLAVORS: Blackberry, black cherry, black plum, chocolate, earth, herbs, mint, plum, raspberry, tobacco

TEXTURE: Fleshy, full; less tannic than Cabernet Sauvignon

Pinot Noir

COLOR: Ruby

AROMAS/FLAVORS: Black cherry, cherry, cinnamon, earth, forest floor, leather, mint, mushroom, raspberry, smoky, spicy, strawberry, truffle, vanilla, violets

TEXTURE: Delicate, round, soft, velvety; less powerful and concentrated than Merlot or Cabernet Sauvignon

Syrah

COLOR: Deep ruby

AROMAS/FLAVORS: Barnyard, blackberry, black pepper/white pepper, black currant, coffee, gamey, leather, licorice, plum, raspberry, smoked bacon, spice

TEXTURE: Moderate tannins

Zinfandel

COLOR: Ruby-purple

AROMAS/FLAVORS: Blackberry, black pepper, berry jam, cherry, coconut, earthy, plum, raspberry, spicy

TEXTURE: Chewy, fresh, rich, velvety; moderate tannins

Pacific Northwest Dessert and Sparkling Wines

Ice Wine

COLOR: Medium to dark straw

AROMAS/FLAVORS: Apple, apricot, citrus fruit, honey, mango, peach, pear

TEXTURE: Viscous

Late-Harvest Riesling

COLOR: Medium to dark straw

AROMAS/FLAVORS: Almond, apricot, caramel, citrus, floral, honey, perfume-y, pineapple, raisin, toffee, tropical fruit

TEXTURE: Medium to viscous

Late-Harvest Semillon

COLOR: Pale to medium straw

AROMAS/FLAVORS: Almond, apricot, butterscotch, clove, fig, honey, nutty, orange peel, pineapple, raisin, spice, toffee

TEXTURE: Medium to viscous

Vintage (Ruby) Port

COLOR: Deep ruby to ruby-brown

AROMAS/FLAVORS: Blackberry, black currant, chocolate, coffee, nutty, plum, spice, violets

TEXTURE: Medium to viscous, velvety

Tawny Port

COLOR: Medium to dark brown

AROMAS/FLAVORS: Dried fruit, caramel, coffee, nutty, prune, raisin, toffee, walnut

TEXTURE: Medium to viscous, velvety

Sparkling Wine/Champagne

COLOR: Pale to medium straw to pale pink

AROMAS/FLAVORS: Almond, apple, biscuit, bread, citrus, dough, floral, strawberry, toast, nutty, vanilla

TEXTURE: Crisp, tart, vivacious

Oysters on the half shell are an iconic food of the Pacific Northwest, which grows five major species—Pacific, Olympia, Kumamoto, European Flat, and Virginica.

In the bedroom suburb of Kirkland, a short drive from Seattle across Lake Washington via one of the region's famous floating bridges, you'll discover the upstairs/downstairs duo of Yarrow Bay Grill and Beach Café at the Point. Downstairs, at the Beach Café, Chef Cameon Orel's eclectic menu offers "food without boundaries," everything from Jambalaya and Chicken Piccata to Baja Mahi Tacos and Chicken Teriyaki Salad. Upstairs, at the Grill, Chef Vicky McCaffree combines the freshest Northwest seafood, produce, and meats with Asian and Italian accents in dishes such as Thai Seafood Stew, American Kobe Beef Tenderloin, and Pan-Seared Monkfish Risotto. There are more than a dozen wines by the glass; the *Wine Spectator* award-winning wine list offers many pleasing Northwest contenders, along with options from California, France, and around the globe. Don't miss dessert—such as Frozen Kahlúa Brownie or Warm Caramel Apple Cobbler—prepared by pastry chef Jessica Maxwell. Collectively, these three talented chefs are known about town as the "three divas." At a media dinner hosted by Allan Aquila, the ebullient general manager/partner of the long-running restaurants, I fell in love not only with the sweeping lakefront views of the Seattle skyline and the snow-capped peaks of the Olympic Mountains beyond, but also with this outstanding recipe from Chef Cameon. That evening, as the sun set over Carillon Point, the lush oyster appetizer formed a magical combination when paired with Chateau Ste. Michelle Sauvignon Blanc from the Columbia Valley (see page 60). The dry, yet fruit-forward, wine (blended with 17 percent Semillon for added richness and concentration) exhibits abundant melon and citrus aromas, plus a hint of oak and spice, characteristics that continue on the palate. The wine's crisp acidity easily cuts through the mineral notes of the bivalves and the rich orange-y sauce, but it would pair nicely with just about any seafood or chicken dish.

**Yarrow Bay Grill/
Beach Café at the Point**

1270 Carillon Point

Kirkland, WA 98033

(425) 889-9052

ybgrill.com

Baked Oysters with Orange-Thyme Beurre Blanc and Citrus Zest

SERVES 8   MAKES 32 appetizers   VARIETAL Sauvignon Blanc

Rock salt

32 large (3- to 4-inch) oysters, such as Imperial Miyagi, Penn Cove, or Pacific, shells scrubbed and patted dry

2 cups freshly squeezed orange juice

Line a rimmed baking sheet with rock salt. Shuck the oysters, reserving as much of the liquid as possible, discarding the top oyster shells. Arrange the shucked oysters cup side down (oyster side up) without crowding over the rock salt.

Place the orange juice in a small saucepan, bring to a boil, and cook, stirring occasionally to be sure it doesn't boil over during the beginning minutes, until it reaches the consistency of maple syrup and about ¾ cup remains, 20 to 25 minutes.

3 teaspoons freshly grated lemon zest

3 teaspoons freshly grated lime zest

3 teaspoons freshly grated orange zest

All-purpose flour

2 cups vegetable oil

8 tablespoons (1 stick) unsalted butter, chilled and cut into 1-tablespoon pieces

½ teaspoon minced fresh thyme, or ¼ teaspoon dried thyme, crumbled

Kosher salt

Freshly ground white pepper

2 cups loosely packed arugula leaves, rinsed, spun dry, and coarsely chopped

While the orange juice is reducing, toss the lemon, lime, and orange zests in a small amount of flour. Place in a fine-meshed sieve and shake off any excess flour. Heat the oil in a large saucepan over medium-high heat. When the oil begins to bubble around the edges, add the floured zest. Cook until crisp and lightly browned, 30 seconds to 1 minute. Drain on paper towels and reserve.

After the orange juice has reduced, remove the pan from the heat and whisk in the butter piece by piece, incorporating well after each addition. Whisk in the thyme and season to taste with salt and pepper. Cover and keep warm.

Ten minutes before cooking, preheat the oven to 400°F. Place the oysters in the oven and bake for 12 to 15 minutes, or until they plump and become firm to the touch. Remove from the oven and top with a small amount of the arugula, the sauce, and the fried zest and serve immediately.

Fruit set is the stage in a grape vine's annual growing cycle that marks the transition from flower to tiny green bunches of grapes, a.k.a. grape berries.

C amaraderie Cellars bills itself as "a craft winery producing fine varietal wines." Located on the Olympic Peninsula in Port Angeles, Washington, Camaraderie claims the title as the farthest northwest winery in the continental United States. Winemaker Don Corson and wife Vicki started more than 20 years ago as "garagistes," making wine in their garage with a motley crew of friends "from just 100 pounds of grapes, free yeast, and a lot of hope," according to Don. Since then, Camaraderie has produced award-winning wines from grapes grown at eastern Washington's top vineyards (such as Artz Vineyard on Red Mountain and Champoux Vineyards at Mercer Ranch). Don creates wines to be full-flavored, yet food-friendly. His varietals include Sauvignon Blanc, Semillon, Cabernet Sauvignon, Merlot, Syrah, and creative blends such as Lake Crescent White (a Viognier/ Semillon blend), Grâce (a red blend), and Storm King Red. Son Steve graduated from the Culinary Institute of America at Greystone in the Napa Valley in 2006 and devises the recipes for the winery's quarterly newsletters. Simplicity is at the heart of Steve's recipe for pork tenderloin, in which the cherry flavors of the sauce are mirrored in the berry flavors of an easy-to-drink wine, such as Camaraderie Merlot. Don describes the wine as being full of blackberry and cherry: "Its beautiful fruit aromas and flavors jump out of the glass, bringing a smile to my face."

Camaraderie Cellars

334 Benson Road

Port Angeles, WA 98363

(360) 417-3564

camaraderiecellars.com

Black Forest Pork Tenderloin

SERVES 6 to 8   VARIETAL Merlot

2 tablespoons olive oil

Two 1-pound pork tenderloins, trimmed of fat and silver skin

2 teaspoons kosher salt

¾ teaspoon freshly ground black pepper

2 cups dry red wine, preferably good-quality Merlot

1 cup cherry preserves

1 tablespoon water (optional)

2½ teaspoons cornstarch (optional)

Heat a large heavy-bottomed skillet over medium-high heat and add the oil. Lightly sprinkle the pork on all sides with the salt and pepper. When the oil is hot, add the pork and cook, turning with tongs, until browned on all sides, a total of 4 to 5 minutes.

Reduce the heat and continue cooking the meat, turning occasionally, until still slightly pink at the center when cut with a paring knife, 25 to 30 minutes. Transfer the meat to a large plate and tent with aluminum foil to keep warm.

Add the wine and preserves to the pan, scraping up the brown bits in the bottom of the pan with a wooden spoon or heatproof rubber spatula. Bring to a simmer and cook until the liquid reduces slightly, 7 to 10 minutes. For a thicker sauce, mix the water and cornstarch and add to the pan, then stir well and simmer for 1 minute, or until thick and shiny.

To serve, slice the tenderloin and spoon the cherry-wine sauce over the meat.

Cook's Hint: For fun and variety, try sprinkling the sliced, sauced pork with fresh chopped herbs such as sage, thyme, or parsley.

Located in Seattle's Madison Valley, Voilà! Bistrot is keeping good company with long-running culinary neighbors such as Rover's, Harvest Vine, Saint-Germain, and Chinoise. Voilà! exemplifies the sort of casual-in-atmosphere, authentic-in-food restaurants that have been popping up in the Northwest so frequently. The Bistrot also offers reasonable prices for the French classics that form the foundation of its small menu— *Assiette de Charcuterie, Coq au Vin, Boeuf Bourguignon,* and *Profitéroles au Chocolat.* The small bar is a good place to sip an aperitif while you wait for one of the dozen café tables. Once seated, oversized French posters, butter-colored walls against dark wood, and the beautiful-people crowd provide a lively, yet serene, ambience. Plate presentations are pretty here, with dots and dashes of sauces and confetti sprinkles of fresh herbs. Chef-owner Laurent Gabrel's mussel dish is an easy, yet inspired, version of the bivalve. Leftover blue-cheese sauce cries out for dipping with crusty artisan bread or (for truly decadent souls) crispy *frites.* Note how perfectly the earthy mussels and bold cheese sauce pair with the big berry flavors of a good-quality Merlot.

Voilà! Bistrot
2805 East Madison Street
Seattle, WA 98112
(206) 322-5460
voilabistrot.com

Blue Cheese Mussels (Moules au Bleu de Gex)

SERVES 2 to 3 as an appetizer   VARIETAL Merlot

¼ cup (1 ounce) *Bleu de Gex* (French blue cheese) or good-quality Northwest blue cheese (such as Oregonzola or Oregon Blue Vein), crumbled

6 tablespoons chopped white onion

¼ cup dry white wine

¼ cup heavy whipping cream

Dash of kosher salt, plus extra for seasoning

Dash of freshly ground black pepper, plus extra for seasoning

2 pounds Northwest mussels, such as Penn Cove or Mediterranean, shells scrubbed and rinsed and mussels debearded just before cooking

2 tablespoons chopped fresh flat-leaf parsley

Heat a stockpot or large saucepan or skillet over medium-high heat and add the blue cheese, onion, wine, heavy cream, salt, and pepper. Bring just to a boil, reduce the heat to medium, and add the mussels, stirring gently. Cover and cook, occasionally shaking the pot back and forth across the burner to redistribute the mussels, until they begin to open, 4 to 6 minutes. Remove the opened mussels to a large mixing bowl. Cover the pot and cook 2 to 4 minutes more, or until the remaining mussels have opened. If using Mediterranean mussels (which have a stronger connective tissue than Penn Cove mussels), pry open any mussels that have not opened. If they smell fresh and are not muddy, add to the other mussels in the mixing bowl. If using Penn Cove mussels, discard any mussels that have not opened.

Arrange the mussels in one large serving bowl or two or three smaller bowls. If you prefer a thin sauce, season the sauce to taste with salt and pepper, stir well, then pour the sauce over the mussels. If you prefer a thicker sauce, reduce the liquid in the pot to the desired consistency. Season to taste with salt and pepper, stir well, then pour the thickened sauce over the mussels. Whichever sauce option you choose, sprinkle the mussels with the chopped parsley just before serving.

Cook's Hint: Penn Cove and Mediterranean mussels are quite different in size. The smaller Penn Cove variety (about the size of the end of your thumb) cooks much more quickly than "Meds" (which can be as long as your forefinger). Visual cues between the two are also different. Penn Coves pop open when they are done; Meds, thanks to a stronger, almost rubber-band-like closure, sometimes don't open without a bit of prompting. So be sure to discard any Penn Cove mussels that do not open, as they might be dead or "mudders" (mussels filled with mud). With Mediterranean mussels that do not open, gently pry them open. Do this well away from the other mussels, not over the cooking vessel, in case they are "mudders." You don't want to contaminate the entire batch! If the mussel inside is plump and cooked, eat it; if shrunken or shriveled, or if it has an "off" aroma, toss it.

Sidnee Suarez samples the many varieties of apples at the local farmers' market.

The Canlis family has offered quintessential Northwest cuisine served in a stunning restaurant perched above Lake Union in Seattle for more than 55 years. Chris and Alice Canlis and sons Mark and Brian focus on cosseting their guests, with a menu that combines Canlis classics (such as the Canlis Salad or the restaurant's famous prawn appetizer, below) with haute moderne cuisine (such as Kampachi Sashimi with Dungeness Crab and Scallion Salad and Blood-Orange Vinaigrette). Canlis Executive Chef Aaron Wright shared this prawn recipe with me, which Shayn Bjornholm, former director of wines at Canlis, Master Sommelier, and Krug Cup trophy winner, suggested pairing with an off-dry Riesling. Shayn specifically recommended two Washington State Rieslings: Eroica (Chateau Ste. Michelle, see page 60) or Poet's Leap (Long Shadows Vintners). "The low alcohol won't intensify the heat from the red peppers, and the sweetness offsets the salty nature of the prawns," Shayn reasoned. Since Shayn's departure, Nelson Daquip has taken over the team of eight sommeliers who oversee Canlis's Wine Spectator Grand Award–winning list made up of 2,000 selections and 15,000 bottles. Chef Aaron says the Prawn Butter, although a bit tricky to make, is worth the effort, as it "takes the dish to another level." I agree, plus it makes a lovely compound butter to melt over simply cooked fish fillets (see the Cook's Hint, right). The red pepper flakes in the sauce make this a very zingy dish (it's back-of-the-throat hot!). If you are chili averse, cut the red pepper flakes in half.

Canlis
2576 Aurora Avenue North at Sixth
Avenue North
Seattle, WA 98109
(206) 283-3313
canlis.com

Canlis Classic Prawns

SERVES 4 to 6 as an appetizer   VARIETAL Riesling (off-dry)

16 Alaskan spot prawns or black tiger prawns (16 to 20 per pound)

2 tablespoons olive oil

Sea salt

Freshly ground black pepper

½ teaspoon minced garlic

½ teaspoon crushed red pepper flakes

¼ cup white vermouth (Lejon Extra Dry brand recommended)

1½ teaspoons freshly squeezed lime juice

¼ cup Prawn Butter (recipe follows)

4 cups loosely packed mixed baby greens, rinsed and spun dry

Rinse and pat dry the prawns. Remove the shells and reserve to make the Prawn Butter. Devein the prawns.

Heat the olive oil in a large skillet over high heat. Just before the oil reaches the smoking point, add the prawns, along with a sprinkle of sea salt and a few grindings of pepper, and cook until opaque on the outside but still translucent on the inside, about 1 minute per side.

Remove the pan from the heat, pour off the excess oil, and add the garlic and pepper flakes, stirring gently. Add the vermouth and lime juice, swirling the pan to deglaze the bottom. Return the pan to the heat and cook until the liquid reduces to about 2 tablespoons, 3 to 5 minutes. Add the Prawn Butter, stir gently, and season to taste with salt and pepper.

To serve, arrange the greens in the center of four small plates. Arrange the prawns around the greens and drizzle with the sauce.

Prawn Butter

Reserved spot prawn or shrimp shells

½ pound (2 sticks) unsalted butter

Preheat the oven to 500°F. Prepare an ice bath (see Techniques section, page 257).

Arrange the shells on an oiled baking sheet without crowding and cook for 3 to 5 minutes, or until the shells turn pink and begin to give off their aroma.

While the shells are roasting, melt the butter in a small saucepan over medium-high heat and bring just to a boil.

When the shells are roasted, add them to an electric blender along with the boiling butter. Pulse until the shells are finely ground, about 2 minutes.

Place a fine-meshed sieve over a mixing bowl and pour the prawn-butter mixture into the sieve. Press the solids with the back of a spoon to drain as much butter as possible.

Place the mixing bowl over the prepared ice bath, whisking to emulsify the butter and prawn stock, until the mixture is chilled.

Cook's Hint: Leftover Prawn Butter can be transferred to a plastic container and frozen for future use. Or spread it on a large sheet of parchment paper or plastic wrap and form it into a log shape. Wrap tightly; place in a large, resealable plastic bag; and freeze. When ready to serve, allow the butter to sit at room temperature until pliable, then slice and melt over cooked fish fillets.

Fran Bigelow is founder and owner of Seattle-based Fran's Chocolates, which celebrates 25 years in business in 2007. During her lengthy career, Fran has authored a cookbook (*Pure Chocolate*) and was named "one of the top ten artisan chocolatiers in the United States" by *Chocolatier* magazine. The acclaimed chocolatier says, "Fine chocolate is like fine wine. The subtle and distinctive flavors are important. But chocolate-making itself is a long, slow process. You think you know everything, then one day you go into the kitchen in a hurry and, 'Oh, no!' You can never be in a rush with chocolate. Chocolate keeps you humble." With this rich, yet airy, chocolate torte, redolent with tannic, earthy walnuts and semisweet chocolate (it reminds me of a brownie on steroids!), she suggests pairing port (either tawny or red works fine—go with your preference or what you have on hand). "Red wine is hard to pair, unless it's aged and has very low tannins, usually an expensive one. But good if you're just finishing a great bottle of wine after dinner." My kind of woman!

Fran's Chocolates, Ltd.
1300 East Pike Street
Seattle, WA 98122
(206) 322-0233
franschocolates.com

Dark Chocolate-Walnut Torte

SERVES 12   VARIETAL Port

8 ounces walnut pieces (about 1¾ cups)

7 ounces semisweet chocolate, finely chopped

8 large eggs, at room temperature, separated

¾ cup plus 2 tablespoons sugar

1 recipe Dark Chocolate Ganache Glaze (recipe follows)

1 cup heavy whipping cream, whipped until soft peaks form, for serving

Place the oven rack in the middle of the oven. Preheat the oven to 300°F. Grease or coat a 9-inch springform pan with nonstick cooking spray and line the bottom with parchment paper.

Spread the walnuts on a baking sheet and lightly toast in the oven for 5 to 10 minutes, or until they begin to give off their aroma. Allow the nuts to cool completely before proceeding. Transfer half of the nuts to a food processor and pulse until finely ground, with pieces no larger than 1/16 inch. Repeat with the remaining nuts. (This should yield approximately 2 cups.)

Stir the chocolate in a double boiler over low heat. Remove when nearly melted and continue stirring until smooth. Return the bowl to the double boiler only briefly if the chocolate begins to set up.

In an electric mixer bowl (use a whisk attachment if available), combine the egg yolks and 7 tablespoons of the sugar. Beat on medium-high speed to combine, then scrape the sides of the bowl and increase the speed to high. Continue beating until the mixture becomes thick and pale yellow in color and the sugar has dissolved, 5 to 6 minutes more. Gently fold the walnuts into the yolk mixture.

In a separate clean mixing bowl, and with a clean and dry whisk or beaters, begin whipping the egg whites on medium-high speed. Increase the speed to high and allow the whites to become quite frothy, slowly adding the remaining

7 tablespoons of the sugar. Continue whipping until the peaks are stiff but not dry; they should appear glossy and smooth.

Gently fold the melted chocolate into the yolk mixture until well blended. Lighten the yolk mixture by quickly folding in one-quarter of the whites. Then gently fold in the remaining whites in three parts. Do not overmix or the egg whites will deflate. Evenly spread the batter into the prepared pan and bake for 45 to 60 minutes, or until a toothpick or wooden skewer inserted in the center comes out with a few moist crumbs.

Transfer to a wire rack and allow the cake layer to cool at room temperature for 15 minutes. To remove from the pan, go around the edge of the cake with a thin-bladed knife, then release the sides of the pan. Cover with plastic wrap and refrigerate until completely chilled. (Once cooled, the layer can be wrapped airtight in plastic wrap and frozen for up to 1 week prior to assembly.)

To assemble the cake, using a large offset spatula, thinly cover the top and sides of the cake with ¼ cup of the glaze. To finish glazing the cake, place it on a wire cooling rack positioned over a rimmed baking sheet. If the glaze becomes too firm to pour over the cake, stir gently in a double boiler over hot water until it softens enough to pour (about 90°F). Beginning 1½ inches from the edge of the torte, slowly and evenly pour the glaze around the circumference of the torte layer, making sure that the sides are covered. Then pour the remaining glaze onto the center of the torte. Using a metal offset spatula and working quickly, spread the glaze evenly over the top, letting the excess run down the sides.

Let the cake sit at room temperature until the glaze sets and becomes slightly firm, about 20 minutes. Once set, slide an offset spatula under the base of the torte, rotating the spatula to release any spots where the glaze has stuck to the rack. Carefully lift the torte off of the pan base and, supporting the cake's bottom with your free hand, slide it onto a serving plate. Slice the cake and dollop with the whipped cream.

Dark Chocolate Ganache Glaze

½ cup heavy whipping cream

4 ounces semisweet chocolate, finely chopped

In a small saucepan, heat the cream on medium-high heat until it begins to boil. Remove from the heat and stir in the finely chopped chocolate until smooth, using a rubber spatula so as not to incorporate any air. Cool the ganache, stirring occasionally, until it thickens and forms ribbons off the end of the spatula, 5 to 10 minutes.

Slow-roasting food on wooden planks made of cedar, alder, or maple gives fish, meat, poultry, and vegetables a distinctive smoky succulence and appealing fresh flavor, according to Sharon Parker, who first fell in love with the planking technique thanks to a Native American family friend. Now Sharon produces and distributes the planks, along with a cookbook titled *Savory Flavors with Wood: Plank-Roasted Foods from Your Oven*, from which this recipe is taken. Much like the oak barrels in which wine is aged, planks can impart different flavors to food. Western Red Cedar is a very durable wood that ranges in color from light amber to deep honey brown. In cooking, it lends a sweet, spicy flavor with a mild smoky edge, according to Sharon. Western Maple, also known as Big Leaf or Pacific Coast Maple, is pale pinkish-brown to almost white in color and is character-ized by a close, fine grain. Perhaps because maple sugar can be produced from the sap of these trees (although Eastern Maple is the preferred variety), planks made from the trees add a sweet, buttery flavor with a mild smoky layering to foods cooked over them. Western Alder is pale yellow to reddish-brown in color with a fine, close grain. Because of its rich, pure smoke flavor it is the "preferred wood" for smoking, as well as the wood traditionally used for smoking food in the Northwest. Its robust smoke flavor is coupled with a light vanilla complement. Shagbark Hickory is a hard, dense wood that burns slowly, producing a lot of heat. Its unique aroma has long been used to give smoked hams and cheeses a distinctive flavor. Sharon suggests a range of wines with this duck recipe—try Semillon, Riesling, or Chardonnay among white varietals; Merlot among red wines.

Nature's Cuisine, Inc.
2144 Westlake Avenue North, Suite E
Seattle, WA 98109
(206) 217-0163
(866) 880-4506
natures-cuisine.com

Duck Breasts with Lemon-Roasted Olives

SERVES 4   VARIETAL Merlot, Chardonnay, Riesling, or Semillon

Four 4-ounce boneless, skinless duck breasts

Kosher salt

Freshly ground black pepper

⅓ cup freshly squeezed lemon juice

1 tablespoon minced garlic

1 teaspoon freshly grated lemon zest

¼ teaspoon lemon pepper

⅓ cup olive oil

20 kalamata or green olives with pits, or a combination

At least 15 minutes before cooking, arrange the oven rack in the upper or middle position. Place the plank on the rack, then preheat the oven to 350°F.

Sprinkle the duck breasts with salt and pepper. Leaving the heated plank on the oven rack, pull out both the plank and rack and arrange the seasoned breasts on the heated plank without crowding. (This eliminates having to move a hot plank around the kitchen.) Roast for 20 minutes.

While the duck is cooking, prepare the dressing by mixing together the lem-on juice, garlic, lemon zest, and lemon pepper in a small bowl. Whisk in the olive oil a few drops at a time, incorporating well after each addition, until the sauce is thick and smooth (emulsified).

Turn the duck breasts over and surround with the olives; drizzle half the dressing over the duck. Roast for 20 minutes, or until the duck is no longer pink when cut into and the juices run clear (for medium).

To serve, divide the duck breasts and olives among 4 dinner plates and drizzle with the remaining dressing.

Cook's Hint: Before using a wood plank for the first time, it is necessary to "season" it—after multiple seasonings, the plank will turn a rich brown color and will no longer need to be seasoned before each use. To season the plank, pour 1 to 2 tablespoons of olive oil (preferred) or vegetable oil into a small bowl. Using a paper towel or soft, clean cloth dipped in the oil, lightly coat the top surface of the plank with the oil. Do not oil the underside of the plank. Always preheat the plank for 15 minutes, following recipe directions, before placing food on the plank to roast. Also, when your plank is new, and as it develops cracks and warps over time, tighten the steel tightening rods that are inserted along the ends of the plank by using the adjustment tool (supplied with most planks) or a $7/16$-inch socket wrench. When planking, do not raise the oven heat above 400°F. Clean the plank with a soft brush, warm water, and mild soap or detergent, never in the dishwasher. And never use a plank designed for use in the oven on a barbecue or grill!

Jesse the vineyard dog roams through the vines at Lopez Island Vineyards, located in Washington's San Juan Islands.

I first enjoyed this playful appetizer at the Columbia Tower Club in Seattle, where it was served as the first course at the 2004 Platinum Dinner. Sponsored by *Wine Press Northwest,* the dinner celebrates the wines chosen as "Platinum winners" in the magazine's annual contest. Crab "BLT" was paired that evening with an amazing White Meritage (a blended white wine made of Sauvignon Blanc and Semillon) created by Holly Turner, the gifted winemaker at Three Rivers Winery in Walla Walla, Washington. "The Platinum," as it is fondly known, is always an intriguing mix of food, wine, and scenery, since the Columbia Tower Club (a private club sometimes open for public events) is located on the 76th floor of the Bank of America Tower, Seattle's tallest building. The club's executive chef, Bruce Ross, who has since moved on to the Tower Club in Dallas, was kind enough to share his recipe with me, which I enjoyed testing on New Year's Day 2006. Its light, lovely flavors (Dungeness crab, lemon, applewood-smoked bacon, and crème fraîche!) were a welcome harbinger of the new year to come.

Columbia Tower Club

701 Fifth Avenue

Seattle, WA 98104

(206) 622-2010

columbia-tower.com

Dungeness Crab "BLT"

SERVES 6 as an appetizer   VARIETAL Chardonnay or White Meritage

Brioche Crisps

3 slices brioche, sliced ¼-inch thick

Extra virgin olive oil

¾ cup crème fraîche

1 tablespoon whole-grain mustard

1 tablespoon freshly grated lemon zest

Kosher salt

Freshly ground white pepper

14 ounces (about 3 cups) Dungeness crabmeat, picked over for shells and cartilage

6 cherry tomatoes, cut in half

3 slices applewood-smoked bacon, cut in 1-inch strips and cooked until browned and crisp

1 cup micro celery, or ½ cup finely chopped celery

Preheat the oven to 300°F.

To make the Brioche Crisps, using a 2½- or 3-inch ring mold, cut 6 discs from the brioche slices. Place the brioche discs on a baking sheet. With a clean pastry brush, lightly brush the bread with olive oil. Bake for 7 to 10 minutes, or until evenly golden brown. Set aside.

With a wire whisk, whip ½ cup of the crème fraîche until soft peaks form. Gently fold in the mustard and lemon zest. Season to taste with salt and white pepper. Gently fold in the crabmeat, being careful to keep the large lumps of meat intact. Gently spoon the crab salad into a 2½- or 3-inch ring mold with a bottom until the salad is about 2 inches high. If using a mold without a bottom, see the instructions in step 4.

Place 2 teaspoons of the remaining ¼ cup of crème fraîche in the center of a chilled serving plate. Top with a Brioche Crisp, pressing down to affix the brioche to the plate. Place the ring mold of crab salad on top of the brioche and lift off the ring. If using a ring mold without a bottom, place the mold on the brioche, spoon in the crab, and remove the mold.

Place two cherry tomato halves on top of the crab. Arrange the bacon over the cherry tomatoes and top with the micro celery or sprinkle with the chopped celery. Repeat with the remaining plates, and serve immediately.

Three Rivers Winery's award-winning winemaker, Holly Turner, is well known for producing distinctive varietal wines, along with outstanding white and red Meritage (Bordeaux blends).

Cook's Hint: Try varying the type of lemon zest you use. I made the recipe with Meyer lemons, which resulted in a very aromatic, floral taste. Lime or even tangerine zest would provide other intriguing options, as well as additional interesting possibilities for wine pairing (for example, try lime and Sauvignon Blanc; tangerine or orange with Viognier).

E tta's Seafood, Seattle über chef Tom Douglas's paean to the region's local seafood bounty, is located just north of the Pike Place Market, but it's close enough to attract tourists and locals alike. Named after his daughter, Loretta, the restaurant has a clubby yet casual feel, along with great people watching as Market shoppers tote their tomatoes and balance their bouquets along Western Avenue. Outstanding dishes include the Dungeness Crab Salad with Lime Vinaigrette, Tom's Tasty Tuna Sashimi Salad with Green Onion Pancakes, and Etta's Rub-with-Love Salmon with Corn Bread Pudding and Shiitake Relish. The latter is the prototypical Seattle salmon dish to try if you have time for only one. Etta's creamy clam chowder is another customer favorite; aficionados have been begging for the recipe for years, but it doesn't appear in any of Tom's books (*Tom Douglas' Seattle Kitchen, Tom's Big Dinners,* and *I Love Crab Cakes!*), only here! Good news: If you don't feel like making your own clam chowder, it's always on the lunch, brunch, and dinner menus at Etta's, where the wine list, devised by Pike and Western Wine Shop owner Michael Teer, leans heavily toward Northwest selections.

Etta's Seafood

2020 Western Avenue

Seattle, WA 98121

(206) 443-6000

tomdouglas.com

Etta's Manila Clam Chowder

SERVES 6 to 8   VARIETAL Semillon

2 cups dry white wine

1 cup bottled or canned clam juice, plus extra as needed

3 pounds Manila or steamer-sized clams, shells scrubbed and rinsed

¼ pound bacon, diced

1 cup finely diced celery

1 cup finely diced leeks (white and light green parts only)

1 cup peeled and diced russet potato

3 tablespoons unsalted butter

4 tablespoons all-purpose flour

2 cups heavy whipping cream, heated to just below boiling

2 teaspoons chopped fresh thyme, or 1 teaspoon dried thyme, crumbled

Add the wine to a large saucepan, bring to a boil over high heat, and boil until the volume is reduced by half to about 1 cup, 8 to 10 minutes. Add the clam juice and bring back to a boil. Add the clams, cover, and cook over high heat just until the clams open, about 4 minutes. Discard any clams that do not open.

Set a colander over a large bowl and pour the clams into the colander, reserving both the clams and all the liquid. Pick the clams out of the shells, discarding the shells, and coarsely chop the clam meat. Set aside. Strain the reserved liquid through a cheesecloth-lined strainer. You should have 4 cups liquid; if not, add more clam juice. Pour the clam liquid into a saucepan and bring to a simmer over medium-high heat.

To finish the chowder, set a large pot over medium-high heat and cook the bacon, stirring occasionally, until it starts to crisp, about 5 minutes. Add the celery and leeks and cook, stirring as needed, until the vegetables are softened, 6 to 8 minutes. Add the hot clam liquid and the potatoes and simmer until the potatoes are tender, about 12 minutes.

Meanwhile, melt the butter in a small saucepan over medium-high heat. Add the flour, 1 tablespoon at a time, whisking until smooth, and cook the roux for 1 to 2 minutes. Ladle about 1 cup of the hot liquid from the chowder

About 2 teaspoons freshly squeezed lemon juice, or to taste

Freshly ground black pepper

Sliced fresh chives, for garnish

and gradually add it to the roux, whisking until smooth. Then scrape the roux into the chowder pot, stirring until smooth. Simmer until the soup thickens slightly, whisking occasionally, 7 to 10 minutes.

Add the hot cream to the chowder and stir until smooth. Add the reserved clam meat and simmer for 1 minute. Add the thyme and the lemon juice and season to taste with the black pepper. (The clams are salty, so you may not need salt.) Ladle the chowder into bowls, garnish with sliced chives, and serve.

Seattle celebrity chef, restaurateur, entrepreneur, and cookbook author Tom Douglas interviews winemaker Kay Simon of Chinook Wines on his radio show *Seattle Kitchen* at the winery in Prosser, Washington.

I n 2003, over the course of the year, the Washington Wine Commission organized a series of "Iron Chef" battles between Seattle's most talented celebrity chefs. During one such battle I was lucky enough to serve as a judge, and I watched in amazement as the dynamic duo of Holly Smith, chef/owner of Café Juanita in Kirkland, Washington, and Erik Tanaka, Executive Chef of Tom Douglas's restaurants (see page 16), created this flank steak recipe from nothing more than a basket of fresh veggies, meat, and seafood they were unfamiliar with until moments before the competition began. They handily beat the opposing team, especially since their wine pairing with Apex Cellars Syrah was such a perfect match. The vibrant, award-winning wine from the Yakima Valley, made by long-time Washington winemaker Brian Carter (see page 24), displayed a deep purple color, with robust berry and plum aromas and flavors and hints of cinnamon and leather. It created a cunning complement for the slightly bitter *gai lan* (Chinese broccoli), pungent mustard and garlic, rare beef, and red-wine sauce in the dish. Though pressed for time, the chefs even whipped up cheese flans as a lush side dish; if you are so inclined, try the recipe for Fallen Cheese Soufflés on page 22.

Washington Wine Commission

1000 Second Avenue, Suite 1700

Seattle, WA 98104

(206) 667-9463

washingtonwine.org

Flank Steak Roulade with Red-Wine Sauce

SERVES 6 to 8   VARIETAL Syrah

2 tablespoons olive oil

1 tablespoon unsalted butter

1 pound *gai lan* (Chinese broccoli) or broccoli rabe, tough stems trimmed and remaining portion coarsely chopped to measure about 6 packed cups (see Cook's Hint, right)

1 tablespoon minced garlic

¾ teaspoon kosher salt

⅛ plus ¼ teaspoon freshly ground black pepper

One 2-pound flank steak, pounded to ¼-inch thickness

2 tablespoons Dijon mustard

Preheat the oven to 425°F. For easy cleanup, line a roasting pan with heavy-duty aluminum foil. Lightly oil the foil.

Heat 1 tablespoon of the olive oil and the butter in a large skillet over medium-high heat. When the oil is hot, add the *gai lan* and cook, stirring often, until tender-crisp, 3 to 5 minutes. Add the garlic and stir until softened but not browned, about 1 minute. Season with ¼ teaspoon of the salt and the ⅛ teaspoon pepper. Remove from the heat and reserve.

Place the steak on a clean work surface and sprinkle on both sides with the remaining ½ teaspoon of salt and the ¼ teaspoon pepper. Spread the mustard on the top side of the steak. Spread the sautéed *gai lan* evenly over the mustard-coated steak. Roll up the steak, jelly-roll fashion, beginning with the long side. Tie with kitchen string every two inches.

Heat a large skillet over medium-high heat and add the remaining 1 tablespoon olive oil. Place the roulade in the skillet and cook, turning to brown all sides, for 3 to 5 minutes. Transfer to the prepared roasting pan and roast for 20 to 25 minutes (for rare to medium rare), or until the desired doneness is reached.

Red-Wine Sauce

5 tablespoons sugar

1 cup dry red wine

3 tablespoons cold unsalted butter, cut into 1-tablespoon pieces

¼ teaspoon kosher salt, or to taste

⅛ teaspoon freshly ground black pepper, or to taste

Meanwhile, to prepare the Red-Wine Sauce, place the sugar in a heavy-bottomed medium skillet over medium-low heat. Stir continuously with a wooden spoon for 4 to 6 minutes, or until the sugar melts and turns light golden in color; watch the sugar carefully, as it can quickly turn dark and burn. Add the wine carefully, as it may splash up and sputter (covering your hand with a long oven mitt is an added precaution!). Cook, stirring, until the caramel is dissolved into the wine, 2 to 3 minutes, then continue to simmer until the liquid reduces to a syrup-like consistency and measures about ⅓ cup, 8 to 10 minutes more.

Remove the pan from the heat and gently stir the butter into the sauce 1 tablespoon at a time, incorporating well after each addition, until the sauce is smooth and glossy. Season with the salt and pepper or to taste. Keep warm until serving.

Remove the roulade from the oven, tent with aluminum foil, and allow to rest for 10 minutes. Cut the roulade into 1-inch slices, drizzle with the sauce, and serve.

Cook's Hint: To reduce the assertive, sometimes bitter, flavor of the *gai lan* or broccoli rabe, blanch the vegetables before sautéing in step 2: Add the cleaned, trimmed vegetables to a large pot of salted boiling water and simmer for 1 minute or until tender crisp. (If using stems, simmer them for 1 minute before adding the leafy tops.) Drain well and pat dry with paper towels. Sauté as described in step 2, reducing the cooking time to 2 to 3 minutes.

Seattle chef Maria Hines landed on the radar screens of national foodies when *Food & Wine* magazine named her one of the best new chefs in the United States in 2005. Back then, she was executive chef at Earth & Ocean, the hip restaurant at the even hipper W Hotel Seattle, where she was known for offering boldly flavored, seasonally inspired, often-organic dishes. In the fall of 2006, Maria decided to strike out on her own, creating Tilth, one of two restaurants in the country to receive organic certification from Oregon Tilth. It's an unpretentious, buttery-yellow space located in a Craftsman-style house in the bustling Wallingford neighborhood of Seattle, a few miles north of downtown. Almost everything on the menu is preceded by the farmers' or fishers' names. Salad greens and veggies are grown at Full Circle Farm. Wild sockeye salmon is trolled by Pete Knutson. Chicken breasts and short ribs come from Skagit River Ranch. The chef's King's Garden Melon Salad is a precise dice of colorful fruit gently flavored with mint, *sel gris,* and a sprinkling of feta. Housemade Ricotta Pappardelle are lacy noodles enrobed in brown butter and hazelnuts. An autumn dessert offering of White Corn Crème Brûlée with a crumble of brown sugar and bacon appeals to both the savory and sweet sides of the palate. The salad below demonstrates Chef Maria's style of cooking simple ingredients and creating bold flavors and beautiful plate presentations. The salad can take on a more rustic look if you simply cut the golden beets into one-inch cubes and toss them with the vinaigrette instead of slicing the beets and drizzling the vinaigrette.

Earth & Ocean
1112 Fourth Avenue
Seattle, WA 98121
(206) 264-6060
earthocean.net

Tilth
1411 North 45th Street
Seattle, WA 98103
(206) 633-0801
tilthrestaurant.com

Golden Beet Carpaccio

SERVES 4   VARIETAL Chardonnay

Herb Vinaigrette

4 sprigs fresh flat-leaf parsley

4 sprigs fresh tarragon

4 sprigs fresh chervil

4 fresh chive stalks

¼ cup extra virgin olive oil

1 tablespoon red wine vinegar

2 medium golden or red beets, scrubbed and tops and root ends trimmed

To make the Herb Vinaigrette, mince the parsley, tarragon, chervil, and chives. Transfer to a small mixing bowl and gently stir in the olive oil and vinegar. Set aside.

Preheat the oven to 400°F. Line a small roasting pan with aluminum foil.

Add the beets and thyme sprigs to the roasting pan and sprinkle with salt and pepper. Fill the pan with water until the beets are almost completely submerged, cover with aluminum foil, and bake the beets for 1 to 1¼ hours, or until they are very tender. To test, insert the tip of a small, sharp knife into the center of one of the beets. Remove the beets from the pan and let cool. When the beets are cool enough to handle, remove the skins (see Cook's Hint, on next page).

5 sprigs fresh thyme, or ½ teaspoon dried thyme, crumbled

Kosher salt

Freshly ground black pepper

¼ cup pine nuts, walnuts, or hazelnuts, toasted (see Techniques section, page 258)

½ cup (2 ounces) fresh, soft goat's-milk cheese (chèvre), crumbled

To serve, slice the beets into very thin rounds. Arrange them on 4 small plates in a spiral pattern, overlapping them to form a circle. Drizzle the beets with the vinaigrette, then sprinkle the pine nuts and goat cheese evenly over the beets. If desired, sprinkle lightly with salt and pepper.

Cook's Hint: Chef Maria uses a clean, dry kitchen towel to remove the beet skins by simply wiping them off, a method that also saves your hands from getting stained by beet juice.

Fresh Bing cherries are a popular purchase at farmers' markets throughout the Pacific Northwest in July and August. Many are also commercially dried for year-round snacking.

Stunning views of the Olympic Mountains and the boat traffic on Shilshole Bay combined with a laid-back Northwest atmosphere and regional seafood done up right have landed Ray's Boathouse on many "best of" lists; indeed, savvy tourists and locals consider it one of the quintessential Seattle dining experiences. Executive Chef Peter Birk oversees Ray's seafood-focused menu, which takes advantage of the season's catch, while maintaining classic signature dishes such as Dungeness Crab Cakes or Sablefish (a.k.a. Black Cod) Marinated in Sake Kasu. Wine is taken seriously here; the restaurant hosts the annual Retrospective of Northwest Wines (see page 72), and the wine list is thoughtfully chosen and Northwest-centric.

Chef Peter is a champion of locally made artisan cheese, and he has offered a totally Northwest/Northern California–based cheese tray in his dining room since 2001.

Ray's Boathouse/Ray's Café

6049 Seaview Avenue Northwest

Ray's Boathouse: (206) 789-3770

Ray's Café: (206) 782-0094

rays.com

At a cooking class at the Boathouse, he made his own ricotta, along with a tasty tomato-and-zucchini cheese gratin and the winning salad combination below. Thanks to the cheese soufflés and roasted red peppers, which act as bridge ingredients, wine pairings with this salad are versatile. Chef Peter suggests everything from Cabernet Franc or Syrah to Riesling.

Mixed Greens with Fallen Cheese Soufflés and Champagne Vinaigrette

SERVES 6 VARIETAL Cabernet Franc, Syrah, Riesling

Champagne Vinaigrette

¾ cup extra virgin olive oil

¼ cup champagne vinegar

Kosher salt

Freshly ground black pepper

½ pound fresh asparagus, woody stems trimmed

1 cup (4 ounces) shredded Samish Bay Montasio cheese or high-quality Parmesan or Parmigiano-Reggiano cheese

1 cup heavy whipping cream

2 large eggs, slightly beaten

To prepare the Champagne Vinaigrette, in a cruet or a container with a tight-fitting lid, combine the olive oil and vinegar. Shake well to combine. Season to taste with salt and pepper and set aside.

Preheat the oven to 325°F. Spray six 4-ounce ramekins or custard cups with nonstick vegetable cooking spray.

Prepare an ice bath (see Techniques section, page 257). Bring a large pot of water to a boil, add the asparagus, and cook, stirring occasionally, until the asparagus turns bright green and becomes tender-crisp, 2 to 5 minutes (depending on thickness). Plunge the asparagus into the ice bath until cool enough to handle. Remove the asparagus, pat dry, cut into bite-sized pieces, and set aside.

In a small saucepan, combine the cheese and cream. Cook over medium-high heat, stirring constantly, until the cheese melts. Heat until small bubbles form around the edges of the cream and steam rises off the top, but do not allow the cream to come to a boil. Remove from the heat and, in a mixing bowl, whisk a very small amount of the cream mixture into the eggs (this is called tempering).

Kosher salt

Freshly ground white pepper

4 to 6 ounces fresh arugula leaves

4 to 6 ounces fresh watercress

½ cup roasted red bell peppers, homemade (see Techniques section, page 257) or store-bought (pat very dry), cut into bite-sized pieces

Continue adding the cream very slowly and whisking constantly, being careful not to scramble the eggs. Season to taste with salt and white pepper.

Divide the cheese mixture evenly among the custard cups (for easier handling, place the custard cups on a baking sheet without crowding). Bake for 20 to 25 minutes, or until they turn golden around the edges and puff. Remove from the oven and allow to cool on a wire rack for 30 minutes at room temperature, then cover and cool for 2 to 3 hours (or up to 2 days) in the refrigerator. Do not worry if the soufflés fall; they are supposed to!

When ready to serve, combine the arugula, watercress, reserved asparagus, and peppers in a large bowl and toss with ¼ to ⅓ cup of the vinaigrette, or more to taste. Divide the salad among 6 salad plates. Run a small knife around the inside of each custard cup to loosen. Carefully invert the cup over the salad and tap gently to release the custard. Position the custard on top of the greens and serve.

Goat cheese comes in a variety of shapes, sizes, and types.

eattle's upscale Madison Park neighborhood is home to an eponymous café that's been pleasing the locals since opening in 1979. Owner Karen Binder has been on the scene since its inception, taking over solo in 1999. Located in a house with sunny yellow walls to match the bright artwork, Madison Park Café offers diners traditional bistro classics along with Executive Chef Amanda Zimlich's updated dishes. Consider Amanda's Carrot Soup with Crème Fraîche and Truffle Oil versus Karen's Onion Soup Gratinée, or Karen's House Cassoulet versus Amanda's Goat-Cheese Gnocchi with Roasted Eggplant, Sofrito Onions, and Lemon-Caper Sauce. Karen's wine list, while concise, is a thoughtful mix of French and Northwest options that pair well with whichever version of French food you choose at the Madison Park Café. Karen is a former chemist who lived in Geneva, Switzerland, speaks fluent French, and is an avowed Francophile. She dates longtime Washington winemaker Brian Carter, of Apex Winery and Brian Carter Cellars (BCC). BCC celebrated its first release in early 2006, and focuses on handcrafted, European-style blended wines, including red blends in the Bordeaux, Rhône, and Super Tuscan styles, plus a white-wine blend.

This mussel dish is a gutsy Mediterranean take on one of the Northwest's favorite foods. Rife with smoky bacon and dill, the mussels pair perfectly with winemaker Brian's Byzance (which translates as "luxurious"), a Southern Rhône-style blend made from 60 percent Grenache and 40 percent Syrah. The almost-black, inky wine features a gamey-rich nose redolent of blackberries and blueberries, spice, and smoke. Fairly light on the palate, the wine has a smooth, well-knit finish with integrated tannins and spicy flavors—the perfect food wine!

Madison Park Café

1807 42nd Avenue East

Seattle, WA 98112

(206) 324-2626

madisonparkcafe.citysearch.com

Mussels à la Grecque

SERVES 2 to 3 as an appetizer   VARIETAL Red blend

½ teaspoon whole coriander seed

¼ cup tomato juice

2 tablespoons dry white wine

½ teaspoon freshly squeezed lemon juice

2 tablespoons unsalted butter

1 tablespoon minced shallots

2 pounds Penn Cove or Mediterranean mussels, shells scrubbed and rinsed and mussels debearded just before cooking

Heat a small skillet over medium heat. Add the coriander seed and toast, shaking the pan occasionally, until the seeds begin to release their aroma, 1 to 2 minutes. Add the tomato juice, wine, and lemon juice, cook until the liquid is reduced by half (about 3 tablespoons), 3 to 4 minutes, and remove from the heat.

In a large skillet, melt the butter over medium heat and cook the shallot, stirring occasionally, until translucent but not browned, 1 to 2 minutes. Add the mussels, bacon, garlic, and tomato-wine mixture. Cover the skillet, reduce the heat to medium, and cook until the mussels begin to open, 2 to 3 minutes. Uncover the skillet, gently stir the mussels, and sprinkle the mint and dill on top. Cover the skillet and cook for 2 to 3 minutes, or until all the

1 slice thick-cut bacon, cut cross-wise into ¼-inch slices and cooked

1 teaspoon minced garlic

5 medium fresh mint leaves, stacked and rolled like a cigar and very finely sliced

1½ teaspoons minced fresh dill

Kosher salt

Freshly ground black pepper

mussels open. If using Mediterranean mussels (which have a stronger connective tissue than Penn Cove mussels), pry open any mussels that have not opened (see Cook's Hint, page 7). If they smell fresh and are not muddy, add to the other mussels in the skillet. If using Penn Cove mussels, discard any that have not opened. Season the mussels to taste with salt and pepper and stir gently.

Transfer the mussels and broth to a large bowl or 2 or 3 individual bowls and serve immediately.

Racks of wine bottles form a geometric pattern.

Chef/owner Ethan Stowell seemingly came out of nowhere in October 2003 when he opened cool, contemporary Union catercorner to the Pike Place Market. John Mariani named the newcomer one of *Esquire* magazine's 20 "Best New Restaurants of 2004." Since then, Stowell has kept the pace with his daily-changing menu, which celebrates the freshest seasonal ingredients from around the block and around the world. While I can't tell you what dishes you'll encounter the day you visit, I can tell you about a few I will never forget. One memorable meal began with a half-dozen Kumamoto oysters dressed with Casa Brina olive oil and fresh lime juice—heaven on the half shell. Seared sea scallops floated in an avocado purée scented with basil. Medium-rare slices of rich Muscovy duck breast drizzled with an ambrosial port reduction formed our main course, while, for dessert, kumquat confit with pomegranate and pineapple sorbet simultaneously cleansed the palate while satisfying the sweet tooth. Chef Ethan also takes his wines seriously, with a dozen options by the glass and 200 bottles on the wine carte. There are also cool cocktails and a separate bar menu, the perfect answer for impromptu visits to the stylish space that overlooks First Avenue, lately known as the "Park Avenue of Seattle."

Union

1400 First Avenue

Seattle, WA 98101

(206) 838-8000

unionseattle.com

Tavolàta

2323 Second Avenue

Seattle, WA 98121

(206) 838-8008

tavolata.com

In early 2007, Chef Ethan opened Tavolàta, a narrow, bustling space in Belltown that attracts a hip, young crowd. Portions are large and made for sharing: Broiled Oysters with Oregano, Bread Crumbs, and Olive Oil are plump and prime; Linguine with Mussels, Garlic, and Parsley is cooked perfectly al dente; Grilled T-Bone with Agro-Dolce Onions is fork tender and pinkish-red in the center. "You're not at Union anymore," Chef Ethan said with a wink the first time I ate at the Italian-inspired Tavolàta. With this supremely simple yet excessively exquisite halibut dish he sometimes serves at Union, Chef Ethan suggests a pairing with Hamacher Chardonnay "Cuvée Forêts Diverses" from the Willamette Valley.

Roasted Halibut with Sherry-Braised Morel Mushrooms

SERVES 4   VARIETAL Chardonnay

2 tablespoons olive oil

Four 5-ounce halibut fillets, rinsed and patted dry

Kosher salt

Freshly ground black pepper

Heat the olive oil in a large skillet over medium-high heat. Sprinkle the halibut with salt and pepper. When the pan is hot, add the halibut flesh side down and cook until golden brown, 4 to 5 minutes. Turn the fish and cook for an additional 2 to 3 minutes. Remove from the pan and keep warm.

Melt the butter in a medium saucepan over medium heat. Add the shallots and cook, stirring occasionally, until the shallots are softened but not brown,

2 tablespoons unsalted butter

2 tablespoons minced shallots

½ pound fresh morel mushrooms, cleaned (see Cook's Hint, page 219) and cut in half

¼ cup manzanilla sherry (see Cook's Hints, right)

2 tablespoons heavy whipping cream, whipped to stiff peaks (see Cook's Hints, right)

2 to 3 minutes. Add the morels and stir well. Add the sherry, stir well, and cook, stirring occasionally, until the liquid is almost completely reduced, 4 to 5 minutes. Fold in the whipped cream and season to taste with salt and pepper.

Divide the braised morels between 4 warm soup bowls. Place the warm halibut on top, and serve immediately.

Cook's Hints: (1) Unlike the cream sherries (such as Harvey's Bristol Cream) that many North Americans are familiar with, manzanilla sherry is a pale, light, very dry, delicate fortified wine with a pungent, slightly salty taste. Considered one of the best among the fino sherries, this astringent and intriguing sipper should be drunk while still young, rather than aged. It's available at the Spanish Table (various locations or online at spanishtable. com) or at better wineshops and liquor stores. (2) The technique of whipping heavy cream until stiff peaks form, then folding it into a reduced liquid to make a sauce, is often used by savvy chefs. The whipped cream adds a lighter texture to the sauce, while saving a few calories compared to sauces finished with unwhipped heavy cream that is then reduced. Try this technique at home with this sauce and others.

A Chardonnay grape cluster

DeLaurenti Specialty Food & Wine is a cornerstone of Seattle's venerable Pike Place Market, where it's been in business since 1928. The Italian specialty store boasts 220 cheeses; 1,800 wines (a strong Italian contingent as well as choice Northwest contenders); a café with fresh pizza by the slice, espresso, and pastries from Seattle's best bakeries; and all manner of olives, olive oil, and balsamic vinegar. It's the "go-to" place when Seattle cooks seek hard-to-find ingredients. Owner Pat McCarthy is a caring, hands-on kind of guy who works his shop like a pro and stays in touch with his customers via a weekly e-newsletter. It updates readers on Pat's latest "finds" (such as fresh black truffles from Italy, Neal's Yard cheeses from England, and charcuterie from Salumi), not to mention the latest Saturday-afternoon wine tasting and occasional cooking classes.

Pat, who sends out a recipe in each e-newsletter, devised this appetizer after a trip to Alaska. He reports it has since become one of his favorites among his large collection, and he suggests pairing it with a chilled rosé. It's the perfect last-minute appetizer—elegant, yet simple to make. Because of his love of cheese, Pat founded the Seattle Cheese Festival in 2005; the three-day celebration features lectures by national cheese experts and cooking classes by local chefs. Pike Place is shut down to automobile traffic, so that the Cheese Concourse, Artisanal Alley, and Wine Garden can be set up. Area restaurants feature Cheese Fest Best dishes on their menus, and children can take part in the Cheese Maze scavenger hunts. In short, the May festival celebrates all things related to artisanal, handcrafted, and farmstead cheese and specialty cheese producers!

DeLaurenti Specialty Food & Wine

1435 First Avenue

Seattle, WA 98101

(206) 622-0141

(800) 873-6685

delaurenti.com

Smoked Salmon Tartare

SERVES 4 as an appetizer   VARIETAL rosé

½ pound thinly sliced cold-smoked salmon (Gerard & Dominique brand preferred)

1 tablespoon extra virgin olive oil

1 tablespoon capers, well drained

1 to 2 teaspoons freshly squeezed lemon juice

3 tablespoons minced fresh chives

1 tablespoon minced fresh lemon thyme, or ¼ teaspoon dried thyme, crumbled, plus ¼ teaspoon freshly grated lemon zest

On a cutting board, stack the salmon slices several slices high and cut into ¼-inch cubes. Using a rocking motion, slice across the cubes until they are slightly smaller, but not puréed, forming ⅛-inch cubes; the salmon should still have some texture. In a medium nonreactive mixing bowl, gently stir together the salmon, olive oil, capers, and 1 teaspoon of the lemon juice. Taste and add more lemon juice if needed.

Add half the chives and half the lemon thyme and season to taste with salt and pepper.

Divide the tartare among 4 small ramekins or ring molds with bottoms. Place a salad plate over the ramekin or ring mold, then invert and turn the tartare out onto the plate. If using ring molds without bottoms, place the mold on

Kosher salt

Freshly ground black pepper

crostini (See Techniques section, page 257) or mild-flavored crackers

the plate, spoon in the tartare, and remove the mold. Sprinkle the remaining chives and lemon thyme over the tartare, cover, and refrigerate for at least 1 hour to allow the flavors to meld and the tartare to chill. Serve with the Crostini.

Just down the hill from DeLaurenti Specialty Food & Wine in the Pike Place Market, John Farias produces 450 to 500 cases of unpretentious wine a year at Market Cellar Winery, in addition to selling home-brewing supplies.

The Big Cheese

Like many small-business owners in the Pike Place Market, Kurt Beecher Dammeier likes to stand at the entryway to his shop hawking his wares.

A tray of Beecher's Handmade Cheese displays (clockwise from top): Flagship, No Woman, and Mariachi.

"Two days ago, this cheese was grass," he boasts as he plies the crowds with fresh cheese curds. The pure white curds are about the size of your thumbnail and "squeak" when you bite into them.

Some people in the crowd stare at the handsome, bearded cheesemonger in disbelief and rush away; many try a sample. Most, drawn in as much by the comforting smells of grilled cheese sandwiches as by Dammeier's pleasant banter, step inside Beecher's Handmade Cheese for a gander around. The 3,000-square-foot space wears a homey patina, with the look and feel of an old-time country store.

The interplay has taken place since 2003, when Beecher's opened for business in a premier location along Pike Place and quickly became one of Washington State's most visible and productive artisan cheese makers. "Artisan" refers to cheese (indeed, most any specialty food product, such as bread, beer, or coffee) made the old-fashioned way with high-quality ingredients, in small batches, and often by hand. Artisan cheese can also be referred to as "farmstead," but only if the cows, sheep, or goats are raised, tended, and milked right on the farm where the cheese is produced.

There's more attention to detail, care, and craft in artisan cheeses than in mass-produced items. The cheese maker's ethnic origins frequently play a part (Washington State cheese makers of Dutch ancestry often produce Gouda, for example, while New England makers produce cheddar), as does the animals' diets. Spring milk is different than fall milk; if the animals have been dining on dandelions or languishing in lavender, you'll taste those flavors in the cheese!

Beecher's artisanal cheeses begin their lives before the crack of dawn, when "Big White," the milk tanker, pumps 1,000 gallons of fresh milk into the gleaming stainless-steel holding tank. The milk comes from healthy, free-range cows, none of which has been treated with the controversial rBST (bovine growth hormone).

Big picture windows overlook the cheese kitchen, allowing visitors to watch Beecher's head cheese maker, Brad Sinko, and his apprentices progress through the entire cheese-making process. The process, which takes seven to eight hours, begins when the pure, raw milk goes from the holding tank into the pasteurizer.

From there, it's cooked and stirred in open steel vats and cultures are added. The cultures determine which cheese is being made. Whey (the watery part of milk) is separated from the curds, salt is added, and the curds are checked for moisture, acidity, and butterfat.

In addition to fresh cheese curds and special seasonal cheeses, Beecher's products include flavored cheeses; Blank Slate, which resembles a young, fresh cheese such as *fromage blanc*; and Flagship, a semi-hard, cheddar-like variety with a creamy finish. Flagship is released with yearly designations, becoming

> "Beecher's artisanal cheeses begin their lives before the crack of dawn, when 'Big White,' the milk tanker, pumps 1,000 gallons of fresh milk into the gleaming stainless-steel holding tank."

more complex and evolved the older it gets. Beecher's also stocks artisan cheeses from the Northwest (Willamette Valley Cheese, Sally Jackson, Quillisas-cut) and Northern California (Cowgirl Creamery, Cypress Grove, Fiscalini).

"Our Northwest palates have become accustomed to the full flavors and freshness of local beers and breads," Dammeier explains. "Additionally, we are becoming more interested in how our food is made and where the ingredients come from. At Beecher's, customers can actually see the cheese coming to life right before their eyes. They appreciate the wholesome ingredients, artful process, and passion for pure food that is evident in our entire product line."

Beecher's Handmade Cheese

**1600 Pike Place
Seattle, WA 98101
(206) 956-1964
beecherscheese.com**

Harvest time is a hectic, but ultimately rewarding, time of the year.

Kurt Beecher Dammeier, owner of Beecher's Handmade Cheese, combined his lifelong love of cheese and his business savvy to become the only artisanal cheese producer in Seattle. Fresh cheese is made every day of the week at the cheese factory and store in the heart of the Pike Place Market.

Beecher's Handmade Cheese

1600 Pike Place

Seattle, WA 98101

(206) 956-1964

beecherscheese.com

Kurt and the resident experts at Beecher's tasted many wines before deciding on the perfect one to pair with their bread salad, a hearty version thanks to the addition of Beecher's fresh cheese curds or fresh mozzarella. Syncline Viognier, a "cult" wine made by Poppie and James Mantone in the Columbia Gorge region of Washington State (see page 114), was the clear winner, while Sauvignon Blanc came in a close second.

Summer Bread Salad

SERVES 8   VARIETAL Viognier or Sauvignon Blanc

5 large heirloom tomatoes, cored and diced, plus any accumulated juice (about 6 cups)

1 teaspoon kosher salt

4 ounces plain homemade or store-bought croutons (see Cook's Hints, below)

1 ripe avocado, peeled, pitted, and cut into ¼-inch cubes

8 ounces Beecher's Plain Fresh Curds, or 8 ounces fresh mozzarella bocconcini (½-ounce balls), or 8 ounces fresh mozzarella, torn into bite-sized pieces

1 tablespoon minced fresh cilantro or flat-leaf parsley

1 tablespoon minced fresh chives

3 tablespoons extra virgin olive oil

1 tablespoon white wine vinegar

Freshly ground black pepper

Place the tomatoes and their juice in a large nonreactive mixing bowl. Add the salt, toss gently, and let rest for 5 minutes. Add the croutons, avocado, cheese curds, cilantro, and chives to the tomato mixture. Add the olive oil, vinegar, and black pepper to taste and toss gently.

Allow to rest at room temperature for up to 1 hour to allow the flavors to meld before serving, or cover and refrigerate for several hours or overnight, allowing the salad to come to room temperature before serving.

Cook's Hints: (1) For enhanced tomato flavor, after salting the tomatoes, drain the tomato liquid into a small saucepan or skillet. Cook slowly over medium heat until the liquid is reduced by half. Cool to room temperature, then pour the reduced tomato juice over the salad mixture before adding the olive oil and vinegar. This adds to the salad's savory flavor without creating excess liquid in the bowl. (2) To make homemade croutons, cut plain, crusty French bread into bite-sized cubes and toss lightly with olive oil. Place on a baking sheet and toast in a 375°F oven, tossing occasionally, for 10 to 15 minutes, or until crisp and golden brown. For oil-free croutons (which work well in poultry stuffings and dressings), simply cut the bread into bite-sized cubes and dry in a 200°F oven, tossing occasionally.

O ne evening, I enjoyed this succulent salmon entrée at the Oceanaire Seafood Room in downtown Seattle over a bottle of Panther Creek Pinot Noir (see page 144). The former executive chef, Kevin Davis, created the recipe to bridge the gap between Oregon Pinot Noir and fatty Alaskan salmon. "Think smoky, nutty, bacon, dried-cherry essence, and salmon. It's all there!" Kevin enthuses. Chef Kevin suggests that if you find yourself craving this dish any other time of the year, it works well with any wild salmon. Fresh Bing or Rainier cherries or dried cranberries (sometimes referred to as "craisins") can be substituted for the dried cherries. For a decidedly Northwest twist, you can substitute Northwest-grown hazelnuts for the smoked almonds.

Chef Kevin and wife Terresa have since opened the Steelhead Diner in an atmospheric space in the Pike Place Market with peek-a-boo views of Puget Sound and the Olympic Mountains. The playful menu, an intriguing combination of Northwest cuisine and Cajun influences, includes a cadre of local specialty foods, many sourced from the Market neighborhood. Beecher's fresh cheese curds are flash fried and served with hot-sweet mustard vinaigrette; Frank's Veggie "Meatloaf" is a hearty terrine of vegetables sourced at Frank's Quality Produce; the batter for the "Fish and Chips" is made with Kilt Lifter Scotch-Style Ale from the Pike Pub & Brewery. The outstanding wine list, comprised entirely of Northwest wines, is overseen by Restaurant Manager Aaron Angelo, who also concocted the cocktail menu. Don't miss the Grand Coulee Martini, named in honor of Washington State's famous Grand Coulee Dam. It's made of white truffle-infused vodka and garnished with Copper River salmon-stuffed olives!

**The Oceanaire
Seafood Room**

1700 Seventh Avenue

Seattle, WA 98121

(206) 267-BASS

oceanaireseafoodroom.com

Steelhead Diner

95 Pine Street, Suite 17

Seattle, WA 98101

(206) 625-0129

steelheaddiner.com

Wild King Salmon with Macerated Cherries and Smoked Almond Beurre Noisette

SERVES 4   VARIETAL Pinot Noir

Macerated Cherries

1 cup dried cherries (Chukar brand preferred)

1 cup port or Madeira

Four 8-ounce Yukon River King salmon or other wild salmon fillets (center cuts preferred)

To prepare the Macerated Cherries, place the dried cherries in a heatproof nonreactive bowl. Bring the port to a boil and pour over the cherries. Cover with plastic wrap and steep for 30 minutes. Cover and refrigerate if not using immediately.

Prepare a medium-low fire in a gas or charcoal grill. Brush the salmon with the olive oil and season with salt and pepper. Place the fillets on the grill skin side down away from direct heat. Cook for 3 to 4 minutes, turn the fish, and cook for 3 to 4 minutes more (for medium rare), or to the desired doneness.

2 tablespoons extra virgin olive oil

Kosher salt

Freshly ground black pepper

8 tablespoons (1 stick) unsalted butter

1 teaspoon chopped fresh rosemary, or ½ teaspoon dried rosemary, crumbled

Freshly grated zest of 1 orange

1 cup smoked almonds, lightly crushed (Blue Diamond Smokehouse brand preferred)

While the fish is grilling, melt the butter in a medium skillet over medium-high heat. Cook until the butter turns brown and gives off a nutty aroma. This is called *beurre noisette* in French, and translates as "brown butter." Remove the skillet from the heat and add the chopped rosemary, orange zest, almonds, and Macerated Cherries (drained and patted dry) in that order, pausing between each addition and stirring gently to allow each ingredient to render its essence into the butter. Be careful when adding the first two ingredients, as the butter may sizzle and pop. Season to taste with salt and pepper.

Place the salmon fillets on 4 dinner plates, top with the brown butter, and serve immediately.

Cook's Hint: Yukon River King salmon has a very high fat content and will tend to flame up if cooked too fast. It's always a good idea to have a water bottle handy, just in case. Don't leave the grill unattended at any time throughout the cooking process. Also, Chef Kevin has an easy way to prevent overcooking fish. Simply turn the grill off when the fish is slightly underdone; this allows the carryover heat to finish cooking the fish.

A Victorian-style mansion houses the tasting room, gift shop, and cellars at Columbia Winery in Woodinville, Washington.

Originally known as Associated Vintners, Columbia Winery was founded in 1962 by ten friends, six of whom were University of Washington professors. David Lake, nicknamed "the dean of Washington wine" by *Wine Spectator* and *Decanter* magazines, came on board as winemaker in 1979. For 20 years, he was the only Master of Wine actually making wine (as opposed to selling it or working in the restaurant industry) in North America. Although Lake retired in 2006 after 27 vintages with Columbia Winery, his erudite thoughts on food-and-wine pairing remain invaluable. I can imagine his cultured British accent as he says, "Wine should enhance the pleasure of good food just as food should enhance the enjoyment of wine. Many modern, international-style wines are made for show, not for drinking.…Columbia Wines are made for drinking and not for show. The dry whites are genuinely dry without a trace of residual sugar, and are designed to finish cleanly and crisply to contrast with and complement the food. Our red wines possess adequate underlying acidity to freshen fruit flavors and balance alcohol and flavor intensity." This arugula salad, developed especially for the winery by longtime local chef Tom Black (Fullers, Barking Frog, see page 48), is a true work of art. The aromatic lemongrass creates a beautiful floral complement to the slightly bitter arugula, while the goat cheese forms a creamy bridge of all the flavors. Pair the salad with Columbia Winery Pinot Gris, which exhibits "aromas of spicy grapefruit with notes of peach and melon. It's fresh, full-bodied, and round with a crisp, lively finish," according to the winemaker's notes.

Columbia Winery
14030 Northeast 145th Street
Woodinville, WA 98072
(425) 488-2776
columbiawinery.com

Arugula Salad with Lemongrass Vinaigrette and Goat Cheese

SERVES 4 to 6   VARIETAL Pinot Gris

Lemongrass Vinaigrette

2 stalks fresh lemongrass or 2 Meyer lemons, skins scrubbed with a soft brush and patted dry

½ cup water

½ cup sugar

1 tablespoon minced shallots

1½ teaspoons white wine vinegar

2 tablespoons canola or vegetable oil

To make the Lemongrass Vinaigrette, remove the tough outer leaves of the lemongrass. Trim about 2 inches from the stem end and 6 inches from the top and discard. (You should have about 8 inches of lemongrass left.) Bruise the remaining portion by tapping quickly with the back of a large kitchen knife 10 to 12 times. Cut one of the lemon grass stalks in half lengthwise. Lay the pieces cut side down and cut each piece in half lengthwise again. Repeat with the remaining lemongrass stalk. Gather the pieces together, line them up, then cut the stalks into ¼-inch slices. (If using Meyer lemons, with a clean vegetable peeler, remove the skins of each lemon. Stack several pieces of peel and cut into fine slices. Repeat with the remaining pieces.)

Place the water and sugar in a small saucepan and add the lemongrass (or lemon peels). Bring to a rolling boil, stir until the sugar is dissolved, and cover. Remove the pan from the heat, and allow the liquid to cool to room temperature.

4 to 6 ounces arugula or baby or regular spinach leaves (see Cook's Hint, below)

½ cup (2 ounces) fresh, young goat's-milk cheese, such as chèvre

Transfer the lemongrass mixture to a fine-meshed sieve placed over a mixing bowl and strain the juice into the bowl, pressing the solids with the back of a spoon to remove as much of the liquid as possible. Remove the sieve and discard the solids.

Add the shallots and vinegar to the bowl and whisk well. Continue to whisk while adding the oil, a few drops at a time, whisking well after each addition, or until the vinaigrette is smooth and pale straw in color. Use immediately or cover and refrigerate for up to 2 days to allow the flavors to meld.

To make the salad, place the arugula in a large mixing bowl and toss with several tablespoons of the vinaigrette, or to taste. Divide the salad among 6 salad plates. Crumble the goat cheese over the arugula and serve.

Cook's Hint: Arugula is grown in sand and can be difficult to clean if you don't buy the kind that is already prewashed and bagged. When buying arugula in bunches, I like to fill a large mixing bowl (or clean kitchen sink) with cold water. Divide the bunch of arugula into quarters and, grasping one of the quarters by the stem end, dunk it until the leaves are clean. Tear off the root ends and discard. Fill the basin with clean water and rinse the individual leaves, then spin them in a salad spinner. (This cleaning method also works well with bunches of fresh spinach, which are also often very sandy.) There is also waste when you buy arugula in bunches; I found that 4 ounces of arugula in a bunch yielded about 2½ ounces of cleaned arugula.

Columbia Winery's long-time winemaker and Master of Wine, David Lake, attends an exhibit at Seattle's Museum of History and Industry that highlighted his many contributions to the development of the Washington wine industry.

The people behind the three Purple Cafés take their wine very seriously; indeed, the restaurants are named for the color of grapes. Café menus are eclectic and Northwest inspired, designed to pair with an extensive global wine selection that includes 75 wines by the glass (including K Vintners Syrah, L'Ecole No. 41 Cabernet, and Tsillan Chardonnay), daily-changing wine flights, and 300 bottle selections. The atmosphere at the café locations, in Kirkland, Woodinville (the heart of Woodinville wine country), and downtown Seattle, is often described as an urban retreat with rustic elements—wrought-iron furniture, brick walls, and concrete tabletops. The Seattle location is particularly dramatic, with a 20-foot, 5,000-bottle spiraling wine tower as the focal point. Since opening, it's quickly become the living room of downtown, the perfect place to drop in for a glass of wine, quick bite, full meal, or after-theater dessert. Purple's Baked Brie is an appetizer designed to share; managing partner Larry Kurofsky reports it is wine friendly, easy to make, and very popular at his restaurants. Larry likes to pair it with a dry Gewürztraminer or Viognier. Other standouts on Executive Chef Robb Kirby's menu include Grilled Flank Steak Skewers with Soy-Honey Marinade; Mixed Greens with Apples, Candied Walnuts, and Stilton with Champagne Vinaigrette; Pan-Seared Duck Breast with Honey-Lavender Sauce; and Chicken Caprese. Winemaker's dinners and wine-education classes are also offered at Purple.

Purple Café & Wine Bar

323 Park Place
Kirkland, WA 98033
(425) 828-3772

14459 Woodinville-Redmond Road
Woodinville, WA 98072
(425) 483-7129

1225 Fourth Avenue
Seattle, WA 98101
(206) 829-2280
thepurplecafe.com

Baked Brie with Candied Walnuts and Caramelized Onions

SERVES 2 to 4 as an appetizer   VARIETAL Dry Gewürztraminer

1 tablespoon vegetable oil

1 small white or yellow onion, very thinly sliced

Pinch of kosher salt

4 sheets phyllo dough

6 tablespoons clarified butter, melted (see Techniques section, page 256)

One 4- to 8-ounce wheel of ripe Brie or Brie-like cheese (such as Camembert), or one 4-ounce wedge of ripe Brie

Heat the oil in a medium skillet over medium heat. When the oil is hot, add the onion and salt and cook, stirring occasionally, until the onions are tender and golden, 25 to 30 minutes; adjust the heat if necessary so the onions don't brown too quickly or burn. Set aside.

While the onions are cooking, arrange the oven rack in the center of the oven. Preheat the oven to 450°F. Spray a baking sheet with nonstick cooking spray or line with parchment paper.

Lay the phyllo dough on a clean, damp kitchen towel on a dry work surface and cover with another damp kitchen towel. Lay a sheet of dough on the baking sheet. Brush the dough lightly with melted butter. Place a second piece of dough across the first piece of dough to form a cross shape and brush lightly with butter. Place a third piece of dough diagonally over the cross and brush

1½ to 2 tablespoons apricot glaze, apricot jam, or orange marmalade (Note: If using jam or marmalade, stir or whisk it until it loosens enough to spread.)

3 to 4 tablespoons Candied Walnuts (recipe follows)

Fresh fruit of your choice, such as red grapes, apple slices, or pear slices

Baguette slices or crackers

lightly with butter. Place the fourth piece of dough diagonally over the third piece of dough (to form an "x" shape) and brush lightly with butter.

Cut the Brie horizontally through the middle to form a top and bottom layer. Place the bottom layer of brie in the center of the phyllo dough. Brush with the apricot glaze, and arrange 2 to 3 tablespoons of the reserved onions and the Candied Walnuts evenly over the glaze. Cover with the top layer of brie.

Form a beggar's purse by gathering all eight ends of phyllo dough, bringing them together over the top of the brie, and pinching them together until the brie is totally encased in dough. Brush lightly with butter. If using a cut piece of brie (as opposed to a round of brie), place the phyllo package in the refrigerator for 30 minutes to 1 hour before proceeding with the next step.

Cover loosely with aluminum foil and place in the oven for 5 minutes. Remove the foil and continue baking for 1 to 2 minutes, or until the phyllo turns golden in color.

Remove from the oven and transfer to a serving plate. Arrange the fresh fruit and baguette slices around the brie and serve immediately.

Candied Walnuts

MAKES 3 cups

1 large egg white

1 cup whole walnuts

¼ cup granulated sugar

2 tablespoons firmly packed light or dark brown sugar

½ teaspoon pure vanilla extract

Preheat the oven to 300°F. For easy cleanup, line a rimmed baking sheet with aluminum foil or parchment paper and spray with nonstick cooking spray.

In a small mixing bowl, whisk the egg white until light and frothy. Add the walnuts and mix well. Sprinkle the nuts with the granulated sugar and brown sugar, add the vanilla, and stir until the walnuts are evenly coated with sugar.

Arrange the walnuts in a single layer on the baking sheet without crowding and cook for 5 minutes. Remove from the oven and stir the nuts. Continue cooking, stirring the nuts every 5 minutes, for a total of 25 to 30 minutes of cooking time, or until the walnuts no longer look moist and are medium caramel in color.

Remove from the oven and transfer the baking sheet to a wire rack. When cool enough to handle, break apart the nuts, then dry completely on the baking sheet on the wire rack. Store in an airtight container at room temperature until serving.

Cook's Hint: You will have leftover Candied Walnuts. They are delicious sprinkled around the Baked Brie, simply eaten out of hand, tossed with salads (Purple adds them to their Apple-Walnut-Stilton Salad), or used as a topping for ice cream or frozen yogurt. Leftover caramelized onions make a nice topping for crostini (see Techniques section, page 257) or simply grilled meats, or they can be added to soups or stews.

Executive Chef Robb Kirby and Wine Director Christine Larsen work together to ensure optimum food-and-wine pairings at the three locations of Purple Café & Wine Bar.

The husband-and-wife team of Chris Upchurch and Theodora ("Thea") van den Beld personify the Northwest lifestyle. Chris is the winemaker and one of the partners at DeLille Cellars in Woodinville, Washington, where he's won numerous awards for his French-styled wines. DeLille currently produces five Bordeaux-styled wines, including Grand Ciel, Chaleur Estate Red, D2, Harrison Hill, and Chaleur Estate Blanc. The Doyenne wines include a classic Northern Rhône-styled Syrah, a Châteauneuf-du-Pape-styled red named Métier, a Provence-styled white named Métier Blanc, a Roussanne, and a Provence-styled red named Aix. Thea is a former longtime Seattle caterer and restaurateur (Baci Catering, Theoz, and the Yakima Grill) and one of the most gracious hostesses in town. This dynamic duo spent two years constructing a new home in Kirkland, Washington, because Chris was tired of "cookie-cutter tract homes" and Thea wanted to create "a winemaker's house." So when Chris and Thea invited us over for dinner to celebrate the Christmas holidays and to see the new house, we accepted with great anticipation.

Chris, who does all of the cooking, runs the gamut of cuisines from "lots of French and some Italian to Thai and Chinese." He's the kind of guy who makes his own breakfast pastries and roasts his own coffee. "Roasting is like oaking wine," Chris explains. "Most people overdo it." Thea more than lived up to her promise of creating "a winemaker's house." The residence includes towering 200-year-old front entryway doors from Pakistan and an eclectic blend of art, including a commanding tapestry from Bordeaux, a South China house god from the 1800s (he "keeps out evil spirits, but not teenagers," Chris quips), an etching by Cézanne, and a 250-year-old Buddha that the couple traded for a case of DeLille wine during a visit to China. While seated around the massive dining-room table (an import from Thea's native Holland), Chris served the soup that follows, Lamb Popsicles with Fenugreek Sauce (a recipe from Vij's, one of the couple's favorite restaurants in Vancouver, British Columbia), and the most decadent "chocolate decadence" cakes I've ever tasted. Chris paired the soup with Chateau Ste. Michelle Eroica (see page 60). The award-winning Riesling is the product of a partnership between the American

DeLille Cellars

P.O. Box 2233

Woodinville, WA 98072

(425) 489-0544

delillecellars.com

winery and Dr. Ernst Loosen, a legendary German winemaker. When I tested Chris's recipe at home, I paired it with DeLille Chaleur Estate Blanc, Chris's skillful blend of Semillon and Sauvignon Blanc. Spencer and I both loved the harmony between the thick, gingery soup and the slightly spicy, viscous wine, which shines with just a hint of petrol in the nose and palate.

Butternut Squash Bisque

2 medium butternut squashes, halved and seeds removed (about 6 cups flesh)

2 tablespoons unsalted butter

2 large leeks (white parts only), cleaned and chopped

2 tablespoons grated fresh ginger

6 cups homemade chicken stock or reduced-sodium chicken broth

1 to 2 teaspoons kosher salt

Sour cream, for garnish

Candied ginger, minced, for garnish (optional)

Preheat the oven to 400°F. Line a baking sheet with aluminum foil and place the squash halves flesh side down on the foil without crowding. Place in the oven and cook for 45 minutes to 1 hour, or until very tender. Scoop out the squash and reserve. Discard the skins.

Heat the butter in a stockpot over medium heat. Add the leeks and cook, stirring occasionally, until translucent, about 3 minutes. Add the ginger, stir well, and cook, stirring occasionally, until the leeks are tender but not browned, about 7 minutes more. Add the squash and 4 cups of the chicken stock, stir well, and cook for 20 minutes. Cool slightly.

Being very careful, transfer the hot soup in batches to a food processor or blender and pulse until smooth. Return to the stockpot and add the remaining 2 cups of chicken stock and 1 teaspoon of the salt. Taste and add additional salt if needed. Cook for 5 minutes, or until heated through.

Divide among 6 soup bowls and dollop with sour cream. If desired, sprinkle with candied ginger.

Chris Upchurch, co-founder of and winemaker for DeLille Cellars in Woodinville, Washington, is an award-winning winemaker who enjoys roasting his own coffee beans almost as much as blending Bordeaux varietals.

John Sarich, Culinary Director at Chateau Ste. Michelle (CSM) winery in the Woodin-ville wine country, is a pioneer in the field of food-and-wine pairing, as well as a beloved culinary icon in the Northwest and around the world. John joined CSM as a winery guide in 1976, the summer the winery first opened its doors. Thanks to his obvious enthusiasm for and knowledge about food and wine, he quickly rose through the ranks by teaching cooking classes, then serving as a food-and-wine consultant for chefs up and down the West Coast. After opening two groundbreaking restaurants in the early 1980s (Adriatica in Seattle and Dalmacija Ristoran in the Pike Place Market), John returned to CSM in 1990 as Culinary Director. "It's incredibly exciting to live in the Pacific Northwest," he says. "Not only do we have an outstanding variety of ingredients from the land and sea, we also have exceptional wines from Washington's Columbia Valley, where long summer days and crisp autumn nights produce ideal conditions for well-balanced wines."

Nowadays, John teaches cooking classes, conducts wine-and-food tastings and winemakers' dinners, presents training seminars, and hosts the nationally and internationally syndicated television show *Best of Taste: Travels With John Sarich*. He's also the author of four cookbooks, including *Entertaining Simply—Celebrate the Season* (Sea Hill Press, 2001). But instead of using a recipe from one of his books, I asked him for a recipe he makes often at home. Almost immediately he sent several options; the halibut (below) was the very dish he was making for dinner that evening! You'll want to make it from the beginning of the fresh halibut season in March to the end of the run in November. It also works well with fresh wild Northwest salmon. John suggests serving this with vine-ripened sliced tomatoes, cooked pasta tossed with olive oil and Par-mesan cheese, a good loaf of bread, and Greek olives. The white bean side dish not only makes a great accompaniment to the halibut, but also for grilled meats such as pork tenderloin or a leg of lamb or lamb chops.

Chateau Ste. Michelle

14111 Northeast 145th Street

Woodinville, WA 98072

(425) 415-3636

ste-michelle.com

Pesto-Glazed Halibut with Puttanesca White Beans

SERVES 6   VARIETAL Sauvignon Blanc or Syrah

Puttanesca White Beans

4 Roma tomatoes, cored and diced

1 bunch green onions, bottom ½ inch and top 1 inch trimmed; remaining portion cut into ½-inch slices

To make the Puttanesca White Beans, in a medium mixing bowl, add the tomatoes, green onions, olive oil, balsamic vinegar, olives, basil, parsley, oregano, capers, garlic, and cumin and mix well. Marinate for up to 1 hour at room temperature or refrigerate for several hours or up to 1 day.

Heat an outdoor grill to medium or an indoor stove-top grill to medium-high.

¼ cup extra virgin olive oil

2 tablespoons balsamic vinegar

2 tablespoons chopped kalamata olives or other good-quality black olives

2 tablespoons chopped fresh basil

2 tablespoons chopped fresh flat-leaf parsley

1 tablespoon chopped fresh oregano or 1½ teaspoons dried oregano, crumbled

1 tablespoon capers

2 teaspoons chopped garlic

⅛ teaspoon ground cumin

Two 14-ounce cans Great Northern (white) or navy beans, rinsed and well drained

½ cup homemade or store-bought basil pesto sauce

½ cup Sauvignon Blanc

¼ freshly squeezed lemon juice

⅛ teaspoon kosher salt

⅛ teaspoon ground cumin

Six 4- to 5-ounce halibut fillets or steaks, rinsed and patted dry

In a small mixing bowl, whisk the pesto, Sauvignon Blanc, lemon juice, salt, and cumin until well mixed. Transfer half of the glaze to another small mixing bowl, cover, and reserve.

Lightly oil the grill, then place the halibut flesh side down (if using fillets) and cook until the fish begins to turn opaque on the outside, 4 to 5 minutes. Turn and brush the fish liberally with one of the small bowls of glaze. Cook for 2 minutes, then brush again. Continue cooking until the fish is opaque on the outside, but still slightly translucent in the middle (for medium-rare fish), 2 to 3 minutes more.

To finish preparing the beans, a few minutes before the fish is finished cooking, heat a large saucepan over medium-high heat. Add the tomato mixture and cook, stirring constantly, until just warmed through (you do not want the tomatoes to cook!), 1 to 2 minutes. Add the beans and stir well.

To serve, place the beans in the center of 6 dinner plates. Arrange the fish over the beans. Pass the reserved bowl of glaze at the table for drizzling on the fish.

Glasses of Chateau Ste. Michelle's Cold Creek Cabernet Sauvignon are lined up for a wine tasting in Cold Creek Vineyard north of the Yakima Valley.

Nestled in the heart of Woodinville wine country, Barking Frog is located 15 miles north of Seattle. Its next-door neighbors include Willows Lodge (an 86-room Northwest-style lodge voted one of the World's 50 Most Romantic Getaways by *Travel + Leisure* magazine) and The Herbfarm (which has garnered four stars from *Mobil Travel Guide,* Fodor's, *Best Places Seattle, The Seattle Times,* and the *Seattle Post-Intelligencer,* plus the coveted AAA Five-Diamond Award). The surrounding area boasts 30 wineries (including Chateau Ste. Michelle, Columbia Winery, and DeLille Cellars), Red Hook Brewery, and Molbak's regional garden center. Woodinville wine country is the perfect place to escape the city and spend the weekend touring, tasting, and relaxing, and Barking Frog is a big part of the region's success. The restaurant has brought home awards for "Most Innovative Wine List" and "Washington Wine First" from the venerable Washington Wine Commission.

In keeping with the wine, dishes on Chef Bobby Moore's menu are earthy and full flavored. Begin your meal with Lamb Loin Carpaccio or Dueling Foie Gras, followed by Pancetta-Wrapped Rabbit Loin or Wild Japanese Sea Bass. Seating around a fire pit at the restaurant's center further punctuates the wine country feeling and the rustic charm of a country lodge. Chef Bobby's lamb burgers make an intriguing alternative to beef burgers, with the added attraction of a peppery bite from the toasted mustard seed. They are great as adult appetizers, or for small children to introduce them to new tastes in an attractive (and kid-sized!) package. Of course, the burgers can also be formed into regular-sized patties, enough to feed four. Leftover marinated onions can be served as a condiment with grilled fish, chicken, or meat dishes, or tossed in salads.

Barking Frog
14582 NE 145th Street
Woodinville, WA
(425) 424-2999
willowslodge.com

Petite Lamb Burgers with Red Wine Onions

SERVES 8 as an appetizer; 4 as a main course   VARIETAL Cabernet Sauvignon

Roasted Garlic Mayonnaise

3 to 4 cloves roasted garlic (see Techniques section, page 258), finely chopped to a smooth paste measuring 2 teaspoons

½ teaspoon freshly squeezed lemon juice

Pinch of ground white pepper, to taste

¼ cup homemade or prepared mayonnaise (Best Foods or Hellmann's brand preferred)

To make the Roasted Garlic Mayonnaise, in a small bowl, stir the garlic, lemon juice, and white pepper into the mayonnaise. Cover and refrigerate until serving.

To make the Red Wine Onions, in a small saucepan, bring the vinegar, wine, and sugar to a simmer. Place the onions in a small nonreactive mixing bowl and pour the hot liquid over the onions, making sure all the onions are submerged in the liquid. Cool to room temperature and set aside.

In a medium mixing bowl, combine the lamb, onion, mustard seed, salt, and pepper. Cover and refrigerate for 1 hour.

Divide the meat into 8 equal portions and form into patties about the same diameter as the dinner rolls you will serve them on. Heat a large heavy-bottomed

Red Wine Onions

½ cup red wine vinegar

½ cup dry red wine

3 tablespoons sugar

1 medium red onion,
very thinly sliced

1 pound lean ground lamb

½ cup minced white or yellow onion

¼ cup mustard seed, toasted
(see Cook's Hint, right)

1 teaspoon kosher salt

¼ teaspoon freshly ground
white pepper

1 tablespoon vegetable oil

8 small dinner rolls (about 2-inch
diameter), cut in half and toasted

½ cup (about 2 ounces) grated
Gruyère cheese

skillet over medium-high heat and add the oil. When the oil is hot, add the burgers without crowding, cooking in batches if needed, until browned, 1 to 2 minutes per side; then reduce heat to medium-low and cook until they reach the desired doneness, turning once or twice, 4 to 5 minutes more.

Spread 1 to 2 teaspoons of the garlic mayonnaise on the bottom half of each roll and top with about 1 tablespoon of the drained onions. Place the burgers over the onions, sprinkle the cheese on the burgers, and top with the remaining roll halves. Serve warm.

Cook's Hint: To toast mustard seed, place the seeds in a small skillet (with a lid) over medium heat. Stir with a wooden spoon until the seeds begin to pop. Cover with the lid, remove from the heat, and allow to cool.

Bobby Moore, Executive Chef at Barking Frog in Woodinville, Washington, puts the finishing touches on one of his signature dishes, Petite Lamb Burgers.

Bob Betz, M.W., winemaker/co-owner of Betz Family Winery in Woodinville, Washington, is an aficionado of his wood-burning oven, where he creates delectable thin-crusted pizzas, such as Pizza Rustica.

The Heart(h) of the Home

It's a long way from managing the Spaghetti Factory in Bellevue, Washington, to becoming one of only 260 Masters of Wine in the world, enjoying a successful 28-year-long career at Ste. Michelle Wine Estates (see page 60), and starting your own family-owned and -managed winery. But Bob Betz has seen and done all those things, well before the age of 60.

Betz Family Winery
P.O. Box 39
Woodinville, WA 98072
(425) 861-9823
betzfamilywinery.com

In addition to his vocational accomplishments, Bob is an excellent home cook. He likes to say that when he cooks, his kitchen "sings to you." One sunny spring evening, Spencer and I were "serenaded" with Bob and wife Cathy's expertly crafted food along with an amazing array of wines.

Dinner *chez* Betz began with flutes of Pol Roger Champagne paired with the winemaker's signature spicy shrimp. The shrimp were cooked in the couple's pride and joy—an Earthstone Model 110 wood-burning oven.

Il forno sits like an inverted Buddha's belly at the back of the Betzes' open his-and-hers kitchen. While Bob readied a trio of pizzas for the oven, we shared stories and sipped a bottle of Betz Family Winery's Beausoleil (bay-so-LAY). The bonny-bright Grenache-based wine with rich strawberry and plummy flavors proved as cheerful and sunny as its name, which translates from the French as "beautiful sunshine."

First out of the oven came a pizza topped with Bob's slowly simmered tomato sauce, fresh chèvre, oil-cured black olives, minced garlic, dried Greek oregano, freshly ground black pepper, and a sprinkling of freshly grated Parmigiano-Reggiano. It was a simple yet satisfying combination, with a nice char and a bit of puff to the crust.

Next came the pizza combo that started it all for Bob—tomato sauce, chunks of "real" mozzarella, minced garlic, dried oregano, black pepper, Parmigiano-Reggiano, and paper-thin slices of prosciutto.

Draped over the pizza immediately after removing it from the oven, the pale pink meat slowly wilted under the heat of the dough and formed a salty-crisp contrast to the melted cheese. Bob and Cathy first tasted this combination of ingredients at Forno al Legno, a modest pizzeria in Italy where foods prepared in the wood-burning oven captured the winemaker's heart and imagination.

Finally came a Northwest-inspired pie topped with fresh porcini mushrooms, sautéed and caramelized onions, olive oil, thyme, and a sprinkling of freshly grated Parmesan. We agreed that a drizzle of truffle oil, a last-minute inspiration, really made this tomato-sauce-free variation "sing."

After several slices of pizza, we moved out onto the Betzes' balcony to stretch our legs and partake of the encompassing views of the sunset and the Sammamish Valley. Rolling farmland spread out below us—a lush green blanket—while tall poplars stood like sentinels and the sweet smoke from the Earthstone scented the air.

Once back inside, Bob set about cooking the evening's entrée, marinated leg of lamb accompanied by giant portobellos. As the lamb and mushrooms sizzled inside *il forno*, Bob opened a bottle of La Serenne, his Syrah-based wine. Its deep color, carefully modulated fruit, and peppery notes proved yet again that Syrah is one of Washington State's premier grapes.

After the meat cooked to perfection, Bob arranged it on one of the rustic ceramic platters he and Cathy have collected during their 30 years of researching the world's finest wine regions. A hush fell over us as the lamb was brought to the table.

> " After several slices of pizza, we moved out onto the Betzes' balcony to ... partake of the encompassing views of the Sammamish Valley. "

Bob raised a bottle of 1998 Châteauneuf-du-Pape skyward and proclaimed, "This is the holy grail we all hope to attain." After sampling the wine's earthy and complex notes, all agreed the "grail" had been found.

Bob, the self-described "rustic cook born of a Neapolitan mother," ended the meal in typical Italian style with fresh strawberries drizzled with 75-year-old balsamic vinegar that Cathy imports through Primavera Imports, her olive oil and vinegar company; biscotti; and a 1983 (yes, 1983!) Sauternes.

From chilled Champagne to sweet Sauternes, a bit of "happy sunshine" had shone on us all that lovely spring evening, an evening of food, wine, and friendship that none of us would soon forget.

Pizza Rustica, one of Bob Betz's signature dishes, fresh from the winemaker's wood-burning oven.

Winemaker, Master of Wine, self-described "rustic cook," and wood-burning oven aficionado Bob Betz, co-owner, with wife Cathy, of Betz Family Winery in the Woodinville wine country just north of Seattle, has developed definite ideas about making pizza over the years. Among his tips are to let the dough fall into shape by stretching it with your fingers, rather than using a rolling pin. And don't worry about a perfect shape for your pizza pie—irregular shapes look and taste better, according to Bob! When choosing a wine to pair with his rustic-style pizza, Bob opts for Betz Family Winery's own Rhône-style blends of Syrah. His La Serenne is described as "meaty and smoky and a hint of wild spice," while La Côte Russe displays "profound blackberry and black cherry aromas, pure and penetrating. Syrah emerges as a roasted meat/violet/spice concerto that carries across to the flavor." Grenache is another good option, according to Bob. Betz Family Winery Beausoleil (bay-so-LAY) is "intense, with ripe strawberry and blueberry fruit aromas, with notes of earth, leather, and gravel."

Betz Family Winery
P.O. Box 39
Woodinville, WA 98072
(425) 861-9823
betzfamilywinery.com

Pizza Rustica with Tomato, Goat Cheese, and Black Olives

MAKES four 10-inch pizzas   VARIETAL Syrah

Tomato Sauce

3 tablespoons olive oil

1½ tablespoons chopped garlic

One 28-ounce can diced tomatoes

2 tablespoons chopped fresh basil, or 1 tablespoon dried basil, crumbled

1 tablespoon dried oregano, crumbled

Dash of kosher salt, plus additional for seasoning

Freshly ground black pepper

4 teaspoons chopped garlic

2 teaspoons extra virgin olive oil, plus extra for drizzling

To make the Tomato Sauce, heat the olive oil in a medium deep saucepan over medium heat. When hot, add the garlic and cook, stirring constantly, until the garlic turns golden brown, 1 to 2 minutes; do not allow the garlic to burn. Add the tomatoes, stir well, and bring to a simmer. Lower the heat and simmer very slowly (with barely an occasional bubble), stirring occasionally, for 1 hour. Add the basil, oregano, and salt and pepper to taste and stir well. Cook, stirring occasionally, until the sauce reduces and darkens slightly, but remains fairly chunky, with a bit of liquid, about 1 hour more.

Remove from the heat and cool slightly, then transfer to a food processor or blender and pulse until still slightly chunky (not entirely puréed). An immersion blender also works well for this job. Season to taste with additional salt and pepper, if needed.

Meanwhile, preheat a wood-burning oven to 550° to 650°F, or a conventional oven to 450° to 500°F.

To make the pizza, in a small bowl, stir together the garlic and olive oil and reserve.

Ten minutes before cooking, take one round of pizza dough and gently stretch it into a circle by holding the top edge of the dough and letting it

Pizza Dough (recipe follows)

Crushed red pepper flakes (optional)

1 to 1½ cups (4 to 6 ounces) soft, fresh goat's-milk cheese, such as chèvre

1 small red onion, very thinly sliced

¼ cup good-quality oil-cured black olives, pitted (Note: Be sure to use oil-cured, as opposed to brine-cured, olives, or they will dry out and wrinkle in the hot oven.)

4 teaspoons dried oregano, crumbled

Freshly ground black pepper

2 tablespoons freshly grated Parmigiano-Reggiano cheese (optional)

droop under its own weight to form a circle, quickly working around the circumference of the dough with your fingers.

Lay the dough on a well-floured flat surface and spread a thin layer of the tomato sauce to within ¼ inch of the edge. Evenly distribute 1 teaspoon of the reserved garlic-and-oil mixture over the tomato sauce. If desired, sprinkle with red pepper flakes to taste. Divide the goat cheese into quarters. Divide one of the quarters into smaller pieces and evenly distribute over the tomato sauce.

Evenly distribute one-quarter of the onion slices and one-quarter of the olives over the pizza. Sprinkle evenly with 1 teaspoon of the oregano and pepper to taste. If desired, sprinkle with 1 ½ teaspoons Parmigiano-Reggiano. Drizzle with olive oil. Repeat this procedure with the three remaining rounds of dough.

If baking in a wood-burning oven, using a pizza peel, transfer the pizzas to the deck of the oven. Cook for 2 to 4 minutes, or until the toppings are slightly browned and bubbly and the bottoms are lightly browned. If baking in a conventional oven, transfer the pizzas onto lightly oiled baking sheets and cook for 10 to 14 minutes, or until the toppings are slightly browned and bubbly and the bottoms are lightly browned.

Remove the pizzas from the oven and serve whole (one per person), or allow to cool 2 minutes before cutting into slices.

Pizza Dough

MAKES enough for four 10-inch pizzas

3¾ cups all-purpose flour

½ cup semolina flour

1 teaspoon active dry yeast

1½ teaspoons kosher salt

½ teaspoon sugar

1½ cups cold water

2 tablespoons extra virgin olive oil

Place 2½ cups of the all-purpose flour, the semolina flour, and the yeast in a large mixer bowl with the dough hooks attached.

In a small bowl, dissolve the salt and sugar in the water. Add this mixture, along with the oil, to the mixing bowl. Combine on medium speed until well mixed, scraping down the sides of the bowl as needed.

Add the remaining 1¼ cups of the flour a few tablespoons at a time, until the dough comes together and forms a ball. (Note: It may not be necessary to use all the remaining flour.) Continue kneading until the dough becomes smooth and silky, 5 to 7 minutes.

Transfer the dough to a well-floured work surface and knead by hand a little longer, adding flour as necessary, until it forms a smooth texture and is easy to manage; it should feel neither too wet nor too dry.

Form the dough into a circle and divide into quarters. Form the quarters into balls and pat down slightly. Arrange without overlapping on a well-floured baking sheet, flour the dough balls well, and cover with plastic wrap so the dough is completely covered (so that the edges do not dry out) but not tightly wrapped (so the dough has room to expand). Place the baking sheet in the refrigerator for at least 18 hours and up to 3 days.

One hour before cooking, remove the dough from the refrigerator. Keep it in its wrapping, but allow to come to room temperature before proceeding.

Farmers' markets are popping up all over the Pacific Northwest; many offer a wide selection of organic fruits and vegetables.

Executive Chef Jerry Traunfeld's Scallops with Spiced Carrot-Dill Sauce is one of the most popular dishes on the menu, and the recipe the most requested, at the venerable Herbfarm in Woodinville, Washington.

C hef Jerry Traunfeld is the James Beard award-winning chef at The Herbfarm restaurant in Woodinville, Washington; the author of two cookbooks; and an all-around nice guy. In his second book, *The Herbal Kitchen: Cooking with Fragrance and Flavor*, the chef sings the praises of using fresh herbs in the home kitchen. The book's premise is that fresh herbs add so much vibrant flavor and aromatic appeal to a meal, they help keep prep time to a minimum. Jerry's latest is a chef's book that isn't "chef-y," with recipes that have been crafted to be easy enough for the home cook, yet enticing enough to serve at a gourmet restaurant. Indeed, a few of the recipes are streamlined versions of those prepared at the legendary Herbfarm, where Jerry creates four-hour, nine-course seasonal dinners that focus on a theme or an ingredient (such as Northwest truffles or Copper River salmon) combined with products from The Herbfarm's own kitchen garden, small local growers, and artisan purveyors. It's all served up in a cozily decorated country home located next door to the Willows Lodge (see page 48) in the Woodinville wine country.

Herbfarm co-owner Ron Zimmerman, a discerning connoisseur and wine collector, conducts a nightly food-and-wine talk, while wife and partner Carrie Van Dyck orchestrates the pre-dinner introduction and garden tour (not to be missed). The Herbfarm has garnered four stars from *Mobil Travel Guide*, Fodor's, *Best Places Seattle, The Seattle Times,* and the *Seattle Post-Intelligencer,* and the AAA Five-Diamond Award. Wine Press Northwest has awarded the restaurant "Best Northwest Wine List" for many years running. When asked about a wine pairing with this vibrantly colored, gently herbed and spiced seafood entrée, Jerry quickly replied, "Without question, this is a Riesling dish!"

The Herbfarm

14590 NE 145th Street

Woodinville, WA 98072

(425) 485-5300

theherbfarm.com

Sea Scallops with Spiced Carrot-Dill Sauce

SERVES 4   VARIETAL Riesling

2 cups fresh carrot juice (available at health-food stores, juice bars, and select grocery stores)

½ cup white wine

¼ cup diced shallots

One 2-inch piece cinnamon stick

2 star anise pods

2 whole cloves

¾ teaspoon kosher salt, plus extra for seasoning

Freshly ground black pepper

Pour the carrot juice and white wine into a medium saucepan and add the shallots, cinnamon stick, star anise, cloves, the ¾ teaspoon salt, and a few grindings of pepper. Bring to a boil, reduce the heat to medium, and simmer, stirring occasionally, until it is reduced to about 1 cup, 25 to 30 minutes. Set it aside while you cook the scallops.

Pull off the small white piece of muscle that is attached to the side of the scallops (some may not have it) and discard. Pat the scallops very dry on paper towels and season with salt and pepper. Heat a large skillet over medium-high heat. Swirl in the olive oil and carefully add the scallops, flat side down, in a single layer without crowding. Cook, without turning, until the bottoms turn a deep brown color, 2 to 3 minutes. Turn and brown on the other side, 1 to 2 minutes more. Transfer the scallops to a warm plate and let them rest while you finish the sauce.

1½ pounds fresh or thawed untreated (dry pack) sea scallops (see Cook's Hint, right)

2 tablespoons olive oil

2 tablespoons freshly squeezed lemon juice

4 tablespoons (½ stick) unsalted butter, cut into 1-tablespoon pieces

¼ cup coarsely chopped fresh dill

Bring the sauce back to a simmer over medium heat and add the lemon juice. Whisk in the butter, 1 tablespoon at a time. Place a fine-meshed sieve over the top of a blender container, and strain the sauce, pressing the solids with the back of a large spoon to remove as much of the sauce as possible. Discard the solids and blend the sauce for 30 seconds, or until smooth. Pour the sauce back into the saucepan and stir in 3 tablespoons of the dill.

Arrange the scallops on 4 warm serving plates. Ladle the carrot sauce around them and sprinkle with the remaining 1 tablespoon dill.

The award-winning Herbfarm restaurant in Woodinville, Washington, features four-hour, nine-course dinners paired with regional wines.

Executive Chef Jerry Traunfeld prepares scallops at The Herbfarm in Woodinville, Washington.

Cook's Hint: Whether using fresh or previously frozen sea scallops, it is important to use "dry pack" scallops, or the scallops will not brown (caramelize) properly, and will instead steam in their own juices. Scallops that have been treated with phosphates during processing absorb water. Not only do they not cook properly, but they also lack the fresh, sweet, and briny sea flavor of their dry-packed cousins. Sea scallops that are uniformly white in color, or that are displayed surrounded by juice, are most likely treated.

A honeybee gets ready to take a sip of nectar from a rosemary flower in The Herbfarm's prolific garden in Woodinville wine country, about 45 minutes from Seattle.

Borage, one of The Herbfarm's Vietnamese potbelly pigs, makes an appearance from behind his coffee bag–curtained doorway. Borage and his buddy Basil are reportedly training to be truffle hunters.

Washington State's oldest winery, Chateau Ste. Michelle (CSM) dates back to 1934 and produces nearly 30 different wines. The company owns 3,400 acres of vineyards in some of the most desirable areas in Washington State's Columbia Valley, including Cold Creek, Canoe Ridge Estate, and Horse Heaven Vineyards. The white wine–making operation, company headquarters, and a magnificent chateau/tasting room/gift shop are located in Woodinville, on 87 wooded acres that were home to Seattle lumber baron Frederick Stimson in the early 1900s. It's the kind of place where ornamental grapevines grow out front and peacocks stroll the palatial lawns. It's also the venue for a long-running summer concert series, cooking and wine-education classes, and numerous charity events, such as PICNIC and the Auction of Washington Wines.

Try these salmon cakes, created by CSM Executive Chef Janet Hedstrom, with CSM Cold Creek Vineyard Riesling. She says, "The Cold Creek Riesling, with its luscious fruit-forward nature, shows very well with the spicy flavors in this dish. Oftentimes the heat in a dish will overwhelm the fruit in a wine, but that is the reason Rieslings are such a great match with this type of food. Also, the Cold Creek Riesling's balance of sweetness and crisp acidity is a great way to showcase the rich, full flavors of our Northwest salmon. The aïoli is added to balance the dish, but it also serves to enhance the more complex flavors in the Riesling."

Chateau Ste. Michelle
14111 Northeast 145th Street
Woodinville, WA 98072
(425) 415-3636
ste-michelle.com

Spicy Salmon Cakes with Ginger Aïoli

SERVES 6 to 8 as an appetizer   MAKES 24 cakes   VARIETAL Riesling

Ginger Aïoli

½ cup homemade or regular or light mayonnaise (Best Foods or Hellmann's brand preferred)

2 tablespoons diced pickled ginger

2 teaspoons freshly squeezed lime juice

Kosher salt

1½ pounds salmon fillets, rinsed, patted dry, and pin bones removed

1 large egg, beaten until frothy

2 cups unseasoned soft (fresh) bread crumbs or panko (Japanese) bread crumbs (see Cook's Hints, right)

Arrange the oven rack in the center of the oven. Preheat the oven to 375°F.

To make the Ginger Aïoli, mix together the mayonnaise, pickled ginger, and lime juice in a small nonreactive mixing bowl and season to taste with salt. Cover and refrigerate until serving.

Using a baking pan with a rack, lightly oil the rack or spray with nonstick cooking spray. Arrange the salmon skin side down on the oiled rack without crowding. Transfer to the oven and bake for 30 to 35 minutes, or until the fish just flakes and is still slightly translucent in the center (medium rare). Allow the salmon to cool completely, then remove the skin and discard and flake the salmon into a large mixing bowl.

Add the egg and mix until thoroughly combined with the salmon. Add 1 cup of the bread crumbs, the cilantro, bell pepper, red onion, lemon juice, soy sauce, brown sugar, *sambal oelek,* red pepper flakes, black pepper, and salt, and mix until thoroughly combined. Do not worry about breaking up the large salmon flakes; it is easier to form the cakes if the salmon is very finely flaked.

1 bunch cilantro, stems removed
and discarded and leaves chopped,
plus extra leaves, for garnish

¼ cup diced red bell pepper

¼ cup diced red onion

3 tablespoons freshly squeezed
lemon juice

2 tablespoons soy sauce

2 tablespoons firmly packed light or
dark brown sugar

1 tablespoon *sambal oelek*
(see Cook's Hints, below)

2 teaspoons crushed red
pepper flakes

1 teaspoon freshly ground
black pepper

¼ teaspoon kosher salt

3 to 4 tablespoons vegetable or
canola oil

Divide the salmon mixture into 24 portions, form into balls, then press down lightly to form cakes. Transfer to a baking sheet, cover, and refrigerate for I hour.

Place several thicknesses of paper towels on a large plate or baking sheet. Place the remaining 1 cup of bread crumbs on a second large plate and coat 6 to 8 cakes with the crumbs, patting firmly so the cakes hold together.

In a large nonstick skillet, heat 1 tablespoon of the vegetable oil over medium heat. When the oil is hot, arrange the cakes without crowding and cook, turning once, until golden brown on both sides, 3 to 4 minutes total. Remove from the pan and drain on the paper towels. Repeat with the remaining cakes, wiping out the skillet with a clean paper towel between batches and adding fresh oil.

Arrange the cakes on a large platter to pass as appetizers, or divide among 6 to 8 salad plates. Pass the Ginger Aïoli alongside the cakes or drizzle it over the cakes and garnish with cilantro leaves.

Cook's Hints: (1) To make unseasoned soft (fresh) bread crumbs, tear slices of white or whole-wheat bread into chunks and place them in a food processor. Process until crumbs of the desired size form. Fresh bread crumbs can be stored in the refrigerator for up to a week; in the freezer, tightly wrapped, they keep for about six months. Panko bread crumbs are used in Japanese cooking. Coarse and crunchy, they are often used to coat foods before frying. (2) *Sambal oelek* is a condiment used in Indonesia, Malaysia, and southern India. It is made of red chiles, brown sugar, and salt, and is available at Asian markets, such as Uwajimaya in Seattle and Portland, and in the Asian section of many grocery stores.

Cherishing Chinook

Since 1983, the husband-and-wife team of Kay Simon and Clay Mackey have been quietly going about their work as winemaker and grape grower, respectively, at Chinook Wines in Washington's Yakima Valley. I first met the couple well over a decade ago when I took a cooking class at the original Herbfarm (see page 57), when it was still located in an atmospheric house in rural Fall City.

The class, billed as "an afternoon with the winemaker," was a real family affair as well. Not only Kay, but also Clay (who only half jokingly calls himself the CFO—chief forklift operator) and his parents were on hand to help. The foursome brought a taste of the Washington wine country to us city slickers by demonstrating their favorite recipes and serving lunch.

The meal began with a glass of Chinook's signature Sauvignon Blanc served with herb-flecked, home-cured cheese spread on yeasty, home-baked bread. The aromatic cheese and supple wine proved a simple, yet winning combination. We were off to a roaring start.

Next came Cornish game hens steeped overnight in a heady mash of crushed Bing cherries and white wine vinegar. As I took my first bite of hen hot off the grill, along with a sip of Chinook Merlot, I marveled at the sweet explosion of tastes and textures—earthy, sweet, succulent.

> "The aromatic cheese and supple wine proved a simple, yet winning combination. We were off to a roaring start."

I quickly realized that although Kay and Clay were passionate eaters and oenophiles, they were (refreshingly) neither food snobs nor cork dorks. While the couple gently tossed a cherry-studded salad and simmered a wine-based syrup for dessert, I sensed they shared a style of cooking I hadn't encountered in Seattle proper. For want of a better term, I deemed it "vineyard cooking." In many ways, the seedling of the idea for this book probably germinated at that very moment.

Vineyard cooking was simple, often only a handful of ingredients— but what ingredients! Fresh fruits and vegetables of the season were grown in Kay and Clay's extensive summer garden or purchased at their local farmers' market. Asparagus was cut the same day they ate it; eastern Washington tomatillos were chopped into salsa; locally grown eggplant, zucchini, and sweet and hot peppers caramelized on the grill; homegrown walnuts were tossed into desserts and breads. Meats came from their favorite meat market, sausage from the sausage maker, seafood (which they picked up during weekly wine deliveries to Seattle) from Mutual Fish Co.

The couple treated the foods gently, often wrapping them in grape leaves or using grape or cherry wood to produce fragrant smoke for grilling. I appreciated that their preparation techniques didn't call for a lot of fats and oils to cover up the inherent goodness of the ingredients. Chinook wines—designed to complement, not to overpower—were thoughtfully paired with each dish.

Over the years, as I ran into the duo at food-and-wine events, I learned that winemaker Kay was brought up in Marin County, California; graduated from the prestigious University of California at Davis enology program; and was the red-wine winemaker at Chateau Ste. Michelle before she and her husband founded Chinook Wines in 1983. Clay, a Navy brat who also went to UC Davis, worked as a vineyard manager in Napa before following the grapes to the burgeoning Yakima Valley wine industry in the late 1970s.

Since their first vintage 24 years ago, Kay and Clay have strived to handcraft well-balanced, fruit-driven wines from grapes grown on their property as well as sourced from leading Yakima Valley vineyards (Carter Family, Boushey, Upland). With a 3,000-case annual output, divided among eight wines, six varieties, and a proprietary blended red wine, Chinook easily fits within the "boutique winery" category. The wines' retail prices, however, do not enter that rarified air.

More than a decade after our initial meeting at The Herbfarm, Kay explained, "Food at Chinook is simple: homemade bread, with no butter; lettuce from the garden with a vinaigrette dressing; meats off the grill, since that is no muss/no fuss; and wine...the health aspects of which are always debated, but the mental-health aspects of which (we would argue) contribute to many relaxing, friendly episodes here at the winery and elsewhere, which makes everyone harmonious and glad to live in the Pacific Northwest."

Chinook Wines
P.O. Box 387, Corner of Wine
Country Road and Wittkopf Loop
Prosser, WA 99350
(509) 786-2725
chinookwines.com

Kay Simon, winemaker and co-owner with husband Clay Mackey of Chinook Wines, enjoys a summer dinner party at the winery's tasting room in Prosser, Washington.

R ock Cornish game hens take on an appealing crimson color when marinated overnight in a crushed-cherry mash. The birds develop even more flavor when cooked over a charcoal fire spiked with grapevine cuttings or moistened cherrywood chips to season the smoke. The dish is optimal for people who don't eat red meat but want a hearty, rich-tasting entrée with which to pair red wines, such as Chinook Merlot.

The hens are easier to split and skin if they are still partially frozen. Use dry paper towels to hold the flesh and skin as you pull it away, then allow the hens to thaw completely before marinating.

Chinook Wines

P.O. Box 387, corner of Wine
Country Road and Wittkopf Loop
Prosser, WA 99350
(509) 786-2725
chinookwines.com

Cherry-Marinated Game Hens

SERVES 6   VARIETAL Merlot

6 cups fresh Bing or sweet cherries (see Cook's Hint, below)

4 to 5 cups white wine vinegar

6 small (less than 1½-pound) rock Cornish game hens, left whole and skin removed, or 3 large (1¾-pound or more) rock Cornish game hens, split in half and skin removed

opposite: Cherry-Marinated Game Hens is one of the innovative dishes created by Kay Simon to go with the food-friendly, reasonably priced wines she crafts at Chinook Wines in the Yakima Valley.

Rinse and pat dry the cherries, then remove and discard the stems. Place the cherries in an extra-large (2-gallon), resealable plastic bag, seal the bag, and mash the cherry flesh (not the pits) with your hands, a meat mallet, or the back of a heavy skillet until the cherries break apart and release their juices. Pour in enough vinegar to cover the cherries and set aside.

Remove the neck and giblets from the hens and reserve for another use. Rinse the hens in cold water, then blot inside and out with paper towels, removing any excess fat from the cavities. Place the hens in the plastic bag, seal the bag, and place it in the refrigerator at least 4 hours or up to 24 hours, turning the bag several times.

Prepare a charcoal grill or position a rack in the center of the oven and pre-heat the oven to 400°F. Grill the birds over indirect heat, covered, until the thickest part of the thigh exudes clear juices when pricked and an instant-read thermometer measures 170° to 175°F, 25 to 35 minutes. Or arrange the hens without crowding on a lightly oiled baking sheet or in a shallow roasting pan and cook for 45 to 50 minutes. Remove the birds to a platter, tent with aluminum foil, and let stand for 10 minutes.

Serve one whole small or one-half large bird per person.

Cook's Hint: If fresh cherries are unavailable, substitute 8 cups of thawed frozen sweet cherries (not pie cherries), crushed and covered with 3 to 4 cups of white wine vinegar, as described above.

C ookbook author Erika Cenci is a chef and co-owner, with husband and general manager Jim, of A Touch of Europe Bed & Breakfast and Fine Dining Establishment in the heart of Washington's Yakima Valley. There's an otherworldly feeling as you drive through the Mansion District of Old Yakima. Lush lawns are studded with graceful maple, sycamore, and tulip trees. The sense of history continues as you enter the Cencis' Queen Anne Victorian home, built in 1889 and on the National Register of Historic Places. The couple's extensive collections of heirloom European silverware, crystal, and porcelain grace the tables and decorate the antique-filled mansion. President Theodore Roosevelt even met with one of the home's former owners, Mrs. Ina Williams, in the library here. She was the first woman legislator in the Washington State House of Representatives.

German-born Erika, a former caterer, and Jim opened the bed-and-breakfast in 1995, and since then it has become *the* place in the Yakima Valley to hold winemakers' dinners, three-course luncheons, and afternoon teas. Erica's cookbook is titled *A Touch of Europe Cookbook: Bringing Fresh to the Table Naturally.* At one of the chef's custom-designed, multi-course dinners in the fall of 2004, I enjoyed this sophisticated dish. Full of vibrant colors and lush textures, the soup features flavors of sweet watermelon, spicy/earthy arugula, and slightly salty crab. It is easy to make, yet elegant enough for company, the perfect dish for summer entertaining. The aromatic, mouth-filling characteristics of Viognier partner well here, while the starker flavors of Pinot Gris form a fitting contrast. The night of our dinner, it paired perfectly with Thurston Wolfe PGV, a very popular and pleasing Pinot Gris/Viognier blend (see page 78) and W. B. Bridgman Viognier, one of my favorite bottlings of one of my favorite varietals.

A Touch of Europe Bed & Breakfast and Fine Dining Establishment

220 North Sixteenth Avenue

Yakima, WA 98902

(509) 454-9775

(888) 438-7073

winesnw.com/toucheuropeb&b.htm

Chilled Yellow Watermelon Soup with Dungeness Crab and Watercress Coulis

SERVES 4 to 6   VARIETAL Viognier or Pinot Gris

Watercress Coulis

Leaves from 2 bunches watercress (about 8 firmly packed cups)

1½ teaspoons extra virgin olive oil

2 to 3 teaspoons water

Pinch of fine sea salt, plus extra for seasoning

To prepare the Watercress Coulis, in a food processor or blender, pulse the watercress leaves with the oil and 2 teaspoons of the water until the watercress is very finely chopped and slightly liquidy, scraping down the sides of the bowl as needed. Place a fine-meshed sieve over a small mixing bowl and strain the watercress, pressing the solids with the back of a spoon to remove as much liquid as possible. Discard the solids and add the remaining 1 teaspoon of water to the coulis as needed to obtain a pourable consistency. Stir in the salt, taste, and add more salt as needed. Cover and refrigerate until serving.

2 cups jumbo crabmeat, picked over for shells and cartilage

¼ cup fresh watercress leaves, chopped

1 tablespoon plus 2 teaspoons extra virgin olive oil

2 tablespoons plus 1 teaspoon aquavit (see Cook's Hint, below)

¾ teaspoon fine sea salt, plus extra for seasoning

½ teaspoon freshly ground white pepper, plus extra for seasoning

6 cups seeded and coarsely chopped yellow or red watermelon

¼ cup diced Walla Walla sweet onion or other variety of sweet onion, such as Maui or Vidalia

2 teaspoons minced garlic

2 tablespoons freshly squeezed lime juice

crostini (see Techniques section, page 257)

In a medium bowl, gently mix the crabmeat with the chopped watercress, 2 teaspoons of the oil, 1 teaspoon of the aquavit, ¼ teaspoon of the salt, and ¼ teaspoon of the pepper. Cover and refrigerate until serving.

Pulse the watermelon, onion, and garlic in a blender or food processor until smooth. Transfer to a large glass bowl. Stir in the lime juice, the remaining 1 tablespoon of the olive oil, and the remaining 2 tablespoons of the aquavit, plus the remaining ½ teaspoon salt and ¼ teaspoon pepper. Refrigerate the soup, uncovered, for about 2 hours. If desired, season with additional salt and pepper.

Place a 3-inch ring mold in the center of a shallow, chilled soup bowl and spoon the crab into the mold until full, packing down lightly with the back of a spoon (a 3-ounce ramekin or custard cup, lined with plastic wrap, can substitute if a ring mold is unavailable). Remove the ring (or the inverted ramekin) and pour the chilled soup around the crab without covering it completely. Drizzle the soup with the coulis and serve with crostini.

Cook's Hint: The soup may be made 1 day ahead, covered, and chilled until ready to serve. Depending on the Scandinavian country in which it is produced, aquavit is a clear, colorless to golden-colored liquor flavored with dill and coriander. It makes a bracing aperitif when served ice cold in small glasses, and in Scandinavian countries is traditionally paired with seafood. But beware the alcohol level (42 percent alcohol and 84 proof), which can sneak up on you when imbibing this smooth, elegant elixir. The national spirit of Denmark, the name "aquavit" translates from Latin as "water of life."

Paul Vandenberg, co-owner with wife Barbara Sherman of the family-owned and-operated Paradisos del Sol winery in the Yakima Valley, calls himself a winegrower, not a winemaker, since his philosophy is to keep the quality of the grape as the driving force in his wines. The rather opinionated winegrower claims his first venture into wine was with blackberries in 1968, he has made his living with fermented grapes since 1983, and he's collected pay from more than 10 Northwest wineries, sometimes working for wine! He went out on his own in 1999, making "mostly estate wine" primarily from grapes grown at Vineyard del Sol near Sunnyside, Washington. *Paradisos* is the Spanish derivative of a Persian word that means "walled garden." Paul says that when he walks through a vineyard, he feels like he's in a paradise.

The winegrower crafts Gerty del Sol (Gewürztraminer), Riesling, rosé, Cabernet Sauvignon, red blends, and Angelica G, a soft, sweet dessert wine, yet he has a particular penchant for Lemberger, a red varietal also known as Blue Franc in Germany, and little known outside Washington State. His Lot 2 Paradisos Red is a lively blend of 70 percent Lemberger (which imparts raspberry, spice, and roundness, according to the winegrower) and 30 percent Cabernet Sauvignon (which adds blackberry and plum flavors, body, and "grip"). Paul likes his Lemberger-based wines paired with Italian and Mexican cuisine, handmade sausages from Glondo's (www.glondos.com) in Cle Elum, Washington, or anything flavored with chipotle peppers. Hence, he created Chocolate Chipotle Cake, a riff on his grandmother's favorite chocolate cake recipe that is kicked up a notch thanks to the addition of red wine, chipotle pepper, and cinnamon. Pair the dark, spicy cake, bursting with the aromas and flavors of musky chipotle and dark chocolate, with an easy-drinking, fruity/spicy wine (such as Lemberger or a Lemberger blend) and indulge!

Paradisos del Sol

3230 Highland Drive

Zillah, WA 98953

(509) 829-9000

paradisosdelsol.com

Chipotle Chocolate Cake

SERVES 8 to 12   VARIETAL Lemberger

3 cups all-purpose flour

1 cup granulated sugar

¾ cup Dutch-processed cocoa powder, plus extra for sprinkling on the cake

2 teaspoons baking soda

1½ teaspoons kosher salt

½ teaspoon ground chipotle chile

Preheat the oven to 350°F.

In a large mixing bowl, sift together the flour, sugar, cocoa, baking soda, salt, chipotle, and cinnamon. In a small mixing bowl, mix together the water, oil, red wine, and vanilla. Make a well in the center of the dry ingredients, add the wet ingredients, and stir until just combined. Do not overmix, or the cake will be tough.

Pour the batter into an ungreased 9 x 12-inch baking pan and bake for 30 to 40 minutes, or until a toothpick or wooden skewer inserted in the middle comes out with just a few crumbs remaining.

¼ teaspoon ground cinnamon

2 cups water

¾ cup canola or vegetable oil

3 tablespoons red wine

1 tablespoon pure vanilla extract

Confectioners' sugar, for sprinkling on the cake

Cool on a wire rack for 10 minutes, loosen the sides of the cake with a knife, and turn the cake out onto the wire rack to cool completely. Sprinkle with confectioners' sugar and additional cocoa powder just before slicing and serving.

Berry-stained feet is the price you pay to participate in the annual grape-stomping contest at Claar Cellars in Zillah, Washington.

Ray's Boathouse's Retrospective of Northwest Wines, which celebrated its 20th year in 2006, is a unique and much-anticipated event. Early in January, Ray's invites local wine experts to do a blind tasting of close to 300 of the region's wines. Winning wines are paired with a menu created by Executive Chef Peter Birk (see page 22), and served as part of a two-night dinner series. In 2005, Hogue Cellars Columbia Valley Gewürztraminer was named the winner in the Riesling/Gewürztraminer category for the second year running. The medium-bodied, slightly sweet wine, with aromas and flavors of lychee and rose water backed by good acidity, was paired with Ray's Pastry Chef Marcia Sisley-Berger's innovative citrus-flavored cake. The cake can be flavored with either orange or lemon and is accompanied by cilantro-spiced pears and the citrus marmalade of your choice. It was no surprise when Hogue Cellars took home the gold; the Hogue family has been farming in the Columbia Valley for more than 50 years, ever since Wayne and Shyla Hogue scraped together enough money to buy 80 acres of hops. Son Gary chose to pursue a career in construction materials in Seattle; son Mike joined his father in farming, and planted his first grapes (six acres of Riesling) in the Genesis Vineyard in the Yakima Valley. He sold the grapes to other wineries, but was certain that Washington wines would one day stack up against those from Europe and California.

In 1981, Mike and a family friend made their first batch of Riesling in Mike's daughter's playhouse; in 1982, Mike informed Gary they were starting a winery and that Gary's sales expertise was needed; in 1983, a vacant building in Prosser was converted into The Hogue Cellars winery and tasting room. The young winery, the 19th bonded winery in Washington, began winning medals in wine competitions, and the number of cases continued to rise, from 2,000 in 1982 to 10,000 in 1984. In 1994, *Wine & Spirits* magazine named Hogue as one of its Wineries of the Year. By 1996, Hogue's production capacity rose to 405,000 cases. In 1998, *Wine & Spirits* again named Hogue as a Winery of the Year. In 2001, Hogue Cellars was purchased by Vincor International, Inc., a multinational wine concern based in Toronto. In 2002, production reached 570,000 cases. Even so, on a research trip to the Yakima Valley during harvest time, Mike Hogue took time out of his busy schedule to fly me and a group of wine writers over his beloved birthplace. Second-generation and ever-ebullient wine-grape grower Bill den Hoed gave running commentary as the beautiful landscape glided past.

The Hogue Cellars
2800 Lee Road
Prosser, WA 99350
(509) 786-4557
hoguecellars.com

Citrus Yogurt Cake with Baked D'Anjou Pears and Meyer Lemon Marmalade

SERVES 8   VARIETAL Gewürztraminer

Baked D'Anjou Pears

½ cup sugar

1 tablespoon ground coriander

4 ripe, firm D'Anjou pears, peeled, cored, and cut in half

1½ cups sugar, plus 1 tablespoon for coating the pan

1½ cups plain whole-milk yogurt (see Cook's Hint, below)

4 large eggs

2½ teaspoons freshly grated orange or lemon zest

1 teaspoon pure vanilla extract

2¼ cups all-purpose flour

1 tablespoon baking powder

Pinch of table salt

¾ cup vegetable oil

½ to ¾ cup Meyer lemon, grapefruit, or orange marmalade

Sweetened whipped cream, vanilla ice cream, or frozen yogurt, for serving (optional)

Preheat the oven to 350°F. Line a large baking sheet with aluminum foil (for easy cleanup) and grease or coat with nonstick cooking spray.

To make the Baked D'Anjou Pears, in a small bowl, mix together the sugar and coriander. Rub the sugar mixture over the pear halves. Arrange the pear halves, cut side down, on the prepared baking sheet. Bake for 12 to 15 minutes, or until a small, sharp kitchen knife is easily inserted, but the pears are not mushy. Allow the pears to cool completely at room temperature.

To make the cake, reduce the oven temperature to 325°F. Grease well or coat with nonstick cooking spray a 5 x 9-inch loaf pan or an 8- to 10-cup fluted tube or Bundt pan. Sprinkle the 1 tablespoon of sugar in the pan and turn to evenly coat the greased surfaces with sugar. Tap out and discard any excess sugar.

Add the 1½ cups of sugar, the yogurt, eggs, zest, and vanilla to a large mixing bowl. Stir with a wire whisk until thoroughly combined. In a separate bowl, stir together the flour, baking powder, and salt. Gradually whisk the dry ingredients into the wet ingredients to make a smooth batter. Do not overmix. With a rubber spatula, add the oil, stirring in gently and turning the mixing bowl as you add the oil (a technique known as "folding").

Pour the batter into the prepared pan and bake for 1 hour and 15 to 20 minutes if using a loaf pan, or 55 to 65 minutes if using a fluted tube or Bundt pan, or until a toothpick or wooden skewer inserted in the center comes out clean. Tent the cake with foil after 1 hour, if needed, to prevent over-browning.

Transfer the cake to a wire rack and cool for 10 minutes in the pan. Run a thin knife around the edge of the pan to loosen the cake. Turn out and cool completely, right side up, on the wire rack.

When the cake has cooled, cut it into individual slices and place one slice in the center of each small plate. Stir the marmalade well to loosen it or warm at 50 percent power in a microwave oven until softened. Spoon about 1 tablespoon of the marmalade over one side of each piece of cake, allowing a bit to overflow onto the plate. Slice each pear in half lengthwise, starting about 1 inch from the top of the pear and cutting into ¼-inch slices. Keep the top portion intact and spread out each sliced pear half to form a fan shape. Place a fanned pear half on top of the marmalade, propping it up against the cake. If desired, add a dollop of whipped cream, ice cream, or frozen yogurt.

Cook's Hint: Chef Marcia suggests that, for the best texture in the cake, choose a brand of yogurt that doesn't contain pectin or gelatin, such as Dannon or Nancy's.

This recipe, from the Chukar Cherry Company's handy cookbook, *The Chukar Cherry Recipe Collection: Year 'Round Northwest Cherry & Berry Classics,* makes use of two prototypical Northwest ingredients—dried cherries and hazelnuts. The nuts form a crispy crust on boneless, skinless chicken breasts, while the cherries are cooked in a white wine–based sauce redolent of thyme and shallots. Chukar's owner, Pam Montgomery (also known as "Ma Chukar"), likes to pair the chicken with white varietals such as Pinot Blanc or Chardonnay. I tried it with a mellow, cherry-scented Merlot with great success. Pam's crush on cherries began in 1986, when she and her young family purchased an 8,000-tree orchard in small-town Prosser, Washington. She formed Chukar Cherry Company in 1988, after experimenting with a dehydrator to dry fruit for year-round use and developing products for family and friends. Located in the heart of the state's fruit and wine country, the company's plant and tasting room is a "must" stop on the Yakima Valley wine trail. Samples of all the delicious cherry, berry, and chocolate creations are free-flowing, both there and at the company's permanent stand in the Main Arcade of the Pike Place Market.

Chukar Cherry Company

320 Wine Country Road

Prosser, WA 99350

(800) 624-9544

chukar.com

Hazelnut-Crusted Chicken in Cherry-Wine Sauce

SERVES 6 VARIETAL Pinot Blanc, Chardonnay, or Merlot

1 large egg white

1 cup hazelnuts or almonds, finely chopped

4 teaspoons olive oil

6 skinless, boneless chicken breast halves, rinsed and patted dry

1½ cups minced shallots

2 teaspoons minced garlic

1 cup dried tart cherries (Chukar brand preferred)

½ cup dry white wine

2 teaspoons minced fresh thyme, or 1 teaspoon dried thyme, crumbled

2 cups homemade chicken stock or reduced-sodium chicken broth

In a shallow dish, beat the egg white until pale and frothy. Spread the hazelnuts evenly over a large plate.

Heat 2 teaspoons of the olive oil in a large nonstick skillet over medium heat. Dip the chicken breasts in the egg, let the excess egg drip off, then lightly coat the breasts in the nuts. When the oil is hot, arrange the chicken in the skillet without crowding, or cook in 2 batches. Cook the breasts until browned on the outside but not cooked through, 4 to 5 minutes on each side. Remove from the heat, cover, and reserve.

While the chicken is cooking, heat the remaining 2 teaspoons oil in a heavy-bottomed medium saucepan over medium-high heat. Add the shallots and garlic and cook, stirring frequently and lowering the heat as needed, until softened but not browned, 5 to 7 minutes. Add the cherries, white wine, and thyme and stir well. Cook until almost all the liquid has evaporated, 1 to 2 minutes. Add the chicken stock and stir well. Add the cherry–chicken broth mixture to the reserved skillet containing the chicken breasts, cover, and simmer until the chicken is cooked through, 10 to 15 minutes. Gently turn the breasts two or three times while they simmer so they cook evenly and completely.

Place a chicken breast in the center of each dinner plate, surround with the sauce, and serve.

A bowl full of cherries from nearby trees mirrors the flavors in many of the award-winning red wines crafted at Chinook Wines in Prosser, Washington.

Hinzerling Winery is the oldest family-owned and -operated winery in the Yakima Valley, established in 1976. Winemaker Mike Wallace, who's been there from the onset, crafts an eclectic mix of wines, ranging from dry Gewürztraminer and Pinot Noir to authoritative Cabs. He's especially well known and regarded for producing yummy ports and sherries with evocative names such as Three Muses Ruby Port, which is used in the recipe that follows, and Rainy Day Fine Tawny Port. Mike bottles the latter, a double gold medal winner, from the oldest tier of a three-tier Spanish-style *solera* system he started 24 years ago, and he limits production to only 500 bottles a year! He even makes balsamic, sherry, and herbed vinegars. Mike and wife Frankie also operate the Vintner's Inn, Restaurant, and Wine Bar next door to the winery in Prosser. The restaurant (open Saturday evenings for reservation-only dining) features prix-fixe menus inspired by garden-fresh Northwest ingredients and local wines. The bed-and-breakfast inn houses two bedrooms with private baths, and a sumptuous continental breakfast is served each morning. But the inn's intentional lack of telephones and televisions is designed to help you "enjoy the quiet," according to Mike. The wine bar is open during harvest season (September and October) for light appetizers and a unique selection of Yakima Valley wines. Mike suggests pairing these jewel-colored poached pears topped with blue-cheese cream with a small glass of his Ruby Port.

Hinzerling Winery and the Vintner's Inn, Restaurant, and Wine Bar

1520 Sheridan Avenue

Prosser, WA 99350

(509) 786-2163

(800) 727-6702

hinzerling.com

Port-Poached Blue-Cheese Pears

SERVES 6   VARIETAL Port

4 cups water

2 tablespoons freshly squeezed lemon juice

6 firm, ripe pears, such as D'Anjou

2½ cups Hinzerling Three Muses Ruby Port or other good-quality ruby port

One 3-inch cinnamon stick

¼ teaspoon whole black peppercorns

About ½ cup (about 2 ounces) blue-veined cheese, such as Oregon Blue, Gorgonzola, Stilton, or Roquefort, crumbled

½ cup light cream cheese (Neufchâtel), at room temperature

In a large mixing bowl, combine the water and lemon juice. Peel the pears and remove the core from the bottom ends (a melon baller works well for this); leave the stems intact. Gently place the pears in the acidulated water. Combine the port, cinnamon stick, and peppercorns in a Dutch oven or stockpot large enough to hold the pears without crowding, and bring to a boil. Reduce the heat and simmer, uncovered, for 5 minutes. Gently add the pears and acidulated water, bring back to a simmer, and cover the pot, leaving the cover slightly askew so the steam can escape. Cook the pears, turning the fruit occasionally, until tender, 15 to 20 minutes. (To test for doneness, insert a small, sharp knife into the center of one of the pears.)

Carefully remove the pears with a slotted spoon and transfer to a shallow baking dish. Bring the cooking liquid to a boil, and cook until reduced to about ¾ cup, 25 to 30 minutes. Watch the pot carefully during the final minutes of cooking. Place a fine-meshed sieve over a bowl, strain the poaching liquid, and reserve. Discard the solids.

Pour the poaching liquid over the pears, cover, and refrigerate for 8 hours, turning the fruit once or twice as it chills.

Ten minutes before serving, in a food processor, pulse the blue and cream cheeses until smooth and creamy, scraping down the sides of the bowl as needed. Spoon the creamed cheese into a pastry bag with a small decorative tip. Divide the sauce (the poaching liquid) among 6 dessert plates. Cut the pears lengthwise into three or four wedges each and arrange on top of the sauce. Pipe the cheese in a decorative pattern onto the pears.

Cook's Hint: If you don't own a pastry bag, substitute a quart-sized resealable plastic bag. Simply spoon the creamed cheese into one corner of the bag, press out the air, cut a small hole in the tip of the bag, and gently squeeze the cheese in a decorative pattern on top of the poached pears.

A worker speeds down a row of vines to dump handpicked grapes into a storage bin.

During a trip to the Yakima Valley, I visited Thurston Wolfe Winery's tasting room and picked up the recipe for this flavorful, easy-to-prepare appetizer that makes a beautiful plate presentation. Since my visit, the winery has relocated to a new facility that features the 20-foot Black Galaxy tasting bar and a wine patio that boasts dramatic views of the Yellow Rose Nursery and the Horse Heaven Hills. Thurston Wolfe is a family-owned winery established in 1987 by Dr. Wade Wolfe and wife Becky Yeaman to realize their shared dream of producing unique, finely crafted wines in small-case lots. Together, they have coaxed outstanding wines from a number of grape varietals not commonly used at other Washington State wineries, such as Lemberger (Blue Franc), Petite Syrah, and Sangiovese. Wade has combined his extensive knowledge of area vineyards with a passion for blending to create truly memorable wines such as Dr. Wolfe's Family Red and PGV, a Pinot Gris/Viognier blend (see page 68). Among my favorite wines in their lineup is not only the PGV, but Sweet Rebecca, a lyrically fragrant and luscious dessert wine made from 100 percent Orange Muscat fortified with brandy during fermentation. Their goal of producing small lots of exceptional wines from the best vineyards in Washington State is fully realized in every vintage and has won them numerous awards; many of their wines sell out quickly.

Thurston Wolfe Winery
588 Cabernet Court
Prosser, WA 99350
(509) 786-3313
thurstonwolfe.com

This recipe comes from caterer Cathleen Williams, an energetic woman who offers cooking classes, runs an event-planning company, and "works a lot of wineries from Walla Walla to Yakima." For red-wine lovers, she recommends pairing her recipe with Syrah; white-wine lovers will prefer an unoaked Chardonnay. Meanwhile, Becky suggests pairing the torte with Lemberger or rosé, which simply goes to show the incredible versatility of Cathleen's recipe.

Sun-Dried Tomato and Pesto Torte

SERVES 16 to 20 as an appetizer   VARIETAL Syrah, Chardonnay (unoaked), Lemberger, or rosé

Three 8-ounce packages cream cheese, at room temperature

½ cup (2 ounces) freshly grated Parmesan cheese

1 tablespoon minced garlic

7 ounces homemade basil-based pesto, one 7-ounce container refrigerated basil-based pesto, or one 6.35-ounce jar basil-based pesto

One or two days before you plan to serve, line a 5-cup mold or medium mixing bowl with pieces of plastic wrap long enough to hang out over the sides (the long pieces will be used to wrap the torte). Place the cream cheese, Parmesan, and garlic in a food processor and pulse until well blended.

Spoon one-third of the cream cheese mixture into the bottom of the mold and smooth the top. Spoon the pesto evenly over the cream cheese layer. Spoon half of the remaining cream cheese mixture over the pesto and smooth the top. Evenly cover the second layer of cream cheese mixture with the sun-dried tomatoes. Spoon the remaining cream cheese mixture on top of the tomatoes and smooth the top.

One 8.5-ounce jar oil-packed sun-dried tomatoes, well drained and minced

2 large fresh basil leaves, for garnish

12 cherry tomatoes, for garnish

1 baguette, cut into ¼-inch slices, for serving

Carefully strike the filled mold on the countertop to pack down the layers. Bring the long ends of plastic wrap up and over the top of the torte to cover completely. Refrigerate for at least 24 hours to allow the flavors to meld.

Just before serving, unwrap the long pieces of plastic wrap, place a serving platter over the mold, hold the platter, and carefully flip the mold and platter. Remove and discard the plastic wrap. Garnish the torte with the fresh basil leaves and cherry tomatoes and serve with the baguette slices.

Cook's Hint: Caterer Cathleen Williams suggests making this torte up to 2 days ahead of time to allow the flavors to develop even further. You can vary the flavor of the torte depending on the type of pesto you choose. Use your own homemade version or try various other varieties, such as arugula or cilantro.

Sandy soil is one of the defining characteristics of the Horse Heaven Hills Appellation, south of the Yakima Valley and home to some of Washington State's best vineyards.

C hef Big John Caudill comes by his name naturally—he's a bigger-than-life personality who's cooked at wineries, charity events, and restaurants (and even owned one of his own) throughout the Washington wine country since 1989. I reconnected with him when I popped my head into the kitchen at Alexandria Nicole Winery's upscale tasting room and café in Prosser's quaint but ever-gentrifying downtown (the winery has since moved into a larger space in the Prosser Business Park). He and I started an e-mail correspondence about recipes he wanted to submit, and I got absolutely ravenous reading the possibilities. "Tenderloins stuffed with chèvre over portobello duxelles and a sweet sherry-balsamic gastrique is a Cabernet lover's dream," according to Big John. "My Walla Walla sweet onion torte with Gruyère and smoked bacon really highlights a buttery Washington Chardonnay. I have a Spanish spice rub that I use often on bone-in cuts of beef, normally a well-marbled rib-eye, and toss on the grill. I serve it with the local sweet gypsy peppers stuffed with cheese, sage, and prosciutto over a bed of wilted escarole. This dish begs for a beefy (pardon the pun) Washington Syrah…Whitman Cellars and Christopher Cellars come to mind." After lots of pleasant back-and-forth, the "Washington wine country chef," as he's known, and I finally decided on this summer sweet corn soup, which Big John likes to serve with grilled bread and a chilled glass of Apex II Sauvignon Blanc. Like the chef who created it, the soup boasts *big* flavors—sweet corn, salt, black pepper, and a piquant note of Tabasco—while the wine "is crisp and refreshing and balances out the creaminess of the soup very well," according to John. Those with timid palates might cut back on the black pepper and Tabasco the first time they make the soup, although I found their presence agreeably tongue-tingling and throat-warming.

Tasting Washington:
The Love of Wine & Food
P.O. Box 676
Outlook, WA 98938
(509) 949-7022
tasting-washington.com

Sweet Corn and Basil Bisque

SERVES 6 as an appetizer   VARIETAL Sauvignon Blanc

6 to 7 ears sweet corn, husks and strings removed and discarded, ears rinsed and patted dry

4 cups chicken stock or reduced-sodium chicken broth

2 tablespoons unsalted butter

¼ cup minced Walla Walla sweet onion or other variety of sweet onion

¼ cup minced shallots

1 tablespoon minced garlic

With a large, sharp kitchen knife, cut the kernels from the corn and save the cobs. Measure 4 cups of kernels and set aside. Save any remaining kernels for use in another recipe.

Bring the chicken stock to a simmer in a medium saucepan, add the corn-cobs (cut in half if needed to fit the pan), cover, and cook, stirring occasionally, until the stock is infused with the flavor of the corncobs, about 20 minutes. Strain the cobs and discard; keep the stock warm.

Melt the butter in a large stockpot or Dutch oven over medium heat. Add the onion, shallots, and garlic and cook, stirring occasionally, until softened but not browned, 4 to 5 minutes. Add the reserved corn kernels, the potatoes, 3

Wine country chef Big John Caudill cooks at a Washington Hills Cellars wine-tasting event in the Yakima Valley.

1 cup peeled and diced russet potatoes

1 teaspoon coarse kosher salt, plus extra for seasoning

1 teaspoon freshly ground black pepper, plus extra for seasoning

½ cup heavy whipping cream

1 teaspoon Tabasco sauce

2 tablespoons fresh minced basil, plus extra sprigs, for garnish

3 tablespoons crème fraîche or sour cream

cups of the warm stock, the salt, and pepper, and stir well. Bring to a simmer, cover, and cook, stirring occasionally, until the potatoes are very tender, 20 to 25 minutes.

Add the cream and Tabasco and stir well. In a food processor or blender, pulse the soup in batches until very smooth, adding the batches back to the stock-pot to re-warm. (An immersion blender also works well to purée the soup.) If needed, add some or all of the remaining 1 cup of chicken stock to thin the soup. Season to taste with salt and pepper, then gently stir in the basil.

Ladle the soup into 6 soup bowls, dollop with crème fraîche, and garnish with fresh basil sprigs.

Rulo Winery's Blue Cheesecake is a rich, creamy companion to both red and white wines, especially Sauvignon Blanc, Viognier, and Syrah.

O ne of Washington State's hottest boutique wineries, Rulo Winery was created by Kurt and Vicki Schlicker, who moved from California to Washington to fulfill their winemaking dream. The couple named their winery in honor of six landmark grain elevators in Walla Walla that Kurt remembered fondly from his childhood. The wine's names (such as Silo and Combine) and label designs continue the agrarian theme. Kurt, the winemaker, crafts gorgeous white wines—Viognier, Chardonnay, and white blends—as well as Syrah and red blends. "I want my wines to have life, each with a personality, wines that make people think a bit," Kurt explains simply. Originally titled Gorgonzola Cheesecake, this recipe originated at Paragon restaurant in Portland, but Kurt and Vicki have personalized it over the years. I've added a few Northwest touches, such as hazelnuts and Oregon Blue Vein cheese from Rogue Creamery (see page 160) to the merry mix. You can serve it as a rustic appetizer with crostini and crackers, but I like slicing it into narrow wedges and serving it with fresh fruits of the season as a savory dessert or cheese course. Pear or quince paste is also a tasty accompaniment. Blue Cheesecake is so versatile, it pairs well with either a red wine, such as Syrah, or a white, such as Sauvignon Blanc or Viognier.

Rulo Winery

3525 Pranger Road

Walla Walla, WA 99362

(509) 525-RULO (7856)

rulowinery.com

Blue Cheesecake

SERVES 12 to 16   VARIETAL Syrah, Viognier, Sauvignon Blanc

1½ cups water

½ cup medium-grind cornmeal

1 tablespoon chopped garlic

1 tablespoon dried basil, crumbled (optional)

1½ teaspoons *herbes de Provence*, crumbled

1½ teaspoons kosher salt

Three 8-ounce packages cream cheese, at room temperature

½ pound Oregon Blue Vein, Oregonzola, Gorgonzola, Roquefort, or other high-quality blue cheese, cut into chunks, at room temperature

3 large eggs

Bring the water to a boil in a small saucepan. Slowly stir in the cornmeal, stirring in one direction to avoid lumps, then add the garlic, basil, if using, *herbes de Provence,* and salt. Reduce the heat to a simmer and cook until smooth and creamy, stirring occasionally and adjusting the heat as necessary so the polenta doesn't overcook or bubble up and splatter, 12 to 15 minutes.

While the polenta is cooking, place the cream cheese and blue cheese in a large mixing bowl. Add the eggs one at a time and mix by hand (if you are very strong!) or beat with an electric mixer until the eggs are thoroughly incorporated. Set aside.

Arrange the oven rack in the center of the oven. Preheat the oven to 325°F. Lightly oil a 9-inch springform pan or spray with nonstick cooking spray.

When the polenta is done, remove it from the heat and stir in the Parmesan cheese. Let cool for 5 minutes. With a rubber spatula, press the polenta into the bottom of the prepared springform pan and set aside.

Pour the reserved cheese filling evenly over the polenta crust. Tap the pan lightly on the counter to remove any air bubbles. Squeeze the garlic cloves

¼ cup (1 ounce) freshly shredded Parmesan cheese

1 head garlic, cloves separated and roasted (see Cook's Hint, below)

½ cup whole hazelnuts, pine nuts, or almonds, toasted (see Techniques section, page 258)

crostini (see Techniques section, page 257) or crackers, for serving (optional)

from their skins and arrange them around the perimeter of the pan at equal distances. Sprinkle the hazelnuts evenly in the center of the cheesecake.

Place the cheesecake on a baking sheet to catch any drips, transfer to the oven, and bake for 1 hour, or until the cake springs back when lightly jiggled and the internal temperature on an instant-read thermometer reaches 160°F. Cool on a wire rack for at least 1 hour.

To serve, release and remove the sides of the springform pan. Serve the cheesecake warm or at room temperature, cut into slices as an appetizer or spread onto crostini or crackers for a more rustic look. The cheesecake can be covered and kept in the refrigerator for up to 1 week (its flavors meld and deepen the longer it sits). If serving from the refrigerator, slice and warm it in a 350°F oven or microwave briefly before serving.

Cook's Hint: To roast individual cloves of garlic, preheat the oven to 375°F. Remove as much skin as possible from each clove, place in a small baking dish without crowding (a pie plate also works well for this), cover tightly with aluminum foil, and bake until the garlic is very tender and easily squeezed from the skin, 35 minutes.

Rulo Winery's winemaker, Kurt Schlicker, enjoys a barrel sample with visitors in the Walla Walla tasting room and winery.

View of a red barn and horse from
Rulo Winery in Walla Walla.

Lunch at the chef's table at the Marcus Whitman Hotel & Conference Center capped off a memorable visit to Walla Walla, Washington. The Marcus Whitman is the kind of place where history meets modern technology in a beautiful and gracious way. Built in 1928, the area's only luxury hotel is named after Marcus Whitman, who established a mission among the Cayuse Indians near Walla Walla until he and his party met with their untimely deaths in 1847. "The Hotel" has hosted numerous dignitaries and celebrities during its lively history, including President Dwight D. Eisenhower, Vice President Lyndon B. Johnson, Louis Armstrong, and Shirley Temple, but had fallen into disrepair. Between 1999 and 2001, local businessman and entrepreneur Kyle Mussman, along with the City and Port of Walla Walla, restored and expanded the grand old building to its original classic elegance and style.

The Marc is the white-tablecloth restaurant at "The Hotel," overseen by Chef Hank ("Bear") Ullman, a gregarious bear of a man who spins art-quality wooden bowls (Bowls by Chef Bear) in his spare time. Bear's menu changes with the seasons, chock-full of the Valley's prime produce, meats, artisan cheeses, and wild Pacific seafood. Local and regional wines are important here; the restaurant has won the Washington Wine First award from the Washington Wine Commission. Along with winemaker Mike Neuffer of Nicholas Cole Cellars (see page 95) and General Manager Mussman, we enjoyed a lunch created by Chef Bear and paired with Mike's outstanding wines. Wild Pacific Salmon Gravlax with Lemon-Zest Brandy and Dill started the meal off in style. Separatist Duck Salad (seared duck breast and Medjool date confit with local organic greens) followed. Lemon Thyme Sorbet formed a nice intermezzo and palate cleanser. Stuffed Loin of Lamb, from which the recipe to the right is adapted, merged Anderson Ranch free-range lamb loin with a rich stuffing of porcini mushrooms, goat's-milk cheese from nearby Monteillet Fromagerie, manchego cheese, and blanched spinach. Choices from the Marc's elegant cheese cart and a final glass of Camille, Mike's Bordeaux-style blend named after his beloved grandmother, rounded out the extraordinary afternoon highlighting the Northwest's bounty in style. Chef Bear suggests serving the chops "with the biggest red in the house," along with roasted baby beets, carrots, and zucchini.

The Marc at the Marcus Whitman Hotel & Conference Center
6 West Rose Street
Walla Walla, WA 99362
(509) 525-2200
(866) 826-9422
marcuswhitmanhotel.com

Broiled Lamb Chops with Mushroom-Spinach-Cheese Sauce

SERVES 6   VARIETAL Cabernet Sauvignon

Twelve 1- to 1¼-inch-thick T-bone (loin), rib, or sirloin lamb chops

Kosher salt

Freshly ground black pepper

¾ pound fresh spinach leaves

2 tablespoons clarified butter (see Techniques section, page 256)

1 tablespoon minced shallot

1 teaspoon minced garlic

1½ teaspoons minced fresh thyme

¾ cup fresh morel or chanterelle mushrooms, well cleaned (see Cook's Hint page 219 for instructions on cleaning fresh wild mushrooms), or ½ cup dried morel or porcini mushrooms, well cleaned (see Cook's Hint, below)

1¾ cups heavy whipping cream

¾ cup (about 3 ounces) grated manchego cheese

3 ounces fresh, young goat's-milk cheese, such as chèvre

Arrange an oven rack on the top level, closest to the heat source. Preheat the broiler. Generously sprinkle the lamb chops with salt and pepper. Arrange the lamb chops on a large broiling pan with a rack large enough to hold the chops without crowding. Set aside.

Bring a large saucepan of water to a boil. Add half the spinach to the boiling water and cook until the spinach just turns bright green, 15 to 30 seconds. With a slotted spoon, immediately transfer the spinach to a bowl of ice water to cool. With a slotted spoon, remove the spinach from the water and transfer to a small mixing bowl. Repeat with the remaining spinach. Gather the spinach into fist-sized balls and squeeze until completely drained of water. When all the spinach is squeezed dry, you should have about 1 cup.

Heat a large skillet over medium heat and add the butter. When the butter is hot, add the shallots and garlic and cook, stirring constantly, until tender, 1 to 2 minutes. Add the thyme and stir well. Add the mushrooms and cook, stirring occasionally, until softened and most of the moisture has cooked out of the mushrooms, 3 to 4 minutes.

Add the cream and cook, stirring occasionally, until it is reduced by half to about 1 cup, 10 to 12 minutes. Watch carefully so the cream does not boil over. Add the spinach, stir well, and bring to a simmer. Remove from the heat and stir in the manchego cheese.

While the cream is reducing, transfer the broiling pan with the lamb chops to the broiler. Broil for 3 to 4 minutes per side, depending on the thickness and doneness preferred. Broiling for 4 minutes per side will yield medium-rare to medium chops.

Just before serving, crumble the goat's-milk cheese into the sauce and stir gently once or twice, just until small lumps of cheese remain. Divide the sauce among 6 dinner plates, arrange the lamb chops over the sauce, and serve immediately.

Cook's Hint: Chef Bear prefers using fresh morels for the sauce, but chanterelles also work, or even dried mushrooms. To substitute dried mushrooms in this recipe, choose morels or porcinis and place them in a small glass bowl. Cover with warm water or chicken or beef stock and let rest until softened, 15 to 30 minutes. Remove the mushrooms from the soaking liquid and agitate in several changes of fresh, cold water, until the water runs clear of grit (it will still be light brown in color). Cut off the tough stems (if needed),

(continued from previous page)

and chop or use whole. The liquid adds additional flavor to soups or stews, but is often sandy. So pour slowly (until you get to the grit in the bottom), or strain through a fine-meshed sieve lined with several thicknesses of cheesecloth before using.

Hank "Bear" Ullman, Executive Chef at the Marc Restaurant in Walla Walla, Washington, sharpens a knife while working the line.

Myles Anderson and Gordon (Gordy) Venneri are the owners of and wine-makers at Walla Walla Vintners, where they have been making award-winning red wines since 1995, including Merlot, Cabernet Franc, Cabernet Sauvignon, Sangiovese, and red blends. They're considered old-timers, since back then they were only the eighth winery to have been bonded in the Valley; now there are more than eighty, with eight to ten more in the planning phase. Before producing wine commercially, the duo made wine at home on a very small scale for years, as nothing more than a hobby. This experience allowed them to practice their winemaking, take their mistakes to the dump, and forge a successful partnership. The affable Gordy, a C.P.A. and former insurance agent, met us for dinner at Whitehouse-Crawford restaurant (see page 98) in downtown Walla Walla one lovely spring evening. Of Italian heritage, he got hooked on winemaking when he visited the mother country in 1981 and met his cousins, who were making their own wine. "I consider wine a food," he says simply. When Myles and his wife joined us later in the evening for dessert, Myles (a retired businessman) told me he loves to cook, everything from rack of lamb and Caesar salads to terrines and pâtés. Considered difficult and time consuming to make by many cooks, soufflés are part of his repertoire, and something he makes at least once a week!

Although Gordy described Cab Franc as "the Rodney Dangerfield of wines," it is perhaps the duo's most celebrated variety. Their 2003 vintage was rated "Outstanding" by *Wine Press Northwest* for its "aromas of black currants, oak, and a hint of smokiness and herbs, followed by flavors of dark, ripe berries and adroitly handled oak. The sweet tannins are there but not aggressive, providing the perfect foil for a grilled T-bone with sautéed mushrooms on the side." It's also a perfect foil for Myles's fluffy, luscious cheese soufflé, served, as the winemaker suggests, with fresh asparagus spears from the Walla Walla Valley. Be sure to have all your ingredients prepped ahead of time, as this recipe goes together quickly once you begin cooking.

Walla Walla Vintners

225 Vineyard Lane

Walla Walla, WA 99362

(509) 525-4724

wallawallavintners.com

Egg White Cheese Soufflé

SERVES 6 to 8   VARIETAL Cabernet Franc

3½ tablespoons unsalted butter, plus extra for greasing the soufflé dish

4 tablespoons freshly grated Parmesan cheese

1 cup plus 2 tablespoons half-and-half

Place the oven rack on the bottom rack of the oven. Preheat the oven to 375°F. Generously butter a 10- to 12-cup soufflé dish, then sprinkle the sides and bottom with 2 tablespoons of the Parmesan cheese, shaking the soufflé dish so the cheese coats the inside of the dish evenly. Tap out any excess cheese.

In a small saucepan, bring 1 cup of the half-and-half just to a simmer, remove from the heat, and cover. Melt the remaining 3½ tablespoons butter in a large saucepan over medium heat. Whisk in the flour a little at a time to prevent lumps from forming. Remove the pan from the heat and add the hot half-and-

4½ tablespoons all-purpose flour

Kosher salt

Freshly ground white pepper

Freshly ground nutmeg

12 jumbo egg whites, separated

2 cups (about 8 ounces) grated Gruyère cheese

Hollandaise Sauce (see page 194)

half all at once, whisking until it is smooth and thickened. Add the additional 2 tablespoons half-and-half if the sauce becomes too thick. Add a pinch or two of salt, several grinds of white pepper, and a couple of gratings of fresh nutmeg and set aside.

With an electric mixer, beat the egg whites until stiff peaks form. (Be sure the mixer bowl and beaters are scrupulously clean or the whites may not whip to stiff peaks.) Stir the Gruyère into the white sauce in the saucepan. When totally incorporated, gently fold one-third of the egg whites into the white sauce. Gently fold the remaining egg whites into the white sauce to form the soufflé mixture. Do not worry if the sauce and egg whites are not totally mixed; you want the whites to retain as much volume as possible to produce a light, fluffy soufflé.

Gently pour the soufflé mixture into the buttered soufflé dish, smoothing the top with a spatula. Place the soufflé in the center of the oven rack and cook for 25 to 30 minutes, or until the soufflé puffs and turns golden brown on top. Quickly open the oven and sprinkle the top of the soufflé with the remaining 2 tablespoons Parmesan cheese. Gently close the oven door and bake the soufflé for another 5 minutes, or until the cheese is lightly browned. Serve immediately with the Hollandaise Sauce.

A Cabernet Franc grape cluster

The Inn at Blackberry Creek in Walla Walla, Washington, offers guests the relaxing ambience of a quiet country setting while affording them proximity to Pioneer Park, Whitman College, a bustling downtown, and award-winning wineries within a five-mile radius. The inn, housed in a beautifully restored Victorian farmhouse (circa 1906), offers three spacious rooms. All include private baths and king-sized beds with puffy down comforters, are decorated with antique furnishings, and boast views overlooking the formal rose gardens or spring-fed creek, where pheasant, quail, raccoons, owls, rabbits, squirrels, goldfinches, and blue jays make frequent appearances. With a vintage radio tuned to old-time standards playing in the parlor, a cookie jar of fresh-baked goodies always ready for raiding, and complimentary hot coffee, tea, and cocoa at any hour, the Inn rivals the best bed-and-breakfast inns found in Napa and Sonoma and parts of Europe. Three idyllic days at the Inn left me hungry for more of innkeeper Barbara Knudson's sumptuous breakfast dishes—Smoked Pork Chops, Housemade Granola, or Egg Dish of the Day—which she prepares to order for her guests every morning. Barbara's quiche, which she likes to pair with fresh melon and French pastries, focuses on a few of the spring vegetables common in the Valley. It reheats well, and also makes a great light lunch when served with sliced melon and tomatoes, along with a glass of Cougar Crest Winery Viognier.

Inn at Blackberry Creek

1126 Pleasant Street

Walla Walla, WA 99362

(509) 522-5233

(877) 522-5233

innatblackberrycreek.com

Fresh Asparagus and Walla Walla Sweet Onion Quiche

SERVES 6 to 8   VARIETAL Viognier

1 large red potato

2 tablespoons unsalted butter, melted

¼ teaspoon kosher salt, plus extra for seasoning

¼ teaspoon freshly ground black pepper, plus extra for seasoning

1 cup (about 4 ounces) grated Jarlsberg cheese

1 teaspoon canola or vegetable oil

Preheat the oven to 375°F. Lightly oil a 9-inch deep-dish pie pan or a 9-inch springform pan. If using the latter, wrap the outside with aluminum foil to catch any drips.

Peel the potato and cut it into paper-thin slices by hand or with a mandoline. Arrange the slices in a swirling pattern on the bottom of the pie pan, overlapping the slices. Brush the potatoes with the melted butter, sprinkle lightly with salt and pepper, transfer to the oven, and cook for 12 to 15 minutes, or until lightly browned and just tender. Remove from the oven and sprinkle evenly with the Jarlsberg cheese.

Meanwhile, heat the oil in a small nonstick skillet, add the asparagus and onion, and cook, stirring often, until the onion is tender and lightly browned and the asparagus turns bright green, 5 to 7 minutes. Lightly season with salt

8 to 10 asparagus stalks, woody stems broken off and discarded, remaining portion cut into 1-inch pieces, enough to measure 1 cup

⅓ cup coarsely chopped Walla Walla sweet onion or other variety of sweet onion, such as Maui or Vidalia

5 large eggs

1½ cups half-and-half

½ cup plus 1 tablespoon freshly grated Parmesan cheese

3 dashes of Tabasco sauce

and pepper and stir well. Arrange the asparagus-onion mixture evenly on top of the cheese and potatoes.

In a medium mixing bowl, whisk together the eggs, half-and-half, the ½ cup of Parmesan cheese, the ¼ teaspoon of the salt, the ¼ teaspoon of the pepper, and the Tabasco. Pour over the asparagus mixture and sprinkle with the remaining 1 tablespoon Parmesan cheese. Place on a baking sheet to catch any drips, and bake for 35 to 40 minutes, or until a knife inserted in the center comes out clean and the sides of the quiche are golden brown and puff slightly.

Transfer to a wire rack and allow to cool for 5 to 10 minutes, then slice and serve.

Since 1983, L'Ecole No. 41, an award-winning Walla Walla Valley winery known for its Semillon, Cabernet Sauvignon, Merlot, and Bordeaux blends, has been producing premium, handcrafted varietal wines in the historic Frenchtown School in Lowden, Washington.

S tanding amid the lush grapevines in his hillside vineyard in the Walla Walla Valley, with nonstop views of Mt. Rainier and Mt. Adams and Leonetti Cellar as a next-door neighbor, winemaker/owner Mike Neuffer feels like a latter-day pioneer. Compared to his fellow winemakers in Napa and Sonoma who have many more years of experience under their belts and in their barrels, Walla Walla is a young grape-growing region. Yet the successful third-generation homebuilder from Reno, Nevada, who's had a lifelong passion for wine and describes himself as "a part-time cellar rat," just felt like he was home when he first discovered the Valley in 2000. He bought his parcel of land in 2001, planted estate grapes, and waited for his first harvest in 2005. Meanwhile, assisted by mentor and friend Chris Camarda of Andrew Will Winery fame, the two used grapes from some of the best vineyards in the state to craft carefully blended, Bordeaux-style red wines. Mike founded the winery—named after his son, Nicholas, and daughter, Michelle Cole—in part with the idea of building an agrarian-based business that could carry over to the next generation. In 2004, Nicholas Cole Cellars 2001 Claret received 93 points from *Wine & Spirits* magazine, and was followed (after a name change to honor his grandmother) with the release of the 2002 vintage of Camille, an ultra-premium blended red wine made of Merlot, Cabernet Sauvignon, and Cabernet Franc, in 2004. GraEagle RedWing, a Merlot/Cabernet Sauvignon blend aged in 100 percent French oak, is Mike's "second-label" bottling, priced for more casual drinking and immediate enjoyment thanks to its soft tannins, ripe fruit, and full flavor.

Nicholas Cole Cellars

705 Berney Drive

Walla Walla, WA 99362

(509) 525-0608

nicholascolecellars.com

The winemaker's lamb stew—a toothsome, Mediterranean-leaning concoction of lamb, sun-dried tomatoes, and large butter beans—is one he has served at all his Holiday Barrel Taste Weekends, although "stew" may be a bit of a misnomer, since it's a refreshingly quick-cooking dish. Mike reports, "It has garnered rave reviews from my customers, some of whom have threatened bodily injury if I refuse to share the recipe with them. The second year I had it printed up and available upon request."

Lamb Loin Stew with Sun-Dried Tomatoes and Butter Beans

SERVES 4   VARIETAL Cabernet Sauvignon

3 tablespoons olive oil

2 cups chopped yellow onion

2 large cloves garlic, minced

1 pound boneless lamb loin, trimmed and cut into 1/3-inch strips

Heat the olive oil in a large skillet over medium heat. Add the onion and cook, stirring frequently, until slightly softened, 5 to 7 minutes. Add the garlic and cook, stirring constantly, until softened but not browned, 1 minute. Increase the heat to medium-high. Add the lamb and sprinkle with the salt and pepper. Cook until browned on the outside but still pink within, 1 to 2 minutes per side.

½ teaspoon kosher salt, plus extra for seasoning

¼ teaspoon freshly ground black pepper plus extra for seasoning

10 sun-dried tomato halves packed in oil, drained and cut into thin strips (San Remo brand recommended)

½ cup chicken stock or reduced-sodium chicken broth

½ cup loosely packed fresh basil leaves, stacked and rolled like a cigar and cut into thin strips, plus extra basil leaves, for garnish

One 15-ounce can butter beans, rinsed and drained

Add two-thirds of the sun-dried tomatoes, the stock, and one-half of the basil and stir well. Cover and simmer over low heat for 10 minutes. Add the beans, the remaining sun-dried tomatoes, and remaining basil and stir well. Cook until heated through, 1 to 2 minutes more. Season to taste with salt and pepper.

Ladle the stew into 4 bowls, garnish with the fresh basil leaves, and serve.

Cook's Hint: Mike suggests that rabbit, duck, beef, or venison can be substituted for the lamb in this dish; chicken and pork are too bland. Home-made lamb stock or store-bought veal demi-glace also works well in place of the chicken stock. The dish is wonderful to serve to company when accompanied by crusty artisan bread and a simple green salad. To extend the stew to serve more than four people, serve it over egg noodles, plain rice, or couscous (in keeping with the Mediterranean flavors), or accompanied by new potatoes roasted with olive oil, garlic, and fresh rosemary.

Marie-Eve Gilla, Forgeron Cellars' winemaker, her husband Gilles Nicault, a winemaker with Long Shadows Vintners, and their dog keep it all in the family.

Mike Neuffer, winemaker/owner of Nicholas Cole Cellars in the Walla Walla Valley, bought his parcel of land in 2001 and harvested his first estate-grown grapes in 2005.

Whitehouse-Crawford restaurant in downtown Walla Walla, Washington, is the kind of place where the local winemakers hang out, exchanging tastes of the wine they've produced, ordering an extra glass or bottle off the Walla Walla–centric wine list, all the while enjoying a beautifully crafted meal brimming with the best in local produce, seafood, and meat. Wine is taken seriously yet lightheartedly here; Napa Valley Cabernets are listed under "Other Reds." Chef Jamie Guerin spent six years at Campagne, a long-running French restaurant in Seattle's Pike Place Market, before heading East (of the mountains). His menu features bright, bold flavors with bursts of heat from the local hot peppers. He follows the seasons with starters such as Walla Walla Asparagus Soup with Fresh Mint or Warm Spinach Salad with Smoked Trout, Bacon, Grilled Onions, and Mustard Dressing. Entrées might include Green Mole Enchiladas Filled with Spinach and Goat Cheese or Roasted Pheasant Breast with Green Apple Risotto.

The restaurant's dining room is the epitome of wine-country décor; a former planing mill (circa 1904 and restored in 2000), it is listed on the National Register of Historic Places and boasts soaring ceilings, distressed rafters, red-fir floors, and sepia-toned photos of the old mill. Whitehouse-Crawford shares space with Seven Hills Winery, which specializes in finely crafted varietal wines and Bordeaux-style blends. Its 100-year-old barrel room is visible through floor-to-ceiling paned-glass doors in the restaurant. Many people think it is difficult to pair wine with salads. But "bridge" ingredients, such as the walnut oil, toasted nuts, goat cheese, and cherries found in Jamie's salad recipe here can help link the greens with the wine. The idea of "bridge" ingredients originated with California chef John Ash, a pioneer of the concept of food-and-wine pairing. The founder of John Ash & Company restaurant in Sonoma County, long-time culinary director for Brown Forman wines, award-winning cookbook author, syndicated writer for the *Los Angeles Times*, and cooking teacher has most recently become known as a winemaker thanks to his participation in Sauvignon Republic Cellars.

Whitehouse-Crawford

55 West Cherry Street

Walla Walla, WA 99362

(509) 525-2222

whitehousecrawford.com

Seven Hills Winery

212 North Third Avenue

Walla Walla, WA 99362

(509) 529-7198

sevenhillswinery.com

Organic Greens with Goat Cheese, Walnuts, and Pickled Cherries

SERVES 4   VARIETAL Riesling (dry), rosé, Sauvignon Blanc, or Semillon

Pickled Cherries

1 cup red wine vinegar

1 cup red wine

To make the Pickled Cherries, combine the vinegar, wine, water, sugar, cinnamon stick, allspice, cloves, peppercorns, bay leaves, and salt in a medium saucepan, stir until the salt is dissolved, and bring to a boil. Turn off the heat, cover, and allow to steep for 15 minutes. Place the cherries in a large mixing

½ cup water

½ cup sugar

1 cinnamon stick

3 whole allspice berries

3 whole cloves

3 whole black peppercorns

2 bay leaves

1 tablespoon kosher salt

1 pound fresh, sweet red cherries, rinsed and with stems left on, or ¼ to ½ cup dried cherries

Walnut Vinaigrette

¼ cup red wine vinegar

¼ cup pickled cherry spice brine (see Pickled Cherries, above) or fresh cherry juice (see Cook's Hint, right)

1½ tablespoons Dijon mustard

1 tablespoon honey

Pinch of kosher salt, plus extra for seasoning

Pinch of freshly ground black pepper, plus extra for seasoning

½ cup walnut oil

½ cup light olive, canola, or grapeseed oil

8 ounces mixed organic salad greens

1 cup (4 ounces) Quillisascut goat's-milk cheese or other fresh (chèvre) or aged goat's-milk cheese

¼ cup walnut halves, lightly toasted (see Techniques section, page 258)

12 pickled cherries or fresh red cherries, pitted and halved

bowl. Strain the spice brine over the cherries, making sure all the cherries are submerged in the liquid. Allow the cherries to sit at room temperature for 3 to 4 hours before using. Place leftover cherries in a clean glass jar, cover with the spice brine, and refrigerate for up to 1 week.

To make the Walnut Vinaigrette, in a medium mixing bowl, whisk the vinegar, spice brine, mustard, honey, salt, and pepper until the honey is dissolved. Whisking constantly, add the walnut and olive oils in a slow, thin stream, until the dressing becomes smooth and shiny, forming an emulsion. Season to taste with additional salt and pepper, if needed.

To prepare the salad, place the greens in a large mixing bowl, add about ¼ cup of the vinaigrette, or more to taste, and toss gently. Divide the salad among 4 plates. Top each salad with one-quarter of the goat cheese and 1 tablespoon of the walnuts. Place 3 pickled cherries on each salad and serve.

Cook's Hint: If using fresh cherry juice in the vinaigrette instead of the spice brine, substitute 12 fresh red cherries, pitted and halved, for the pickled cherries.

Rick Small and Darcey Fugman-Small founded Woodward Canyon Winery in Washington's Walla Walla Valley back in 1981, and it has since become one of the finest wineries in the country. Woodward Canyon is known for producing premium, award-winning Cabernet Sauvignon and Merlot, as well as barrel-fermented Chardonnay. Production has increased gradually over the years, from 1,200 cases in 1981 to current production of 13,000 cases. In addition to being excellent winemakers, the Smalls are experts at wood-oven cooking. In fact, they have two ovens at their beck and call! During Walla Walla's annual Holiday Barrel Tasting Weekend, you'll often find Rick, a vibrant, muscular man in designer eyeglasses, baking bread to pair with locally made tapenades and spreads.

Darcey, a dark-haired, fashionable woman, gave me her recipe for hearty vegetarian lasagne, but admits that for those who prefer a bit of seafood with their pasta, bay scallops and/or shrimp make nice additions. (This is probably not necessary, as even my husband, an avowed carnivore, thought this dish was outstanding.) As a shortcut, you can use homemade or store-bought tomato sauce, but Darcey's sauce, a riff on one created by famed vegetarian chef and cookbook author Deborah Madison, is much more flavorful and works particularly well if you cook the lasagne in a wood-fired oven. Darcey says her dish is "great with fresh, crunchy bread and Woody [Woodward Canyon] 'Artist Series' Cab." The Artist Series started in 1992, when Rick and Darcey decided to create a special label to set apart the Cabernet Sauvignon made from the Canoe Ridge Vineyard.

Woodward Canyon Winery

11920 West Highway 12

Lowden, WA 99360

(509) 525-4129

woodwardcanyon.com

Since 1997, Cabernet from other vineyards has been added to the blend. Posters of the beautifully designed labels (each year featuring a different artist) are available for sale on the Woodward Canyon Web site. Woodward Canyon also produces a "second-label" wine called Nelms Road, which features the same beautifully crafted wine at everyday-drinking prices.

Spinach Lasagne

SERVES 8   VARIETAL Cabernet Sauvignon

1½ pounds fresh spinach

Kosher salt

12 lasagne noodles

2 tablespoons unsalted butter, plus extra for greasing the pan

1 cup cremini or wild mushrooms, well cleaned (see Cook's Hint page 219 for instructions on cleaning fresh mushrooms)

Prepare a steamer basket over boiling water. Add the spinach and cook, lifting and turning the spinach once or twice with kitchen tongs, until it turns bright green and just wilts, 2 to 3 minutes. Drain well, squeeze out the excess water, pat dry on paper towels, and coarsely chop.

Bring a large pot of water to a boil. Add enough salt so the water tastes like sea water. Add the lasagne noodles. Cook until al dente (until the pasta just becomes tender, but not soft or mushy). Drain, rinse in cool water, and set aside.

½ cup chopped shallots

2 teaspoons minced garlic

2 large fresh basil leaves, stacked and rolled like a cigar and cut into thin strips

1 large egg

1 pound ricotta cheese

Herbed Tomato Sauce (recipe follows)

12 ounces buffalo mozzarella, thinly sliced

½ cup (about 2 ounces) freshly grated Parmesan cheese

Preheat the oven to 400°F. Lightly butter a 9 x 13-inch lasagne pan.

Melt the 2 tablespoons butter in a medium skillet. Add the mushrooms, shallots, and garlic and cook, stirring occasionally, until the mushrooms begin to lose their juice and soften, 5 to 7 minutes. Remove from the heat and stir in the spinach and basil.

In a mixing bowl, blend the egg with the ricotta and add to the spinach mixture. Stir to blend well.

Spoon half of the tomato sauce on the bottom of the prepared lasagne pan. Cover the sauce with 3 noodles, followed by one-third of the spinach mixture, and one-quarter of the mozzarella. Repeat the layering of noodles, spinach, and mozzarella twice. Top with the remaining 3 noodles, the remaining one-quarter of the mozzarella, and the remaining half of the tomato sauce. Sprinkle with the Parmesan.

Place the lasagne pan on a baking sheet to catch any drips. Cover with lightly greased aluminum foil and bake for 25 to 30 minutes. Remove the foil and bake 10 to 15 minutes more. Remove from the oven and let stand for 10 to 15 minutes (so the lasagne can set up) before serving.

The artwork on the distinctive labels of Woodward Canyon Winery's "Old Vines" Cabernet Sauvignon has featured local historical figures since 1981. The winery's "Artist Series" Cab has been labeled with artwork from predominantly Northwest artists since 1992.

Herbed Tomato Sauce

MAKES about 2 cups

2 cups whole or low-fat milk

¼ cup finely diced white or yellow onion

3½ tablespoons unsalted butter

3½ tablespoons all-purpose flour

¾ teaspoon kosher salt

½ teaspoon freshly ground black pepper

Big pinch of freshly ground nutmeg

1 cup cored, seeded, and chopped ripe tomatoes, or ½ cup sun-dried tomatoes packed in oil, drained and coarsely chopped

⅓ to ½ cup chopped mixed fresh marjoram, parsley, and oregano

Heat the milk and the onion in a small saucepan over medium heat until small bubbles form around the edges of the milk. Turn off the heat just before the milk boils, cover the pan, remove from the heat, and set aside to steep for 15 minutes.

In a medium skillet over medium heat, melt the butter. Whisk in the flour a little at a time, whisking well after each addition, and cook, stirring constantly so lumps do not form, for 2 minutes. Remove from the heat and slowly add the warm milk and onion, whisking constantly to blend. Return to the heat and stir until the sauce thickens and comes to a boil.

Reduce the heat to low and simmer gently, stirring often, for 8 to 10 minutes. Remove the sauce from the heat and add the salt, pepper, and nutmeg, stirring well. Stir in the tomatoes and herbs and allow to cool completely before using as directed for Spinach Lasagne.

Cook's Hint: For a creative twist on the Herbed Tomato Sauce, try using half fresh and half sun-dried tomatoes. This creates an interesting contrast, since the sun-dried tomatoes provide a sweet-tart flavor and chewy bite.

Legendary Northwest winemaker Gary Figgins, who in 1978 produced his first vintage at Leonetti Cellar in Walla Walla, Washington, today works with son Chris making only red varietals—Cabernet Sauvignon, Merlot, and Sangiovese.

A beja (pronounced "ah-BAY-ha") is Spanish for "bee," and the name of this boutique Walla Walla winery/bed-and-breakfast inn was chosen for its simple beauty and the owners' concern and respect for the land and desire to work in tandem with nature. Abeja's setting is one of the most bucolic in the Northwest: a century-old (circa 1903–1907) farm with beautifully restored buildings in the rolling foothills of the Blue Mountains. Three luxurious cottages (the Chicken House, Summer Kitchen, and Bunk House) and two suites (the Locust and Carriage House) outfitted with fully equipped kitchens, antiques, and eclectic furnishings, Riedel glassware, and field guides and binoculars nestle between the outbuildings of the working winery. The barrel-tasting room is housed in the former mule barn, while the tasting room is the former dairy! The gray buildings have a weathered New England feel; birds chirp, bees pollinate, and lavender scents the air. Guests are invited to stroll the 25 acres of estate vineyards, gardens, creeks, and lawns.

The beauty of the wines made here matches the beauty of the setting. Winemaker and native Oregonian John Abbott always figured he'd end up making Pinot Noir, but instead launched his winemaking career in the Napa Valley in 1989. He moved to Walla Walla in 1994 to begin Canoe Ridge Vineyard, where he was winemaker for nearly 10 years and was best known for his award-winning Merlot, Cabernet Sauvignon, and Chardonnay. Ken and Ginger Harrison, longtime supporters of the wine industry during Ken's more than 35 years in the business community of Portland, Oregon, founded Abeja in 2000. John joined Abeja in 2002, along with life companion and public-relations expert Molly Galt, who now helps with Abeja's marketing and hospitality. At Abeja, John crafts 4,000 cases a year of some of the state's best Cabernet Sauvignon, along with small quantities of Chardonnay and estate-grown Viognier. John's goal is to produce wines that are a companion to food.

Abeja and the Inn at Abeja

2014 Mill Creek Road

Walla Walla, WA 99362

(509) 526-7400 (winery)

(509) 522-1234 (inn)

abeja.net

He and Ken believe that Cabernet Sauvignon will increasingly be recognized as the icon varietal of Washington State. This recipe, an Abbott family tradition, pairs perfectly with John's Cabernet Sauvignon. It comes from Betty Abbott, the winemaker's mother. Pheasant has the flavor of dark-meat chicken, but the texture of white; this recipe is definitely an upscale riff on fried chicken. The morels, after long cooking in butter, turn dark and leathery, like raisins or dried fruit—the true essence of morels.

Spring Pheasant with Morels

SERVES 4   VARIETAL Cabernet Sauvignon

1 cup all-purpose flour

2 teaspoons kosher salt

1 teaspoon freshly ground black pepper

Lightly oil a large roasting pan and set aside. Combine the flour, salt, and pepper in a 1-gallon resealable plastic bag. Seal the bag and shake well. Open the bag, add the pheasant pieces, seal the bag, and shake until the pieces are lightly coated with flour.

2 young farm-raised or wild pheasants (2½ to 3 pounds each), thawed if frozen and cut into serving-sized pieces

¼ cup vegetable oil

2 tablespoons unsalted butter

¾ cup water

6 cups (about 1¼ pounds) fresh morel mushrooms, well cleaned (see Cook's Hint page 219 for instructions on cleaning fresh wild mushrooms)

4 to 8 tablespoons salted butter

Heat the oil in a large skillet over medium to medium-high heat and add the unsalted butter. When the butter is melted, add half of the pheasant pieces. Brown well on one side, 4 to 5 minutes. Turn all the pieces and brown on the second side, reducing the heat if needed and checking often so the pieces do not burn, 4 to 5 minutes. Transfer the browned pieces to the prepared roasting pan. Repeat with remaining pheasant pieces.

Ten minutes before the pheasant is browned, preheat the oven to 300°F. When the oven is preheated, add the water to the roasting pan and cover tightly with aluminum foil. Transfer to the oven and cook for 25 to 35 minutes, or until the pheasant is tender and the leg juices run clear when pierced with a skewer. (Poultry is done when the thickest part of the thigh is 170° to 175°F when measured with an instant-read thermometer. Poultry at 180°F is considered well done.)

Remove from the oven, uncover the pan, tent loosely with aluminum foil, and allow the birds to rest for 10 to 15 minutes.

About 30 minutes before serving the pheasant, prepare the mushrooms. Slice large morels in half; leave small and medium morels whole. Melt 4 tablespoons of the salted butter in a large skillet over medium-low heat until foamy. Add the mushrooms and cook, stirring often and adding more salted butter as necessary to keep the pan moist and the butter from browning, until they turn dark and leathery, resembling raisins or dried fruit, 25 to 40 minutes; the cooking time varies so much because mushrooms vary greatly in their moisture content.

Arrange the pheasant pieces on a large serving platter, sprinkle with the mushrooms, and serve family-style.

Cook's Hint: Pheasant has been farm raised for centuries, and, in its farm-raised version, it is one of the few "exotic" meats that really does taste like chicken! Wild pheasant, however, possesses that unmistakable "gamey" flavor, especially if aged. If you don't hunt for your own pheasant, a good source is Exotic Meats, located in Bellevue, Washington, (800) 680-4375, exoticmeats.com.

Bottles are ready for sampling at the tasting room at Abeja winery in the Walla Walla Valley.

left: The vineyards and barn at Abeja winery in Walla Walla.

below: The five cottages and suites available for rent at the Inn at Abeja definitely offer rooms with a view, as well as fully equipped kitchens, Riedel glassware, and eclectic antique furnishings.

Mike Davis wanted to be a cook from the time he was just nine years old. Indeed, he wrote a letter to the late Julia Child telling her of his plans, and still proudly shows off the letter of encouragement and list of culinary schools her assistant sent back. At 33 years old, the boyish chef has accomplished a lot, having worked in New Orleans, Colorado, California, and many restaurants in Seattle before landing at the venerable Salish Lodge and Spa in Snoqualmie Falls, Washington. But after he went to small-town Walla Walla, Washington, to prepare a winemaker's dinner, and realized there were 50-plus wineries but only a handful of restaurants to service industry workers and tourists, he decided to move. 26brix opened in June 2004, a white tablecloth restaurant that Executive Chef and co-owner Mike dreams will one day be regarded as Walla Walla's answer to Napa Valley's French Laundry. So far, he's not far off the mark, having expanded the restaurant once and appeared at the venerable James Beard House in New York City twice. During his first appearance there, he prepared a 10-course feast titled "Walla Walla Extravaganza" accompanied by wines chosen by his wife, Krista McCorkle, former Executive Director of the Walla Walla Valley Wine Alliance. The couple met, married, and had their first child in the Valley. "People say we're the ultimate food-and-wine pairing of Walla Walla," Mike says with a laugh.

At the beginning of 2007, after closing their doors for nearly two months, Mike and Krista reopened 26brix as an upscale bistro that offers diners (particularly the locals) a more casual experience and dressed-down comfort with a reasonably priced menu, new artwork on the walls, and creative options for the kids. Mike's beloved tasting menus (foie gras!) are still available upon request, and the couple's dream of operating the "French Laundry of eastern Washington" may blossom within the next few years in a smaller, more intimate space.

Meanwhile, this busy chef also serves as spokesperson for the Walla Walla Sweet Onion Commission, making appearances and demonstrating recipes at the annual Walla Walla Sweet Onion Festival. The sweet onions, in season from June to September, were declared the official state vegetable of Washington State in early 2007. The recipe he shared with me is one he likes to prepare for friends on his days off. It incorporates Walla Walla sweets, as well as the fresh herbs he and Krista grow in their home garden. Krista, who devised the wine pairings with the recipe, advises if you don't like Chardonnay to try substituting a "dry rosé, a crisp Sauvignon Blanc, or a big, fat Semillon."

26brix Restaurant
207 West Main Street
Walla Walla, WA 99362
(509) 526-4075
twentysixbrix.com

Walla Walla Sweet Onion Frittata

SERVES 6 to 8   VARIETAL Chardonnay (oaked)

12 large eggs

¾ cup whole or low-fat milk

1 cup firmly packed mixed fresh herbs, minced, preferably parsley, thyme, marjoram, basil, and chives

Pinch of kosher salt

Freshly ground black pepper

1 tablespoon unsalted butter

1 tablespoon olive oil

1 small Walla Walla sweet onion, minced

3 ounces fresh, young goat's-milk cheese (chèvre), or ½ cup (about 2 ounces) grated Asiago or Parmesan cheese

Preheat the oven to 350°F.

In a mixing bowl, whisk together the eggs, milk, mixed herbs, salt, and a sprinkle or two of pepper, and set aside.

Place a large nonstick, ovenproof skillet over medium to medium-high heat and add the butter and oil. When the butter has melted, add the onion and cook, stirring occasionally, until tender, 5 to 7 minutes.

Add the egg mixture to the skillet and continue to cook. When the egg begins to form a light crust on the bottom, lift the sides and allow the liquid eggs to run into the bottom of the skillet. Continue cooking until another crust forms, and repeat the procedure until almost all the liquid eggs are cooked.

Remove the skillet from the heat and slide the frittata onto a plate. Using pot holders, place the skillet over the plate and carefully invert the frittata back into the skillet. Place the skillet in the oven and cook until the frittata puffs slightly and is cooked throughout, 3 to 5 minutes.

Break the chèvre into small pieces and sprinkle evenly over the top of the frittata, or sprinkle evenly with the Asiago or Parmesan cheese. Cut the frittata into equal portions and serve immediately.

Charles Smith is the renegade winemaker and owner of K Vintners and the Magnificent Wine Co. in Walla Walla, Washington, where he's known as much for his eccentric lifestyle as his award-winning Syrahs and red blends. Here he's shown on his 1947 Harley Davidson Knucklehead motorcycle with a suicide shift, a.k.a., the Marlon Brando bike.

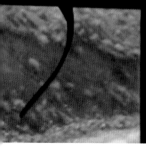
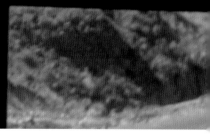
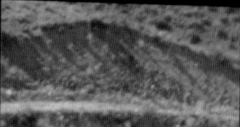

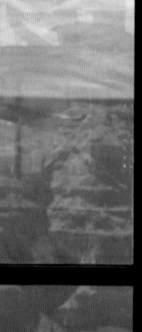

Columbia Gorge

With a monumental site next door to Maryhill Museum of Art, sweeping views of the Columbia Gorge and Mt. Hood, and an expansive outdoor patio, tasting room, and shop, Maryhill Winery in Goldendale, Washington, is *the* destination winery in the region. During a multi-course dinner in the winery's private dining room, we enjoyed nonstop views of the Gorge along with Chef Chad Lovewell's inspired cuisine paired (naturally!) with Maryhill wines. Among the springtime offerings were Mixed Spring Greens with Fresh Chèvre, Toasted Almonds, and Cherry Vinaigrette (served with Gewürztraminer); Copper River King Salmon with Lemon Risotto and Chardonnay Wine Butter (served with Reserve Sangiovese and Pinot Noir); and "Fifteen-Hour" Cherry Cheesecake (an inspired pairing with Reserve Zinfandel). Chad's mushroom soup, composed of wild morels the chef had hand picked earlier in the day, was a silky-rich version redolent of the earthy fungus and dry sherry. It formed the perfect pairing with winemaker John Haw's Proprietor's Reserve Chardonnay. From the highly regarded Connor Lee Vineyard near Othello, Washington, the wine is carefully crafted in the "sur lies" style, wherein the wine stays on the lees (settled yeast) for 10 months and is stirred twice a month. This process creates the wine's silky mouthfeel and toasty, hazelnut flavors.

Maryhill Winery

9774 Highway 14

Goldendale, WA 98620

(509) 773-1976

maryhillwinery.com

Cream of Morel Soup

SERVES 6 as an appetizer   VARIETAL Chardonnay (oaked)

3 tablespoons unsalted butter

1 pound fresh morel mushrooms, well cleaned (see Cook's Hint page 219 for instructions on cleaning fresh mushrooms) and coarsely chopped

½ cup diced shallots

3 cups heavy whipping cream

2 teaspoons minced fresh chives, plus extra for garnish

Kosher salt

Freshly ground black pepper

2 to 3 tablespoons dry sherry (optional)

3 tablespoons crème frâiche or sour cream

Melt the butter over medium-high heat in a large heavy-bottomed saucepan. Add the morels and shallots and cook, stirring often, until the mushrooms begin to release their juice and aroma and the shallots soften, 5 to 7 minutes, lowering the heat if necessary so the shallots do not brown. Add the cream and bring to a simmer, stirring occasionally. Cook, stirring occasionally and watching so the cream doesn't boil over, until slightly thickened, 4 to 6 minutes.

Transfer the soup to a food processor or blender and pulse until only very small pieces of mushroom remain. Place a fine-meshed strainer over a mixing bowl and add the soup, pressing on the solids with the back of a spoon to remove as much liquid as possible. Discard the solids and return the soup to the saucepan.

Add the 2 teaspoons chives and stir well. Season to taste with salt and pepper. Divide the soup among 6 soup bowls and drizzle with the sherry, if desired. Dollop with crème frâiche and sprinkle with chives.

above: Maryhill Winery's vineyards, the Stonehenge replica war memorial, and Mt. Hood offer panoramic views to visitors in the Columbia Gorge area that sits astride both Washington and Oregon.

left: John P. Haw was the winemaker at Maryhill Winery for several years and now consults with wineries throughout the Columbia Gorge.

A s the founder of Seattle's venerable Grand Central Baking Company, Gwen Bassetti is the *grandmère* of Northwest bakers, a cookbook author (*Cooking with Artisan Bread*), and an accomplished farmer/rancher. Her ranch in Goldendale, Washington, is one of the most remote spots in the world I've ever traveled to, reached over sharply angled farm roads, across gravel, and finally up the bumpy hill to the Bassetti complex. Gwen and husband Fred stay there for weeks, often joined by their extended family of children and grandchildren, a group "that fills the house up," according to Gwen. She and Fred manage a 10-year-old orchard, where they graft their own apple trees to produce Spokane Beauties. The heirloom apples are as big as your head, with endearingly imperfect, bumpy surfaces and the haunting taste of apples from a long-ago childhood. The kitchen, "a family farm kitchen that's cooked a lot of food over the years," is truly the heart of this home, with an antique potbelly stove, old-time refrigerator saved from a Girl Scout camp, and nonstop views over neighboring wheat fields. A pot of homemade soup, a pan of oven-warmed bread, a plate of freshly baked cookies, and a pitcher of pear-apple cider the family pressed themselves stand ever at the ready for impromptu meals. After walking the orchard with Gwen and Fred, it seemed only fitting that this Renaissance baker/farmer/rancher gave me her French apple tart recipe, which she likes to pair with either "a bright Late-Harvest Riesling or (in wintertime) a nice slice of cheddar and a little Port."

Grand Central Bakery

Various locations in Seattle and Portland

(503) 232-0575

grandcentralbakery.com

Tarte Tatin (Apple Tart) with Cider Cream

SERVES 6 to 8   VARIETAL Dessert wines (Late-Harvest Riesling)

Cider Cream

1 cup good-quality apple cider, or ¼ cup apple juice concentrate, thawed

1 cup heavy whipping cream

1 sheet (half of a 17.3-ounce package) frozen puff pastry, thawed according to package directions

2¾ pounds (about 8 medium, 2½-inch-diameter) Granny Smith, Newton, or Golden Delicious apples, peeled, cored, and cut into quarters

To make the Cider Cream, bring the apple cider to a boil in a small saucepan. (If using apple juice concentrate, skip this step and begin with the next step.) Cook until the mixture is reduced to about ¼ cup, 7 to 10 minutes. Remove from the heat and allow to cool.

In a chilled mixing bowl, whisk the cream until stiff peaks form. Fold in the reduced cider (or the apple juice concentrate). Use immediately, or keep refrigerated until ready to use, up to 3 days.

To make the tart, roll the puff pastry on a lightly floured surface to about ⅛-inch thickness and cut it into a 12-inch circle. Discard the scraps. Cover and chill the pastry dough until ready to use.

In a large bowl, toss the prepared apples with the lemon juice.

Melt the butter in a 10-inch ovenproof skillet (such as cast iron) over low heat. Sprinkle the sugar evenly over the melted butter. Increase the heat to medium-low or medium and cook slowly, stirring once or twice with a

1½ tablespoons freshly squeezed lemon juice

6 tablespoons unsalted butter

1 cup sugar

1 teaspoon pure vanilla extract

wooden spoon or shaking the pan occasionally, until the mixture begins to turn a light golden color, 3 to 5 minutes. Remove the skillet from the heat and carefully stir in the vanilla.

Place a baking sheet on the middle rack of the oven and preheat the oven to 425°F.

Starting at the outside edge of the skillet, arrange the apple quarters on their sides, in two concentric circles so they fit in as tightly as possible. Return the skillet to the stove top and cook over medium heat until the juices thicken and turn a light golden brown, 15 to 20 minutes.

Remove the prepared pastry circle from the refrigerator. Drape the pastry over the apples and tuck the edges around the edge of the skillet. Place the skillet on the baking sheet in the oven and bake until the pastry is a rich, golden brown, 20 to 30 minutes.

Remove from the oven and let cool in the skillet for 15 minutes. Run a thin knife around the edge of the skillet to loosen the pastry. Place a serving plate over the skillet and invert the tart onto the plate. If the apples stick to the pan, arrange them back on the tart. Serve the tart warm or at room temperature with a dollop of the Cider Cream.

Columbia Gorge: A World of Wine in 40 Miles

The Columbia River Gorge is known for its breathtaking beauty and bountiful orchards, and as one of the world's top sites for windsurfing. But the focus may soon shift from windsurfing to "winesurfing," thanks to the efforts of the region's dedicated winemakers and grape growers.

"Within forty miles we have five microclimates," says Lonnie Wright, who owns the Pines 1852 Vineyard & Winery. "You would have to travel 1,300 to 1,400 miles in Europe to experience that."

The miniature world of wine that Lonnie Wright describes—the Columbia Gorge American Viticultural Area, or AVA—stretches across 280 square miles beginning about 60 miles east of Portland. It runs roughly from Stevenson, Washington, to The Dalles, Oregon; spans both sides of the Columbia River; and runs up the Hood River and White Salmon River Valleys.

As the only sea-level passage through the Cascade mountain range, the Columbia River provides a unique environment where wine grapes thrive. Grapes grown in the Columbia Gorge AVA range from Pinot Gris, Gewürztraminer, and White Riesling in the cooler, wetter west end to Merlot, Syrah, and Cabernet Sauvignon in the dry, high-desert conditions of the eastern end. Grapes also vary according to where they're grown in relation to the Columbia River and at what elevation. In total, these varied microclimates are capable of producing quality wine grapes from more than two dozen varietals.

The Columbia Gorge Wine Growers Association (CGWGA) is made up of both winery owners and grape growers who are in the appellation or who sell wines made

from Columbia Gorge AVA grapes. Only wines made with 85 percent grapes grown in the Gorge can put the words "Columbia Gorge" on their labels.

The Columbia Gorge winemakers are fun-loving, laid-back people who share a common passion for wine-grape growing, wine-

making, and their region. Despite increasing interest in the Columbia Gorge and recent prosperity, it wasn't always so easy. Although historical records show that some of the earliest settlers planted grapes and made their own wine and that growers have raised grapes in the Gorge for over 100 years, it wasn't until the 1980s that grapes from some of the long-standing vineyards were rediscovered and experimentation began.

Today, in addition to Lonnie Wright, whose Old Vine Zinfandel has been traced to 1914, leading winemakers and grape growers in the Columbia Gorge include Rick Ensminger, who has farmed the world-famous Celilo Vineyard since 1976; James Mantone, the winemaker and co-owner of Syncline Wine Cellars, which has attained cult status for its Rhône

varietals; Joel Goodwillie, who makes award-winning wines at Wind River Cellars; and John Haw, winemaker/consultant.

Maryhill, which opened in the fall of 2000, remains the largest and most ambitious of the wineries in the area. Chosen for the unique microclimate, the

"You meet so many neat people. It's all about lifestyle—good friends, good food, and good wine. The best things are yet to come."

winery's grounds command a sweeping view of the Columbia River Gorge and Mt. Hood while providing the vineyards with unparalleled protection and nourishment for fully ripened harvests.

Wine is celebrated in a *big* way here. Visitors are invited to taste Maryhill's award-winning wines in the 3,000-square-foot tasting room. Or experience a summer concert featuring such big-name artists as Bob Dylan, ZZ Top, or Amy Grant in a 4,000-seat outdoor amphitheater built into the natural slope. Or simply soak in the views over a picnic and glass of wine on the spacious outdoor patio.

Owners Vicki and Craig Leuthold and their talented staff strive to produce and sell the highest-quality wines at the lowest-possible prices. Working with 22 varietals, they produce 37,500 cases a year. The Viognier, an almost over-the-top example of the variety, is an award winner and Maryhill's top-selling wine, while Zinfandel is the best-selling red.

Winemaker Haw is a playful man whose motto is, "Live what you love, and love what you live." He doesn't think wine has to be aged for years to be palatable, and is not above suggesting that customers add a couple of ice cubes or a splash of 7Up to his Cabernet Franc Rosé for easy summer sipping.

"I've been doing this [winemaking] for 30 years, since I was age 12 years old in Michigan," he said. "Every morning I wake up and ask myself, 'Am I gonna dig ditches or do this?'

"You meet so many neat people. It's all about lifestyle—good friends, good food, and good wine. The best things are yet to come."

The Pines 1852 Vineyard & Winery

5450 Mill Creek Road
The Dalles, OR 97058
(541) 298-1981
thepinesvineyard.com

Syncline Wine Cellars

111 Balch Road
Lyle, WA 98635
(509) 365-4361
synclinewine.com

opposite: A rainbow crosses Highway 14 alongside the Columbia River Gorge. below left: A small herd of buffalo evokes earlier times as the animals graze beside Highway 14, alongside the Columbia River Gorge. below right: James Mantone, winemaker at Syncline Wine Cellars, juggles both tasting-room duty and taking care of his 18-month-old daughter, Ava Elena Mantone, at the Columbia Gorge winery.

Joel Goodwillie is the ebullient winemaker and owner of Wind River Cellars in Husum, Washington, as well as the founder of the Bad Seed Cider Co., which he describes as "his guilty pleasure." Wind River, established in 1997, is located atop a narrow, winding road high in the hills. Signs are posted along the way with encouraging words such as "Chardonnay Ahead," "Merlot Ahead," and "Winery 100 Yards." A family of wild turkeys even crossed our path en route. But once you make the pilgrimage, you find a rustic, homey tasting room with some of the best views in the Northwest overlooking Mt. Hood and towards Mt. Adams. Joel and his wife, Kris, formerly made wine in Oregon's Umpqua Valley. Today they're known for their boldly delicious wines crafted from a wide range of varietals. Joel's light white wines, such as Gewürz and Riesling, are full of fruit, yet crisp and acidic—they are great for sipping alone or with food. His Pinot Noir is clean and berry filled; the Cab Sauv dark and authoritative. He began producing his Port of Celilo in 1995. The rich, raisin-y wine, rife with notes of chocolate, is made using the *solera* method (similar to Spanish sherry) from Lemberger grapes specially grown on Celilo Vineyard by Rick Ensminger (see page 115), and is one of the most lauded wines in the Northwest. Yet instead of stuffiness, there's a bit of a surfer-dude aesthetic about this winemaker, who kayaks the raging waters around his winery every day and plays in a rock band in his spare time. He's the kind of self-deprecating guy who prefers a plastic turkey baster (purchased at the Dollar Store) to a glass wine thief for sharing barrel samples. When I asked him where he learned to make wine, he replied, "I'll let you know when I learn it."

When I asked him to share a recipe, he was quick to submit his legendary "Pizza on the BBQ." Joel's pizza is a "guy's dish" that's piled high with Italian sausage slices, bell peppers, and red onion and is actually cooked on an outdoor gas grill for ease of preparation. Thanks to all the bold flavors, it's a breeze to pair with wine. Lemberger is a German varietal also known as Blue Franc. It's Joel's favorite wine with food, and pairs well with pizza because of its "crushed black pepper character." Wind River's Tempranillo "pairs well with any barbecue dish, especially one with goat cheese, thanks to its smoky flavors." His third choice is Syrah. "The recipe is actually versatile enough to pair with everything from Gewürztraminer to Pilsner," Joel says!

Wind River Cellars

196 Spring Creek Road

Husum, WA 98623

(509) 493-2324

windrivercellars.com

Wind River Pizza

SERVES 4 as a main course MAKES four 8- or 10-inch pizzas VARIETAL Lemberger, Tempranillo, Syrah, Gewürztraminer

1 cup warm water

1 tablespoon sugar

1 packet active dry yeast

To make the pizza dough, mix the water and sugar in a large mixing bowl until the sugar dissolves. Stir in the yeast and let rest for 10 to 15 minutes, or until the yeast begins to foam. Stir in the 3 tablespoons of oil and the salt. Gradually stir in enough of the flour to make a soft dough.

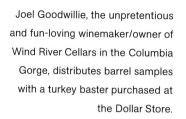

Joel Goodwillie, the unpretentious and fun-loving winemaker/owner of Wind River Cellars in the Columbia Gorge, distributes barrel samples with a turkey baster purchased at the Dollar Store.

3 tablespoons extra virgin olive oil, plus extra for oiling the bread bowl

1 tablespoon kosher salt

3 to 3½ cups all-purpose flour, plus extra for kneading

1 tablespoon chopped fresh rosemary

Italian Sausage Topping

½ cup olive oil

¼ cup balsamic vinegar

4 teaspoons chopped fresh rosemary

2 tablespoons minced garlic

1 pound spicy Italian sausage links, separated

1 yellow bell pepper, cored and cut lengthwise into 1½-inch wedges

1 red bell pepper, cored and cut lengthwise into 1½-inch wedges

1 large red onion, sliced horizontally into ½-inch slices

2 cups (about 8 ounces) shredded mozzarella cheese

½ cup (about 2 ounces) freshly grated Parmesan cheese

2 cups soft, fresh goat's-milk cheese, such as chèvre, crumbled

4 Roma tomatoes, seeded and chopped

¾ cup thinly sliced green onions (green parts only)

Form the dough into a rough ball and transfer to a clean, lightly floured work surface. Sprinkle the dough with the rosemary and knead for 5 minutes, or until the rosemary is evenly distributed and the dough is smooth and elastic, sprinkling with additional flour as needed. Form the dough into a ball. Rub the inside of a large mixing bowl with olive oil, place the ball of dough in the bowl, and then flip the ball of dough so both sides are lightly covered with oil. Cover the bowl with a clean kitchen towel or plastic wrap and let it rest in a warm place for 1 hour, or until doubled in size.

When the dough has risen, gently punch it down. On a clean, lightly floured work surface, divide the dough into 4 pieces. Form each piece into a ball and roll each out into an 8- or 10-inch circle. Place on two lightly oiled baking sheets. Cover with a clean kitchen towel and let rise for 30 minutes.

While the dough is rising, prepare the Italian Sausage Topping. Preheat an outdoor gas grill to medium heat. Whisk the olive oil, vinegar, rosemary, and garlic together in a small mixing bowl. Pour about ½ cup of the vinaigrette into another small bowl and reserve for topping the pizzas.

Arrange the sausages, bell peppers, and onion slices on the grill and brush with the remaining (about ¼ cup) vinaigrette. Cook until the sausages and vegetables are tender and slightly charred, turning once or twice, 10 to 12 minutes. Discard any remaining vinaigrette used on the grilled foods. Remove the sausages from the grill, put on a large plate, and cut into ½-inch-thick slices. Transfer the pepper pieces and onion slices to the same plate.

Before proceeding, wipe down the grill, then raise the heat to medium-high. Place two of the dough pieces on the grill and cook until the underside is crisp, 2 to 4 minutes. Turn the dough, and grill for 1 to 2 minutes. Remove from the grill and place the crusts on a baking sheet with the crispy side up. Repeat this procedure with the remaining two pieces of dough.

Divide the mozzarella and Parmesan cheeses evenly over the tops of the pizzas. Divide the sausage pieces, bell pepper pieces, and onion slices from the Italian Sausage Topping evenly over the pizzas, then divide the goat cheese, tomatoes, and green onions over the pizzas. Drizzle with the reserved bowl of vinaigrette.

Carefully place the pizzas on the grill and cook until the cheeses are melted and the dough is cooked through, 3 to 5 minutes more. Serve warm.

Portland

With a prime location at the base of the 200 Market Building and across from the Keller Theater in downtown Portland, Carafe counts among its customers nearby office workers; opera, ballet, and Broadway-show fans; and students from Portland State University, located just up the hill. The inviting space, with its checkerboard-tiled floor, maroon-and-yellow colors, and large outdoor seating area (well protected with wind and rain covers), offers diners authentic French bistro cuisine ("a little bit of Paris in Portland") filtered through the sensibilities of chef and co-owner Pascal Sauton, a gentle bear of a man whose roots lie in the Lyon region of France. Wife Julie Hunter, an all-American lass with porcelain skin and a dark ponytail, runs the front of house. On their *carte* you'll discover cocktails such as Le Poire (a heady concoction of Champagne and Clear Creek Pear Brandy) or Carafe Cidercar (fresh-pressed Oregon apple cider mixed with Calvados and a touch of lemon). Salade Carafe is a huge plate of local greens with perfectly roasted chicken breast, spiced hazelnuts, and a rich Roquefort dressing. Sandwich Marseille highlights the street food of Marseille that Pascal fondly remembers: a baguette stuffed with *pommes frites*, merguez (spicy sausage), and potent harissa

Carafe

200 Southwest Market Street

Portland, Oregon 97201

(503) 248-0004

carafebistro.com

sauce. The wine list draws heavily from the wine regions of France, along with selections from Northwest wineries. As you might expect, many beverages (iced tea, water, wines by the glass) are served in miniature carafes. As the fun-loving Pascal often says, "Vive le foie gras, vive le vin, and vive l'amour!"

Cervelle de Canut (Herbed Goat Cheese with Walnut Crostini)

SERVES 6 to 8 as an appetizer   MAKES 2 cups   VARIETAL Chardonnay (unoaked) or Syrah

8 ounces Juniper Grove Fromage Blanc or soft, fresh goat's-milk cheese (chèvre)

½ cup crème fraîche

¼ cup minced shallots

Juice and freshly grated zest of 1 lemon

2 tablespoons extra virgin olive oil

1 tablespoon minced fresh flat-leaf parsley

With a whisk or in a food processor, whip the fromage blanc and crème fraîche with the shallots, lemon juice and zest, olive oil, parsley, and chives. Season to taste with salt and pepper.

To serve, spread the herbed goat cheese on the toasted walnut bread and arrange on a serving plate. Top with frisée leaves.

1 tablespoon minced fresh chives

Fine sea salt

Freshly ground black pepper

12 to 16 slices artisan
walnut bread, toasted

½ head frisée, torn into
bite-sized pieces

above: *Cervelle de Canut,* a signature appetizer served at Carafe in downtown Portland.

left: Pascal Sauton preps *Cervelle de Canut* in Carafe's kitchen.

Paley's Place is that most unexpected, yet welcome, of restaurants: unpretentious and inviting in atmosphere, yet sophisticated and secure in its cuisine and wine list. As you cross the threshold of the 50-seat converted house in the Northwest neighborhood of Portland, soothing celadon walls surround you, and you feel the cares of the day melt away. Chef/Owner Vitaly Paley, who won the James Beard Best Chef of the Northwest award in 2005, operates the restaurant with his flamboyant wife, Kimberly. The chef's *carte de cuisine* runs the gamut, with French, Middle Eastern, American, and Continental offerings. But the outstanding dish the day we stopped by was his Fresh Farm Egg & Goat Cheese Raviolo with Spring Morel & Asparagus Stew. The fist-sized single raviolo was tender and golden, filled with herbed goat cheese and a perfectly poached egg. A "stew" (which was more like a light, buttery broth) of the Northwest's best spring morels and asparagus tips surrounded the pasta. Cutting into the raviolo causes the yolk of the egg to burst open, creating a creamy texture and brilliant explosion of saffron color. Not unlike the restaurant itself, the dish managed to be at once inventive and comforting. Dungeness crab, or *Cancer magister*—"big crab"—is the prize catch of the oldest shellfish fishery in the North Pacific. It is named after Dungeness, a small fishing village on the Strait of Juan de Fuca on the northern coast of Washington State, where it was first commercially harvested. In the recipe that follows, Chef Vitaly combines "Dungies" in a rich, creamy chowder redolent of bacon, earthy spices (cumin and coriander), heat from cayenne pepper, and sweet crab. It sings of Northwest seas and oceans and pairs well with unoaked Chardonnay or a fruity, aromatic Viognier.

Paley's Place

1204 Northwest 21st Avenue

Portland, OR 97209

(503) 243-2403

paleysplace.citysearch.com

Dungeness Crab Chowder with Cheddar Cheese Biscuits

SERVES 8   VARIETAL Chardonnay (unoaked) or Viognier

2 to 3 precooked Dungeness crabs in the shell (4½ to 5½ pounds total), cracked into pieces suitable for picking (see Techniques section, page 257)

¼ cup olive oil

1 cup smoked bacon cut into ½-inch dice (5 to 6 slices)

1 cup leeks, cut into ½-inch semicircles (white and light green parts only)

Pick the crabmeat out of the shells, cover, and refrigerate until using. Reserve the shells.

In a stockpot or Dutch oven, heat the olive oil over medium heat. When the oil is hot, add the bacon and cook, stirring occasionally, until browned around the edges, 10 to 12 minutes. Add the leeks and cook, stirring often, until they turn bright green, about 2 minutes. Remove the leeks and bacon (leaving the fat in the pan) and set aside.

Add the reserved crab shells and cook, stirring frequently, for 5 minutes. Do not worry if the bottom of the pan becomes a bit brown in color; this is just

1 cup diced white or yellow onion

1 cup diced carrots

2 sprigs fresh thyme

¼ teaspoon whole cumin seed

¼ teaspoon whole coriander seed

¼ teaspoon cayenne pepper

¼ teaspoon freshly ground
black pepper

2 cups dry white wine

8 cups water

1½ cups diced new potatoes

2 cups heavy whipping cream

¼ teaspoon kosher salt

2 tablespoons chopped fresh
flat-leaf parsley

Cheddar Cheese Biscuits
(recipe follows)

the caramelization of the shells taking place (frequent stirring will keep the pan from burning). Add the onion, carrots, thyme, cumin, coriander, cayenne, and black pepper and cook, stirring frequently, until the vegetables are softened but not browned, 6 to 8 minutes.

Add the white wine, bring to a boil, then reduce the heat and simmer, stirring occasionally, until the liquid is reduced by half, to about 1 cup, 8 to 10 minutes. Add the water, bring to a boil, then lower the heat and simmer, stirring occasionally, until the liquid is reduced to about 4 cups, 60 to 70 minutes.

Place a fine-meshed sieve over a large mixing bowl and add the contents of the stockpot. Press the solids with a large spoon to extract as much liquid as possible. Discard the solids and return the chowder base to the pot.

Add the potatoes and the reserved leeks and bacon. Stir in the cream and salt and bring to a gentle simmer. Cook, stirring occasionally, until the potatoes are tender, 7 to 10 minutes.

To serve, add the reserved crabmeat and cook, gently stirring once or twice, until the crabmeat is just warmed through, 1 to 2 minutes. Divide the chowder among 8 soup bowls and sprinkle with the parsley. Serve immediately with the Cheddar Cheese Biscuits.

Cheddar Cheese Biscuits

MAKES 16 biscuits

7 tablespoons unsalted butter,
chilled and cut into
1-tablespoon pieces

1 cup diced (¼-inch dice) white or
yellow onion

2 teaspoons whole fennel seed

2 cups all-purpose flour

2 teaspoons baking powder

½ teaspoon table salt

¼ teaspoon baking soda

1 cup buttermilk

¾ cup (3 ounces) grated
cheddar cheese

Preheat the oven to 450°F. Line two baking sheets with parchment paper.

In a medium skillet, melt 2 tablespoons of the butter over medium-high heat. Add the onion and fennel seed and cook, adjusting the heat as necessary and stirring occasionally, until the onion is softened but not browned, 5 to 7 minutes. Remove the pan from the heat and cool.

Place the flour, baking powder, salt, and baking soda in a medium mixing bowl and stir until mixed (a whisk works well for this). With a pastry blender or two dull knives used in a criss-cross motion, cut the remaining 5 tablespoons butter into the flour mixture until ¼-inch crumbs form. Add the cooled onions and stir well. Add the buttermilk and cheese and stir until just combined. Do not overmix, or the biscuits will be tough.

Drop the dough by heaping tablespoons onto the prepared baking sheets. Bake for 14 to 17 minutes, or until the biscuits are golden brown and tender. Cool on wire racks for 10 minutes, then remove from the baking sheets and cool completely on wire racks before serving.

Philippe Boulot, executive chef at the venerable Heathman Restaurant (adjacent to the Heathman Hotel in downtown Portland) is the kind of guy who thinks nothing about doing a 10-course dinner at the venerable James Beard House in New York City—in which every course incorporates oysters! The classic dish below—oysters baked in a creamy cheese sauce—could well have been in the lineup, it is so rich and satisfying to the soul. Philippe absorbed a lot about cooking while growing up in his native Normandy, France. Today, his culinary philosophy remains intertwined with the seasons, as he showcases local and regional ingredients in a very traditional French manner with a few Pan-Asian accents. The chef came to Oregon in 1994 at the age of 35, about the same time he noticed an upsurge in the state's wine industry.

Today the Heathman proudly serves 600 different wines and boasts Oregon's largest selection of Champagne and sparkling wines. The restaurant's audience is divided equally between locals and hotel guests, and there's a "come-as-you-are" ambience, so much so that Armani-clad businessmen and -women rub elbows with the Eddie Bauer and Birkenstock set. I've always loved the way the 100-seat restaurant is situated, with big picture windows embracing the streetscape, a busy bar at one end, and the restaurant and demonstration kitchen forming the bulk of the narrow space that is painted a sunny yellow to counteract the often-overcast Oregon skies. The Heathman Restaurant falls under the corporate wing of the McCormick & Schmick group, which owns many restaurants throughout the Northwest region, including Jake's Famous Crawfish just a few blocks down the street. The stuffed shirts understand Philippe's philosophy and don't run roughshod. "We're big enough to have fun, but not so large it's an industry," the graying chef explains in his soft French accent, a twinkle in his eye.

The Heathman Restaurant
1001 Southwest Broadway
at Salmon
Portland, OR 97205
(503) 790-7752
heathmanhotel.com

Oysters Gratinée

SERVES 4 as an appetizer   VARIETAL Semillon

20 fresh Pacific Northwest oysters, such as Westcott Bay European flats, Kumamoto, Kushi, or Pacific

Rock salt

1 pound leeks, chopped (green parts only)

1 cup heavy whipping cream

1½ cups (6 ounces) grated Swiss cheese

1 large egg yolk

With an oyster knife, shuck the oysters over a mixing bowl to catch all the juices. Reserve the bottom (cupped) shell from each oyster. Set the oysters aside. To prepare the reserved oyster shells for stuffing, rinse the shells in hot water, drain, and pat completely dry. Place a layer of rock salt on a rimmed baking sheet and arrange the oyster shells cup side up without crowding. Set aside.

Add the oyster juice, leeks, and cream to a small saucepan over medium-low heat. Cook, stirring occasionally, until the leeks are tender, 5 to 7 minutes. Add the Swiss cheese, stir well, and allow to cool. Once cool, whisk in the egg yolk.

Ten minutes before cooking, preheat the oven to 450°F.

Executive Chef Philippe Boulot meets with the kitchen staff before the Heathman Restaurant opens for dinner.

Divide half the leek mixture among the prepared oyster shells, cover with an oyster, and divide the remaining leek mixture over the tops of the oysters. Cook for 5 to 7 minutes, or until the oysters are cooked through but still tender and the sauce is slightly browned.

Place a fresh layer of rock salt on a decorative platter or 4 individual plates. Arrange the oysters over the rock salt and serve immediately.

Cook's Hint: The Pacific Northwest is the nation's leading oyster-producing region. Species range from the large, meaty Pacific to the delicate native Olympia (about the size of a quarter). European flat oysters, known as Belons in France, are usually round and fairly flat. The Kumamoto is a small Pacific oyster with a deep-cupped shell. The Virginica originated in East Coast waters and is noted for its briny-smooth crispness and pronounced mineral finish. In addition to these broad species of oysters, dozens of varieties named after their growing areas beckon the oyster lover.

Sustainability and Cory Schreiber's name go hand in hand; indeed, the founder of and visionary behind Portland's popular Wildwood restaurant has been singing the praises of fresh seasonal ingredients from local farms and purveyors since his restaurant opened in 1994. In 1998, he was named Best Chef of the Northwest by the James Beard Foundation. In 2000, his heartfelt and lushly photographed cookbook, *Wildwood: Cooking from the Source in the Pacific Northwest*, was published to wide acclaim. As he says in the introduction, "Practicing the philosophy of 'cooking from the source' opens new dimensions in the kitchen, as it moves the cook one step back in the process to the abundant garden, the saltwater oyster or clam bed, the damp indigenous forest, and all other places where foods are found and produced." The chicken recipe Cory shared with me exemplifies the type of hearty, homespun dishes we experienced at Wildwood on a Sunday evening—"family night"—when the tablecloths came off and the starred items on the menu could be ordered as individual portions or as larger servings for sharing. We enjoyed a family-style supper of Draper Valley chicken with wild rice griddle cakes, pear butter, and braised escarole. Pan-seared halibut was the best of earth and ocean, served in a pool of Manila clam stew laced with Carlton Farms bacon and sourdough croutons. Sautéed Squid and Artichokes also magically merged the bounty of farm and sea. Wild Nettle and Mozzarella Pizza featured the harbinger of spring (stinging nettle), while it showed off the kitchen's prowess with its ovens—both wood-burning and clay. Sommelier Randy Goodman notes that while he would usually pair chicken preparations with Pinot Noir, in this case the lentil/celery/caper components of the dish need a more assertive flavor profile. He recommends Andrew Rich Vintner Columbia Valley Cabernet Franc for its leafy, herbal aromatics; ripe, rich fruit; and medium tannins. Brick House Wine Company Gamay Noir, from the Willamette Valley (made from organically grown estate grapes), shows black cherry and plummy fruit, soft tannins, and a hint of spice, and also works well with this dish.

Wildwood Restaurant and Bar

1221 NW 21st Avenue

Portland, OR 97209

(503) 249-9663

wildwoodrestaurant.com

Roasted Breast of Chicken with Lentil Vinaigrette, Cracked Walnuts, and Wilted Spinach

SERVES 4   VARIETAL Cabernet Franc or Gamay Noir

½ cup plus 2 tablespoons olive oil

3 tablespoons Dijon mustard

At least 7 hours before you plan to serve, place the 2 tablespoons olive oil and 2 tablespoons of the Dijon mustard in a 1-gallon, resealable plastic bag and mix well. Season the chicken breasts lightly with salt. Place the chicken breasts in the bag, seal, and rub with the marinade. Place in the refrigerator and marinate for 6 hours, or overnight, turning the bag occasionally.

4 chicken breasts with wing bone and skin on (a special-order cut of chicken known as the "airplane cut"–ask your butcher to prepare it for you, or substitute bone-in chicken breasts)

Kosher salt

1 cup petite green lentils

3 tablespoons freshly squeezed lemon juice

2 tablespoons sherry vinegar

1 cup minced celery

1 cup coarsely chopped celery leaves

¼ cup capers, rinsed well, drained, and patted dry

2 tablespoons minced red onion

Freshly ground black pepper

1 tablespoon unsalted butter

¼ pound fresh spinach, stems removed

¼ cup water

¼ cup walnuts, toasted (see Techniques section, page 258) and coarsely chopped

Place the lentils in a medium-mesh sieve, rinse well with cold water, and drain. Fill a medium saucepan with water and season the water with salt until it tastes like salt water. Bring to a boil, add the lentils, and reduce the heat to a simmer. Cook until the lentils are slightly soft to the bite, 15 to 20 minutes. Drain the lentils and set aside to cool.

To prepare the vinaigrette, add the remaining ½ cup olive oil, the lemon juice, vinegar, and the remaining 1 tablespoon mustard to a small mixing bowl. Whisk to blend. Add the celery, celery leaves, capers, red onion, and cooked lentils. Season to taste with salt and pepper. Set aside. (The lentils can be made one day in advance and kept refrigerated.)

Ten minutes before cooking the chicken, preheat the oven to 375°F.

Arrange the chicken breasts on a roasting pan with a rack without crowding and bake for 35 to 40 minutes, or until the chicken is cooked through and the juices at the thigh bone run clear when pierced with a sharp knife or skewer. Transfer the chicken to a plate, tent with aluminum foil, and allow to rest for 10 minutes.

Melt the butter in a large skillet over medium heat. Add the spinach and season to taste with salt and pepper. Add the water and cook, stirring occasionally, until the spinach is wilted, 1 to 2 minutes. Place a fine-meshed sieve over a mixing bowl and pour the spinach into the sieve to drain.

Divide the spinach among 4 dinner plates. Place a chicken breast on each bed of spinach. Spoon a generous amount of the lentil vinaigrette over the top, sprinkle with walnuts, and serve immediately.

Cook's Hint: This recipe yields 4½ cups of the lentils. Leftovers make a lovely side dish or salad when spooned inside "cups" formed from butter lettuce leaves.

A Fantasy Fulfilled: Urban Wine Works

In a bulky, terra-cotta-colored warehouse on the outskirts of Portland, Oregon, I fulfilled one of my lifelong fantasies. I blended my first bottle of wine.

The scene smacked of a high-school science project as I perched at the end of the long tasting bar at Urban Wineworks. A paper placemat, four small glass beakers, and five wineglasses sat in front of me. The beakers were filled with equal measures of Cabernet Sauvignon, Cabernet Franc, Merlot, and Syrah sourced from Bridgeview Vineyards in Oregon and Abeja and Three Rivers Winery in Washington. Excellent raw materials to start with!

Megan, the helpful tasting-room assistant, advised us to taste each of the samples alone to judge the way they might best be blended. The wines ranged from fresh-from-the barrel wild and wicked to prim and proper examples of each varietal. Suddenly wine blending didn't seem as easy as I thought. How could I ever knit such divergent components into something not only drinkable, but desirable?

I began in what I reasoned was the most logical way—by blending equal portions of my two favorite samples, the Cabernet and Merlot. The result was good but not great. I knew I could do better.

Since I preferred the taste of the Cabernet to the Merlot, my next blend consisted of 75 percent Cab and 25 percent Merlot.

The resulting blend was much better than my first attempt, but lacked a certain *je ne sais quoi.*

Next I tried 25 milliliters of Cab to seven of Merlot and five of Syrah. "Mmmm," I said as I swirled, sniffed, and tasted. For the first time, I liked the result. Those sitting around the bar agreed that my latest blend was mellow and lush without being overly ag-

gressive. I knew it would partner well with lots of different dishes.

Megan noted the blend, mixed a batch, and transferred it into an elegant carafe. She placed a small tag around the neck of the carafe that recorded the date the wine was bottled and the final blend: 70 percent Cabernet Sauvignon, 20 percent Merlot, 10 percent Syrah. I walked out of Urban Wineworks like the proud parent of a newborn, the crystal carafe safely nestled in the crook of my arm. It was cheap thrills for $30, not to mention the experience of a lifetime.

In addition to wines you blend yourself, rich, earthy wines under

the Bishop Creek Cellars label are also for sale at Urban Wineworks, where one of the goals is to take the stuffiness out of wine. The ambience of Urban Wineworks alone dispels any sense of pretense. Sixty-gallon oak wine barrels rise in stacks around the back wall of the warehouse. The barrel heads are brightly decorated by local artists with portraits of winemak-

"The wines ranged from fresh-from-the-barrel wild and wicked to prim and proper examples of each varietal."

ers, still lifes of wine bottles and wineglasses, and rural landscapes.

Urban Wineworks, which is one of Portland's most popular spaces for special events, truly fulfills its mission: "Wine country without the drive."

Urban Wineworks

407 NW 16th Avenue
Portland, OR 97209
(503) 226-9797
(888) GO-PINOT
urbanwineworks.com

Mushroom Madness: The Joel Palmer House

While I was growing up in the suburbs of Philadelphia in the 1960s, one of my parents' passions was discovering the newest restaurants about town. Mom and Dad thought nothing of driving to "Jersey" or anywhere else within a hundred-mile radius of our home for a good meal.

The Joel Palmer House in Dayton, Oregon, is on both the Oregon and National Historic Registers.

I don't remember what year it was, or even how old I was (perhaps 15), when my parents heard about a place in Reading, Pennsylvania, called Joe's Restaurant. Run by a husband-wife team of Polish descent and located in the heart of a blue-collar neighborhood, Joe's must have seemed an especially intriguing dining pursuit to my straitlaced parents, a physician and a stay-at-home mom.

Mom made reservations weeks in advance, and we trekked to Reading in the big Buick Roadmaster. Dinner at Joe's consisted of many courses, all of which revolved around wild mushrooms gathered in the Pennsylvania woods. There were lots of dark, rich, long-simmered sauces and real crystal, china, and flatware. Dad even had a few glasses of red wine. Somehow, I knew this was a *big deal*.

I later learned that Joe's was a legendary establishment. Opened as a Polish workingman's saloon in 1916 by Joseph Czarnecki and his wife, Magdalena, it evolved into a nationally recognized fine-dining establishment thanks to the efforts of Joseph's son, Joseph, Jr., and his wife, Wanda. Once son Jack and wife Heidi took over in 1974, the restaurant started raking in even more accolades. In 1987, the James Beard Foundation named Jack one of the top 16 chefs in the country, along with other soon-to-be-famous chefs such as Dean

Fearing and Robert Del Grande. Jack also authored three cookbooks: *Joe's Book of Mushroom Cookery, A Cook's Book of Mushrooms,* and *Portobello Cookbook.*

Along about 1996, I heard through the foodie grapevine that a world-renowned mushroom expert had moved to the Willamette Valley, put two and two together,

"We love it out here; it's the end of the rainbow."

and realized it was Jack! He and Heidi opened the Joel Palmer House, which is on both the Oregon and the National Historic Registers, in Dayton, Oregon, in 1997.

"We love it out here; it's the end of the rainbow," according to Jack, a bright-eyed, roly-poly man in his fifties. "Running a restaurant in Pennsylvania was like watching the sun set. Here the sun is rising."

I can only say that my second dinner chez Czarnecki was like traveling back in time. Jack and Heidi are the perfect hosts, positioning plates, pouring wine, and conversing with guests like the seasoned pros they are. Son Christopher marks the fourth generation of Czarneckis to work in the family business.

Cooking at the Joel Palmer House focuses on wild mushrooms and locally raised ingredients prepared in a style that Jack characterizes as "freestyle," since it combines the cuisines of Mexico, China, Thailand, Po-

land, and India. Dishes are created to showcase and match the wines of Oregon: Pinot Gris, Pinot Noir, and Chardonnay.

The soups we sampled, especially Joe's Wild Mushroom Soup, from a 50-year-old family recipe, were outstanding. They paired nicely with an Oregon Brut Rosé. Heidi's Mushroom Tart was the essence of wild mushroom, a perfect pairing with Oregon Pinot Noir. Signature main dishes included Filet Mignon with Pinot Noir Sauce and Wild Mushrooms and Beef Stroganoff with Oregon White Truffles (another famous family recipe). Seafood options ranged from Wild Salmon with Porcini Duxelles to Crabcakes with Portobello-Mustard Vinaigrette. Dessert featured tiny, maple-flavored candy-cap mushrooms infused into ice cream and candied in simple syrup. The dainty candied 'shrooms were served over creamy cheesecake with a dollop of real whipped cream.

"I'm the biggest homeboy there is," Jack told me. And from Pennsylvania to Oregon, I'm the first fan to agree.

The Joel Palmer House
600 Ferry Street
Dayton, Oregon 97114
(503) 864-2995
joelpalmerhouse.com

Jack Czarnecki is mad for mushrooms! The world-renowned mushroom expert, chef, oenophile, and bon vivant, along with wife Heidi and son Chris, runs the Joel Palmer House in Dayton, Oregon. With its white-wood siding, dark hardwood floors, lacy curtains, and family antiques, the restaurant offers a beguiling dining experience. And practically everything on the menu contains mushrooms! This is an adaptation of the deep-fried mushroom recipe found in Jack's wonderful *A Cook's Book of Mushrooms: With 100 Recipes for Common and Uncommon Varieties*. I've given it more of a Northwest twist by replacing the original walnuts with hazelnuts, combining Chinese oyster sauce with the chipotle purée for a milder and more Pan-Asian flavor, and using chanterelles instead of oyster mushrooms. If chanterelles are out of season, white or cremini mushrooms are readily available and equally satisfying. Whatever type of mushroom you use, deep-dried mushrooms are the ultimate hot and spicy, crunchy-good finger food!

The Joel Palmer House

600 Ferry Street

Dayton, OR 97114

(503) 864-2995

joelpalmerhouse.com

Deep-Fried Chipotle-Hazelnut Mushrooms

SERVES 4   VARIETAL Gewürztraminer or Pinot Gris

1 quart vegetable or canola oil, for deep frying

One 7-ounce can chipotle peppers in adobo sauce

7 tablespoons oyster sauce

12 fresh chanterelle mushrooms, ends trimmed (if using medium to large chanterelles, slice lengthwise from top to bottom into halves or quarters, so the stem of the mushroom can act as a "handle" for the fried mushroom), or 12 medium white or cremini mushrooms

All-purpose flour

3 large eggs, beaten

1 cup hazelnuts, crushed

Edible flowers, such as nasturtiums, marigolds, or chive flowers, for garnish (optional)

In a large heavy-bottomed saucepan, heat the oil to 340°F.

Place the chipotle peppers plus the adobo sauce in a food processor or blender and pulse until smooth. Pour half the chipotle purée into a small nonreactive mixing bowl and combine with the oyster sauce. With a clean pastry brush, "paint" the mushrooms with the purée, coating lightly. There will be purée left over (see Cook's Hint, below).

Using 3 small dishes, place some flour in one, the eggs in another, and the crushed hazelnuts in the third. Coat the painted mushrooms with the flour, then dip into the egg mixture. Finally, coat the mushrooms with the hazelnuts, gently pressing the nuts into the mushrooms until they adhere. (When "crusting" food, it helps to designate a "wet" hand to dip and a "dry" hand to sprinkle or pat on the flour and nuts.)

Carefully place 3 to 4 mushrooms in the hot oil. Cook, turning once, until the mushrooms are golden brown, 30 to 60 seconds. Remove with a slotted spoon and drain on paper towels to absorb any excess oil. Repeat until all the mushrooms have been fried.

Divide the mushrooms among 4 small plates and garnish with edible flowers, if desired.

Cook's Hint: The leftover chipotle purée can be used for another recipe, and it makes a fiery marinade or rub when blended with your favorite

left: Deep-Fried Chipotle-Hazelnut Mushrooms at the Joel Palmer House.

below: Jack Czarnecki is chef and co-owner, along with wife Heidi, of the Joel Palmer House.

barbecue sauce. Or I like to add a couple of tablespoons of extra virgin olive oil and a few tablespoons of an assertive herb, such as tarragon or rosemary (chopped), and use the mixture as a marinade for large portobello mushrooms. After marinating for 15 to 20 minutes, cook the mushrooms over an indoor or stove-top grill. (To tenderize the mushrooms and achieve prominent grill marks, place a large heavy skillet over the mushrooms as they cook.) Jack also notes that while the mushrooms do not need a dipping sauce, you may want to use a cooling herb-based mayonnaise to quench the fire. Roasted Garlic Mayonnaise (see page 48) or Ginger-Cilantro Mayonnaise (see page 164) fit the bill.

Behind a modest storefront on the main drag in downtown McMinnville, Oregon, lies one of the Northwest's longest-running and most sincerely heartfelt restaurants, Nick's Italian Café. It's like stepping back into a diner/café from the 1970s; indeed, owner Nick Pierano will not allow even so much as a "newfangled" espresso machine to invade its lost-in-time ambience. Still, what the place may lack in upscale appointments it more than makes up for in food, specifically five-course, Northern Italian/Northwest dinners inspired by the Oregon winemakers who have patronized Nick's for three decades. Many of the items on the menu pay tribute to feasts and celebrations during Nick's youth. Don't miss his grandmother's minestrone, a long-simmered soup presented in a big bowl, ladled into soup bowls, and drizzled with pesto just before serving. Pasta dishes rise to new levels here; all are made from Nick's handmade egg pasta, which is as light and airy as the proverbial cloud. To keep things simpler, it's okay to substitute freshly made store-bought pasta in this Dungeness crab recipe, or even dried noodles in a pinch; just don't tell Nick. His seafood pasta features lasagne noodles in a rich, creamy sauce with a light touch of cheese that doesn't overwhelm the crab, plus pine nuts as the crowning touch. Pair it with Pinot Noir or Pinot Gris. Once you move past the pasta on the menu, Rabbit Braised in Oregon Pinot Gris and Rosemary features chanterelles and sweet baking spices—cinnamon and cloves—in the succulent sauce. Salt-Baked Salmon Steak is another signature dish. And don't miss the multi-layered Tiramisù (which translates from the Italian as "pick me up") served straight up in a goblet. The wine list reads like a who's who of Oregon winemakers: Erath Vineyards, Rex Hill, Sineann, and St. Innocent. Some of the Oregon Pinot Noirs that Nick has cellared over the years go back as far as the 1970s, including the legendary Eyrie 1975 South Block Reserve.

Nick's Italian Café

521 Northeast Third Street

McMinnville, OR 97128

(503) 434-4471

nicksitaliancafe.com

Dungeness Crab and Pine Nut Lasagne

SERVES 8   VARIETAL Pinot Noir or Pinot Gris

8 cloves garlic, peeled

1 teaspoon extra virgin olive oil

10 tablespoons plus 1 teaspoon unsalted butter

½ pound white mushrooms, stemmed and thinly sliced

¼ cup sifted all-purpose flour

4 cups hot whole milk

Preheat the oven to 375°F. Place the garlic cloves in the center of a medium piece of aluminum foil, drizzle with the oil, fold the foil into a packet, and roast for 45 minutes, or until the garlic is soft. Mash the garlic into a paste and set aside.

Melt 2 tablespoons of the butter in a large skillet over medium to medium-high heat. Add the mushrooms and cook, stirring occasionally, until the liquid has evaporated, 5 to 8 minutes. Remove from the heat and set aside.

Melt 8 tablespoons of the butter in a medium saucepan over medium heat. Whisk in the flour and cook, stirring constantly, for 1½ minutes. Whisk in the hot milk and simmer gently, stirring often and reducing the heat if needed, until the sauce is as thick as heavy cream, 30 to 35 minutes.

¾ pound fresh or dried lasagne noodles

1½ teaspoons freshly grated lemon zest

¾ teaspoon kosher salt

9 to 12 ounces Dungeness crabmeat, picked over for shells and cartilage and patted dry on paper towels to remove excess liquid

¼ cup (1 ounce) freshly grated Parmigiano-Reggiano cheese

¼ cup (1 ounce) freshly grated Pecorino Romano cheese

½ cup whole-milk ricotta cheese

¾ cup pine nuts

About 15 minutes before the béchamel is finished cooking, bring a large pot of salted water to a boil. Add the fresh lasagne noodles and cook until barely tender, 3 to 4 minutes. If using dried noodles, cook as the package directs. Drain and separate the noodles and set aside.

To finish the sauce, stir in the garlic paste, lemon zest, and salt. Remove the pan from the heat and cover the surface of the béchamel sauce with plastic wrap to prevent a skin from forming.

To assemble the lasagne, grease a 13 by 9-inch baking dish with the 1 teaspoon butter. Line the bottom of the dish with one third of the lasagne noodles. Scatter the crab over the noodles, spread one-third of the béchamel on top, then sprinkle with half the grated Parmigiano-Reggiano and Pecorino Romano cheeses. Cover with another one-third of the noodles, scatter the reserved mushrooms on top, add dollops of ricotta (use all the ricotta), and spread another one-third of the béchamel on top. Cover with the remaining noodles, spread the remaining béchamel on top, sprinkle with the remaining grated cheeses, and scatter the pine nuts on top.

Bake for 30 minutes, or until bubbling and golden brown on top. Allow to rest for 10 minutes (so the lasagne can set up), then slice and serve.

The underground barrel room at Adelsheim Vineyard in the Willamette Valley.

ed Ridge Farms is a small, family-owned herb and specialty plant nursery and garden shop located on a prime site with sweeping views of the Red Hills of Dundee. For half of her life, owner Penny Durant managed her family's property—Durant Vineyard—which sold grapes to such esteemed Oregon wineries as Domaine Drouhin Oregon, Sokol Blosser, Ponzi, and Argyle. In her new endeavor, Penny produces more than 300 types of herbs, including 100 kinds of lavender, and many other culinary, medicinal, and landscaping plants. Penny and husband Ken also nurture a block of 2,000 olive trees, and one day hope to grow enough olives to make olive oil, like producers have done in California for years. For now, she bottles a smooth, yet peppery, unfiltered California oil under the Red Ridge Farms label, although potted olive trees—the Spanish Arbequina variety—are available for purchase by growers and the general public.

The nursery also features a fully furnished country-inn apartment with two balconies, a full kitchen, and floor-to-ceiling windows that's become a favorite getaway for Northwest chefs and winemakers. Don't miss a browse through the garden shop, with an unusual selection of gifts, tools and gardening resources, floral wreaths, and specialty foods. Occasionally, Penny offers classes on creative ways to use herbs in art, crafts, and cooking taught by a local artist, craftsperson, or chef. Class topics include container gardening, wreath making, herb preservation, and cooking with herbs. Red Ridge offers a break from wine touring and a good complement to any traveler's mix of activities. Penny's recipe is as healthy as the lifestyle she represents; it serves as the perfect light, summer appetizer on its own, or as a main course with the addition of chilled cooked Alaskan spot prawns, shrimp, or Dungeness crabmeat. An unoaked Chardonnay, with its citrusy notes, works well, although red-wine lovers may prefer a light, slightly chilled red, such as Lemberger or Gamay Noir.

Red Ridge Farms

5510 Northeast Breyman
Orchards Road
Dayton, OR 97114
(503) 864-8502
redridgefarms.com

Garden-Fresh Gazpacho with Garlic Croutons

SERVES 6 to 8   VARIETAL Chardonnay (unoaked)

1½ pounds heirloom tomatoes, cored, peeled, and coarsely chopped (2½ cups), plus any juice that accumulates (see Techniques section, page 258)

1 large cucumber, peeled and coarsely chopped (2 cups)

1 small white or yellow onion, coarsely chopped (1 cup)

At least 2 hours before you plan to serve, in a food processor or blender, pulse about half of the tomatoes, cucumber, onion, and bell pepper, along with the jar of pimientos and half of 1 can of the tomato juice until smooth, 15 to 30 seconds. Pour into a large mixing bowl. Repeat the blending procedure with the remaining vegetables and the other half of the can of tomato juice. Pour into the mixing bowl.

Stir together the puréed vegetables with the remaining 1 can tomato juice, 3 tablespoons of the olive oil, the vinegar, salt, Tabasco, and pepper. Cover and refrigerate until well chilled, at least 2 hours and preferably overnight to allow the flavors to meld. Refrigerate 6 to 8 soup bowls.

1 medium green bell pepper, seeds and membranes removed and coarsely chopped (1 cup)

One 4-ounce jar pimientos, drained

Two 11.5-ounce cans tomato juice

6 tablespoons extra virgin olive oil

⅓ cup red wine vinegar

1½ teaspoons kosher salt

¼ teaspoon Tabasco sauce, plus extra for seasoning

⅛ teaspoon coarsely ground black pepper

3 large cloves garlic, peeled and cut in half lengthwise

2 cups day-old artisan sourdough bread cubes (½-inch cubes)

¼ cup chopped fresh chives

When ready to serve, rub the inside of a small skillet with the cut garlic. Reserve the garlic. Add the remaining 3 tablespoons olive oil to the skillet and heat over medium heat. When hot (the oil should bubble around the edges of the cubes when you put them in), cook the bread cubes, turning periodically with kitchen tongs so all the sides are coated with oil, until toasted, 6 to 8 minutes. Remove from the heat and drain on paper towels.

Crush the reserved garlic and add it to the chilled soup, mixing well. Ladle the soup into the chilled bowls, float a few croutons in each bowl, and sprinkle with the chives.

The view from Red Ridge Farms encompasses the vineyards at Domaine Drouhin Oregon, whose parent company is Maison Joseph Drouhin, headquartered in Burgundy, France.

How do two high-powered insurance executives who spent 30 years in glittery Las Vegas end up raising goats and running a bed-and-breakfast in small-town Carlton, Oregon? Meet Judi Banks-Stuart and John Stuart, a husband-and-wife team who made just such a life change in 2003. "I fell in love with goats at a bed-and-breakfast in Maine," Judy explains. "When the owner asked if anyone wanted to milk the goats at 6:30 one evening, I raised my hand!" After learning the technical side of the trade at Washington State University's renowned "cheese school" in Pullman, Judi visited Caprine Estates Willow Run Dairy in Ohio, the largest goat farm in the United States, for further pointers. Today, the engaging, energetic proprietor of Abbey Road Farm in the heart of Oregon wine country (Yamhill County) produces a super-creamy fresh goat's-milk cheese. The 82-acre property also boasts an atmospheric bed-and-breakfast inn housed in three former grain silos converted by John, who always seems in search of another project to tackle. With views of the rolling hills and the gentle bleating of the goats to lull you to sleep, the inn provides a bucolic respite to harried travelers. Judi's cheese is also gentle; without the pronounced "goat-y" flavor or tanginess common to many, it's more akin to a full-flavored, lushly textured cream cheese. See if you can find one with similar characteristics when buying the ingredients for Judi's cheesecake. (I like to use California cheesemaker Laura Chenel's creamy-soft version, which falls in the mid-range of flavor.) Judi recommends serving with a sweet-styled Gewürztraminer or—for the more adventurous—Muscat Canelli. Muscat is one of the oldest grapes known to man; it exhibits ripe-grape characteristics and perfume-y, musky aromas and flavors.

Abbey Road Farm

Abbey Road Farm Bed & Breakfast

10501 Northeast Abbey Road

Carlton, OR 97111

(503) 852-6278

abbeyroadfarm.com

Goat's-Milk Cheesecake

SERVES 12 to 16   VARIETAL Gewürztraminer

1½ cups sour cream

1¼ cups sugar

2½ teaspoons pure vanilla extract

10 honey graham crackers

⅛ teaspoon ground cinnamon

⅓ cup unsalted butter, at room temperature

Two 8-ounce packages cream cheese, at room temperature

In a small bowl, stir together the sour cream, ⅓ cup of the sugar, and 1½ teaspoons of the vanilla until the sugar dissolves. Cover and refrigerate.

Preheat the oven to 350°F. Adjust the oven rack to the center of the oven.

Place the graham crackers in the bowl of a food processor and process to measure 1½ cups crumbs. Add ¼ cup of the remaining sugar and the cinnamon to the bowl along with the crumbs and pulse until blended. Add the butter and pulse until well mixed and crumbly.

Measure out ¼ cup of the crust mixture and reserve for topping the cake. Press the remaining crumbs into the bottom and 1 inch up the sides of a 9-inch springform pan. Bake for 7 to 10 minutes, or until the crust is lightly

8 ounces soft, fresh, goat's-milk cheese (chèvre), at room temperature

3 large eggs, at room temperature

1 tablespoon freshly squeezed lemon juice

browned. Remove from the oven and allow to rest on a wire rack while preparing the cheesecake. Reduce the oven temperature to 300°F.

Combine the cream and goat cheeses in an electric mixer bowl. Beat on medium speed, scraping the bowl occasionally with a rubber spatula, until smooth. On low speed, gradually beat in the remaining ⅔ cup sugar. Add the eggs one at a time, beating in completely after each addition and scraping the bowl. Beat in the lemon juice and the remaining 1 teaspoon vanilla.

Pour the batter evenly over the crust in the springform pan and bake for 45 to 60 minutes, or until the cheesecake is almost set in the middle. Turn the oven off, leave the door ajar, and let the cake cool for 1 hour. Remove from the oven and cool completely on a wire rack.

Spread the sour cream topping evenly over the cheesecake and sprinkle the reserved graham-cracker crumbs evenly over the topping. Cover and chill for 4 hours or up to overnight before serving.

One of the baby goats at Abbey Road Farm in Carlton, Oregon, where the owners of the bed-and-breakfast inn make a small amount of goat cheese to share with guests.

L inda and Ron Kaplan lived many an oenophile's dream when they gave up successful careers in Iowa as a newspaperwoman and lawyer to buy Panther Creek Cellars and follow the grapes to Oregon in 1994. Their experiences with everything from errant earwigs to unloading and sorting truckloads of Pinot Noir into the wee hours inspired Linda to write *My First Crush: Misadventures in Wine Country.* Although Ron trained at the famed La Varenne in Burgundy, he retired his toque when he went into winemaking. So this recipe comes from Linda, who reports it arrived by word of mouth from a Norwegian couple who visited McMinnville. The Kaplans like to serve it for a late brunch paired with croissants from the local bakery and summer tomatoes drenched in balsamic vinaigrette. I was skeptical when Linda suggested it could be paired with Pinot Noir, but the earthiness of the dill and the salmon (be sure to use wild fish, not farm raised!) works well with similar notes in the wine. Pinot Gris and sparkling wine are other suggested pairings, although Melon is a more intriguing possibility. According to the Panther Creek Web site, "The Melon grape is the same as France's Muscadet, and is also known as Melon de Bourgogne. Until the early 1980s, Melon in the United States was often misidentified as Pinot Blanc. Panther Creek's Melon comes from the 28-year-old vines of De Ponte Vineyard near Dundee, Oregon. The dry yet fruity wine finds a passionate following among lovers of shellfish and seafood. In the nose of this varietal you'll often find pear, citrus, and peaches. On the palate, it's richly textured, with flavors of pear, peach, and apricot, and just a touch of sea salt." Linda opines that it's the wine's slight salinity that makes it pair beautifully with seafood, especially the Northwest's own native fish, salmon.

Panther Creek Cellars

455 Northeast Irvine

McMinnville, OR 97128

(503) 472-8080

panthercreekcellars.com

Scandinavian Salmon

SERVES 6 to 8   VARIETAL Pinot Noir, Pinot Gris, Melon

1 English cucumber

3 pounds wild salmon fillet, rinsed, drained, and patted dry

2 lemons, very thinly sliced

1 large bunch of dill

Kosher salt

Freshly ground black pepper

Preheat the oven to 400°F.

With a vegetable peeler, peel the cucumber in long strokes and save the skins. Cut the cucumber into thin rounds and reserve.

Line a large baking sheet with heavy-duty aluminum foil, placing one sheet of foil crosswise across the baking sheet, allowing enough excess foil on both sides to be folded across the fish. Run another sheet of foil lengthwise, again allowing enough excess foil to fold over the fish. Place the salmon skin side down in the center of the foil. Cover the fish with the cucumber skins, placing the white portion of the skins toward the fish. Cover the cucumber skins with half of the lemon slices and top with half of the dill. Bring the ends of the lengthwise foil up around the top and bottom of the fish, fold neatly to seal the fish, then repeat with the other ends of foil until the fish, cucumber, lemon, and dill are completely enclosed.

Place the baking sheet on the center oven rack, and cook for 50 to 55 minutes, or until the fish is opaque throughout, depending on the thickness of the fish and the desired doneness. Remove the packet from the oven and let rest for 10 minutes. Open the foil carefully to allow the steam to escape. Scrape off and discard the cucumber skins, lemon, and dill. Using a long, thin spatula, position the side edge of the spatula against the fat layer between the salmon flesh and skin. Move the spatula through the fat layer so that the flesh comes away from the skin. Transfer the salmon to a large serving plate and discard the skin and foil.

Just before serving, season the salmon to taste with salt and pepper. Garnish with the reserved cucumber slices and the remaining lemon slices and dill, and serve family style.

Cook's Hint: If desired, the salmon can also be cooked on a gas grill over medium heat.

Panther Creek Cellars, which is known for its Pinot Gris, Pinot Noir, and Melon, is located in downtown McMinnville's historic former power station.

Chef Gilbert Henry and wife Susan Barksdale, proprietors of Cuvée, like to brag that they operate "the best fine-dining restaurant in Carlton, Oregon." Of course, they're quick to add that they operate the only fancy restaurant in the tiny town, but that's beside the point. Before opening Cuvée in October 2004, the oh-so-French Gilbert and the oh-so-American Susan were the faces behind Portland's popular Winterborne for 13 years. The restaurant, which enjoyed an incredible run of 26 years, was one of the best seafood restaurants in the city. In Carlton, Cuvée bills itself as "French Dining in the Oregon Wine Country." The destination restaurant continues the seafood theme with such classic French dishes as *Moules Marinière* (mussels steamed in garlic, parsley, and white wine), *Coquilles St. Jacques* (scallops in cream sauce), and the fresh catch of day listed alongside *Bifteck avec Pommes Frites* (rib-eye steak and French fries) and escargots baked in garlic-butter sauce.

The wine list is divided equally among local wines (with familiar names such as Ken Wright, Cuneo, and Solena) and French wines from regions such as Alsace, Bordeaux, and the Côtes du Rhône. Next door to the atmospheric 49-seat restaurant, which looks as if it were lifted lock, stock, and barrel from a town in Provence, Susan runs Lulu. The narrow, light-filled shop features rustic furniture, scented soaps, and fine linens imported from France. In this recipe, Gilbert proves skeptics who think red wine and fish don't mix wrong when he pairs Petrale sole, the Northwest's number-one flounder, with Pinot Noir, Oregon's favorite varietal, in a dense, pale-pink cream sauce. He suggests serving the sole with long-grain white rice or steamed baby new potatoes and buttered carrots. And, of course, you'll want to finish the bottle of Pinot Noir you cooked with at dinner. *Bon appétit!*

Cuvée
214 West Main Street
Carlton, OR 97111
(503) 852-6555
cuveedining.com

Petrale Sole with Pinot Noir Cream Sauce

SERVES 4   VARIETAL Pinot Noir

Four 6-ounce Petrale sole fillets, skins removed, gently rinsed, and patted dry (see Cook's Hint, next page)

Kosher salt

Freshly ground black pepper

1 tablespoon unsalted butter

1 cup fish stock

1 cup Pinot Noir

Preheat the oven to 350°F.

Roll the sole fillets jelly-roll fashion and secure with 3 toothpicks per fillet. Lightly season the fish with salt and black pepper. Melt the 1 tablespoon of butter in a large ovenproof skillet over medium heat. Place the rolled sole fillets in the skillet without crowding. Pour the fish stock and Pinot Noir over the fish and sprinkle with the shallots. Bring to a gentle simmer, then transfer the skillet to the oven and cook until the rolls just turn opaque at the thickest part of the roll, 7 to 10 minutes. To check, cut into one of the rolls with the tip of a small, sharp knife. Transfer the fillets to a plate, tent with aluminum foil, and reserve.

1 cup diced shallots

1 cup heavy cream

2 tablespoons unsalted butter, cut into 4 pieces

Ground white pepper

2 tablespoons minced curly-leaf parsley, for garnish

4 lemon slices, for garnish

Place the skillet back on the stove top over medium-high heat and cook until the liquid in the pan is reduced to about 1 cup, 5 to 7 minutes. Add the cream, stir well, and cook until reduced to about 1 cup, 3 to 4 minutes.

Place a fine-meshed sieve over a mixing bowl and strain the sauce, pressing the solids with the back of a wooden spoon to remove as much liquid as possible. Discard the solids and return the sauce to the skillet over low heat. Slowly whisk in the 2 tablespoons of cut-up butter, adding it piece by piece and incorporating well after each addition.

Remove the toothpicks from the sole and discard. Pour any juices that have accumulated from the fish into the sauce and stir well. Season the sauce to taste with kosher salt and white pepper. Divide the sole fillets among 4 dinner plates, pour the sauce over the fish, and garnish each plate with parsley and a slice of lemon.

Cook's Hint: Petrale sole is a large flounder found from Baja California to Alaska. It resembles a small halibut and ranges in weight from two to eight pounds. Petrale is tender and lean, and its flesh has a larger flake than most soles. Next to the renowned Pacific halibut, the Petrale sole has always ranked as the number-one flounder in the Northwest because of its thicker flesh and sweeter flavor. It is well suited to poaching, sautéing, baking, broiling, and steaming. If Petrale sole is not available, substitute Dover or English sole fillets.

Fog, oak, and vines are part of the landscape at Witness Tree Vineyard, which was named after an ancient oak tree that served as a surveyor's landmark in the 1850s, during the Oregon Trail era.

Twin brothers Terry (the winemaker) and Ted (the vineyard manager) Casteel run Bethel Heights Vineyard, in Oregon's Eola Hills, with the help of Terry's wife, Marilyn; Ted's wife, Pat Dudley; and Pat's sister, Barbara. The family began planting vines in 1977, and established the winery in 1984. Bethel Heights specializes in Chardonnay, Pinot Gris, Pinot Blanc, and Pinot Noir; most of the fruit still comes from the 50-acre estate vineyard. The Casteels are well known in Oregon as some of the best vineyard cooks around. This plush dish, created by Marilyn, invigorates the taste buds by pairing the sweet-musky flavor of scallops with the bracing edge of orange and the astringency of fennel. Pair it with Bethel Heights 2004 Pinot Gris, in which "rich aromas of Asian pear, tropical fruits, and hints of orange rind give way to stone fruits with a powerful core of minerality. Firm acidity provides balance and a crisp, dry finish," according to the winemaker's notes. You will have about a cup of marmalade left over after making this recipe; it keeps in the refrigerator for up to a week or freezes well for later use. It is excellent paired with a small block of cream cheese and crackers as a quick appetizer, as a dipping sauce for shrimp, or as a chutney or salsa with pork tenderloin. If serving the marmalade with pork tenderloin, pair the dish with a good-quality Oregon Pinot Noir.

Bethel Heights Vineyard

6060 Bethel Heights
Road Northwest
Salem, OR 97304
(503) 581-2262
bethelheights.com

Sea Scallops with Fennel-Orange Marmalade

SERVES 10 to 15   MAKES 30 appetizers   VARIETAL Pinot Gris

1 fennel bulb, diced (about 2¼ cups), plus the feathery green tops, minced, for garnish

2 tablespoons diced shallots

2 oranges, peeled, segmented, and diced, plus any juice that accumulates

1 tablespoon freshly grated orange zest

4 cups freshly squeezed or store-bought orange juice

¼ cup white wine

¼ cup firmly packed light or dark brown sugar

1 tablespoon whole fennel seed

¼ cup Cointreau or other orange-flavored liqueur

Granulated sugar

Heat a medium heavy-bottomed saucepan over medium-high heat. Add the diced fennel, shallots, orange segments and their juice, zest, orange juice, white wine, brown sugar, and fennel seed and stir well. Bring to a rolling boil, reduce the heat, and simmer, stirring occasionally, until the liquid is reduced to about 2 cups, 30 to 35 minutes. At the beginning of the cooking time, watch the pan carefully so the orange juice does not boil over.

Remove the pan from the heat and stir in the Cointreau. Taste the marmalade; if it is too tart, add sugar to taste. Return the pan to the heat and cook, stirring often, until it reaches the consistency of chutney, 3 to 5 minutes. In the last minutes of cooking, watch carefully and stir often so the marmalade doesn't burn. Transfer half of the marmalade to a small nonreactive bowl or jar, allow to cool completely, cover, and save for another use (see headnote). Keep the remaining marmalade warm until ready to serve.

In a large heavy-bottomed skillet (nonstick works best for this), heat the olive oil and butter over medium to medium-high heat until the butter foams. Working in batches, add the scallops without crowding. Cook the scallops, turning only once, until golden brown on the outside and still translucent in the middle (see Cook's Hint, right), 1 to 2 minutes per side. Add more butter and oil if needed.

A sweeping shot of the vineyards at Bethel Heights Vineyard in Salem, Oregon.

1 teaspoon extra virgin olive oil, plus extra as needed

½ teaspoon unsalted butter, plus extra as needed

30 fresh or thawed untreated (dry pack) sea scallops, rinsed, drained, and patted very dry (see Cook's Hint, right)

30 good-quality whole-wheat crackers

To serve, place a cooked scallop on a cracker and top with a scant teaspoon of marmalade. Garnish with the minced fennel greens.

Cook's Hint: Scallops (like many types of seafood) are delicate and will continue to cook even after they are taken off the heat. It is always preferable to undercook rather than overcook scallops so they don't become tough and rubbery. When using the sauté method described above, many chefs prefer the scallops cooked medium rare (still translucent in the middle). To learn more about "dry pack scallops," see the Cook's Hint on page 59.

The Dundee Bistro, located in downtown Dundee, is a "must" stop on the Oregon wine trail for its creative food and inviting, casual ambience. Weather permitting, diners can choose outdoor courtyard seating, or indoor fireside dining in the airy dining room, where the walls are painted in shades of mustard, avocado, and claret and punctuated with colorful, primitive paintings of people drinking wine. Chef/owner Jason Smith celebrates fresh Willamette Valley cuisine and bold Northwest flavors in dishes such as Manila clams simmered in Chardonnay, shallots, garlic, flat-leaf parsley, butter, and cream. Or his famous Cascade All-Natural Burger, with smoked cheddar and horseradish aïoli. Or hand-tossed pizzas, such as the House Sausage Pizza with tomato sauce, *cavolo nero*, and ricotta.

More than 100 wines are available, along with a dozen wines by the glass. These include predominantly Oregon options from Ponzi, Argyle, Tyrus Evans, and boutique wineries. Don't miss a trip next door to Your Northwest specialty store and the Ponzi Wine Bar, an offshoot of Ponzi Vineyards in Beaverton, Oregon. Ponzi Vineyards is a venerable Oregon winemaker, started in the late 1960s and still owned and sustainably farmed by its founders, Dick and Nancy Ponzi, and their children. The family produces between 12,000 and 15,000 cases of wine per year and maintains 100 acres planted with Pinot Noir, Pinot Blanc, and Pinot Gris (from the nation's first commercial plantings of this grape, in the mid 1970s); Chardonnay; and White Riesling, along with rare Italian varietals such as Arneis and Dolcetto. Luisa Ponzi was one of the first female American winemakers to study in Burgundy; her formal training merges with her father's long experience to produce award-winning wines.

The Dundee Bistro
100-A Southwest Seventh Street
Dundee, OR 97115
(503) 554-1650
dundeebistro.com

Tuscan Pork Ribs (Rosticciana)

SERVES 4 to 6   VARIETAL Cabernet Franc or Dolcetto

4 large cloves garlic

2 firmly packed tablespoons fresh rosemary leaves

¼ cup extra virgin olive oil

3½ pounds country-style pork ribs, cut 1 to 2 inches thick (see Cook's Hint, right)

2½ teaspoons kosher salt

1 teaspoon freshly ground black pepper

The day before you plan to serve, with a large kitchen knife, mince the garlic together with the rosemary. Place in a large mixing bowl and stir in the olive oil. Add the ribs and rub thoroughly with the herbed olive oil. Cover the bowl and refrigerate the ribs for 12 to 24 hours, turning occasionally.

Preheat a gas grill or prepare a hot fire in a charcoal grill. Sprinkle the ribs all over with the salt and pepper. Grill the ribs over high/direct heat to brown, 4 to 5 minutes per side. Move to low/indirect heat, cover, and continue to slowly cook until tender and cooked through, 40 to 45 minutes (see Cook's Hint, right).

Cook's Hint: Country ribs are the meatiest of all ribs, with delectable, toothsome knobs of pork flesh. They are the blade ends of the pork loin. To cook the ribs on a gas grill, heat all the burners to high heat to preheat the grill, and do the initial searing in the center of the grill. For indirect heat, turn off the middle burner, turn the other burners to low, cover the grill, and cook until done. The grill temperature should measure 275° to 325°F during this indirect cooking time. The resulting ribs will be toasty brown in color with a rich rosemary-garlic flavor, especially after a full 24 hours of marinating time, and a crunchy exterior; it's the perfect melding of smoky/fatty/salty flavors.

A worker at Archery Summit winery shows his muscle as he punches down the cap of grape skins on a fermenting tank of red wine.

Lynn Penner-Ash was the first woman winemaker in Oregon, and now boasts more than 25 years in the industry. She graduated from the University of California at Davis with a degree in enology, began her career at Domaine Chandon in the Napa Valley in 1981, worked her way up at several California wineries, and served as winemaker and president/chief operating officer at Oregon's Rex Hill Winery until 2002. In 2001, while still at Rex Hill, she and husband Ron, a former schoolteacher, started making wine under their own label at the Carlton Winemakers Studio. The couple and two close friends opened the stunning Penner-Ash Wine Cellars in 2005. Designed with the latest ergonomics and environmental awareness in mind, the Newberg, Oregon, winery offers commanding views of the Chehalem Valley, the Red Hills of Dundee, and Mt. Hood. The 15-acre Dussin Vineyards, which is planted with Pinot Noir, celebrated its first vintage with estate-grown grapes in 2005.

Lynn, the mother of two young children, likes to keep things simple in the kitchen. She's known around the Penner-Ash household as "the clean-up cook," with one "creative" meal a week and the other six dinners being simpler preparations. She uses her large vegetable garden, makes frequent trips to the Lake Oswego farmers' market, and cooks on the outdoor grill to facilitate meal preparation. Whenever "the cleanup cook" has leftover sparkling wine, white wine, or Pinot Noir (her winery's star product), she makes this vinaigrette. The simple dressing can be served over mixed greens, spinach, or steamed vegetables and paired with either red or white wine, depending on which wine you use as its base. Lynn suggests that if you make the vinaigrette with Pinot Noir and toss it with fresh greens, the salad is best paired with a main dish of lamb (rubbed with garlic, sea salt, and fresh rosemary) served hot off the grill.

Penner-Ash Wine Cellars

15771 Northeast Ribbon Ridge Road

Newberg, OR 97132

(503) 554-5545

pennerash.com

Versatile Vinaigrette

SERVES 4 to 6 MAKES about 1⅓ cups dressing VARIETAL Pinot Noir, Pinot Gris, or sparkling wine

¼ **cup Oregon Pinot Noir, sparkling wine, or dry white wine**

1 to 2 teaspoons sugar

¼ **cup freshly squeezed lemon juice**

1 clove garlic, peeled and gently mashed with the back of a large chef's knife

1 tablespoon Dijon mustard

¾ **cup virgin olive oil**

Kosher salt

Freshly ground black pepper

In a medium nonreactive mixing bowl, whisk the Pinot Noir with 1 teaspoon of the sugar until dissolved. Add the lemon juice, garlic, and mustard and whisk until blended.

Whisking constantly, add the olive oil in a slow, steady stream, blending well after each addition, until the dressing becomes smooth and shiny, forming an emulsion. Remove the garlic clove and season to taste with salt, pepper, and the remaining 1 teaspoon sugar, if needed, whisking well.

Cook's Hint: Winemaker Lynn Penner-Ash notes that sometimes the addition of sugar to the Pinot Noir will not be necessary depending on the bitterness inherent to the wine; I found the dressing made from the Pinot Noir I used could have benefited from a bit more sweetness. The moral: adjust the sweetness to suit the leftover wine you use and your own personal taste.

right: Views of the vineyards and an old barn from Penner-Ash Wine Cellars, a sustainable, gravity-flow facility.

below: Penner-Ash Wine Cellars is surrounded by the estate's 15-acre Dussin Vineyard and encompassing views of Mt. Hood, Mt. Jefferson, and the Chehalem and Wapato Valleys.

White Truffle Fondue, one of the signature appetizers at Bistro Maison in downtown McMinnville, Oregon, oozes seductively.

During a research trip to Oregon's Willamette Valley, we stopped in McMinnville to visit Panther Creek Cellars's funky new tasting room in a converted electrical substation (see page 144). It's an atmospheric space with floor-to-ceiling arched windows, exposed brick walls, and massive rough-hewn tables where bottles of wine are aligned like toy soldiers, just waiting to be poured. After our tasting, we walked a few blocks to Bistro Maison, just off the main drag in the downtown area. The jaunty French flag outside the small converted house immediately caught my eye; once inside, the bright saffron-and-burgundy wallpaper, black-and-white tiled floors, gilt mirrors, and shadow boxes filled with Oregon wines continued the cheerful ambience. Everything we sampled was authentic French bistro fare, artfully prepared, and the wine list was an homage to outstanding Oregon wineries, with selections from Hamacher, Domaine Serene, Ken Wright, and Brooks, among others. But we were especially curious about and excited to try the restaurant's legendary White Truffle Fondue, which had been recommended to us by the tasting-room manager at one of the Willamette Valley's most beautiful wineries, Archery Summit. Bistro Maison owners—Chef Jean-Jacques Chatelard and his wife and front-of-house person, Deborah—created this flavorful fondue when they needed a romantic appetizer to serve on their Valentine's Day menu. I think it makes for good interactive eating with your sweetheart (or just about anyone) any time of the year. Deborah was torn between recommending Cabernet Sauvignon or Cabernet Franc with this dish, but finally went with the Franc. She wanted to pair a wine

Bistro Maison

729 East Third Street

McMinnville, OR 97128

(503) 474-1888

bistromaison.com

"that is a bit more vegetal and mushroom-y, with earthy aromatics to enhance the white truffles." I've adapted Jean-Jacques's original recipe to make it a bit easier for the home cook, but still in keeping with the original version's mellow, soothing flavors.

White Truffle Fondue

SERVES 4   VARIETAL Cabernet Franc

Fondue Accompaniments

Crusty artisan bread or baguette (two-day old preferred)

Fresh pears and apples

Ham fillet

Roasted red beets and carrots

Cornichons (small French pickles)

Cherry tomatoes

To prepare the Fondue Accompaniments, cut the bread into bite-sized pieces. One- or two-day-old bread is preferable, as it will stay on the fondue forks more easily and soak up more of the cheese. Core the fruit and cut into ¾-inch pieces. Cut any fat from the ham and cut into ¾-inch pieces. Arrange the accompaniments on 4 small plates or one large platter and set aside.

To make the fondue, place the Gruyère, Emmentaler, and cheddar cheeses in a medium mixing bowl and toss with the cornstarch.

Heat the wine in a fondue pot over medium heat until hot, but not boiling. Stir in the cheese a handful at a time, stirring constantly with a wooden spoon in a zigzag rather than a circular motion, to help break up and combine the

2½ cups (about 10 ounces) coarsely grated Gruyère cheese

1 cup (about 4 ounces) coarsely grated Emmentaler cheese

½ cup (about 2 ounces) coarsely grated Tillamook (Oregon) white cheddar cheese or other good-quality white cheddar cheese

4 teaspoons cornstarch

1 cup Oregon dry white wine

1 tablespoon Clear Creek Distillery Kirschwasser or other good-quality cherry brandy

Pinch of ground nutmeg

2 tablespoons homemade or store-bought white truffle butter (optional; see Cook's Hint, right)

1 tablespoon white truffle oil

cheeses. Wait for each handful of cheese to melt before adding another. Once all the cheese is melted, stir in the kirschwasser and nutmeg. The fondue should bubble gently and have the appearance of a light, creamy sauce. Do not allow the fondue to come to a boil.

Add the white truffle butter, if using, to the pot and stir until it dissolves into the cheese mixture. Remove from the heat and drizzle in the white truffle oil, stirring constantly.

Place the fondue pot on its stand over a heat source at the table. Adjust the burner flame so the fondue bubbles gently. Serve with the prepared accompaniments.

Cook's Hint: When Oregon white truffles come into season in December and January, and Chef Jean-Jacques gets an ample supply from local foragers, he makes his signature White Truffle Butter. To make the compound butter at home, put cleaned Oregon white truffles in the food processor along with just enough truffle oil so that the truffles form an almost paste-like consistency when they are processed. Next, fold the truffle paste into room-temperature butter until well incorporated. Transfer the butter to a piece of parchment paper or plastic wrap and form it into a cylinder or log about 1½ inches in diameter. White truffle butter is also sometimes available at upscale grocery stores and specialty markets, or through catalogs and online (Amazon.com sells the D'Artagnan brand).

opposite page: Orchards, wineries, lavender farms, country stores, and farm stands blossom along the "Fruit Loop" near Hood River, Oregon, while Mt. Hood shines in the background.

right: Dave Schweitz, a crew member at the Northwest Wine Summit held at Timberline Lodge in Oregon, samples some of the 1,000-plus Northwest wines submitted for judging, while he enjoys views of the wall of snow leading up to the summit of Mt. Hood.

Rogue, Umpqua, and Applegate Valleys

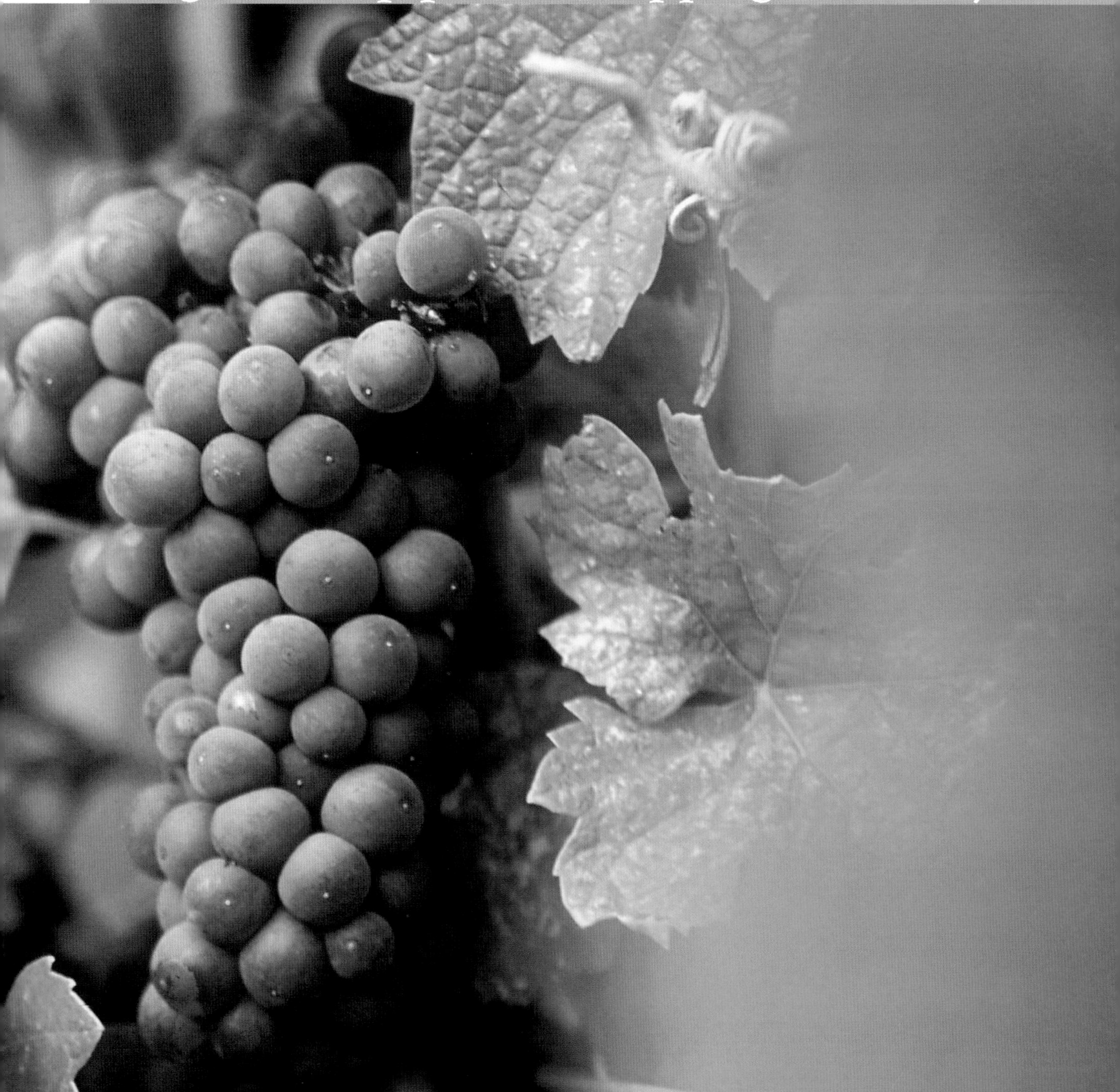

You'd never suspect that an unassuming cinder-block building in the tiny town of Central Point, Oregon, houses one of the finest artisan cheese-making operations in the world. The Rogue Creamery began in 1935, when Thomas Vella, an Italian immigrant known for successfully producing cheese in Sonoma, California, expanded his operations north to Oregon. He produced vast quantities of cheese for the war effort during World War II, traveled to France in 1956 to learn the art of blue cheese–making, and returned to Oregon to produce Oregon Blue Vein, a mild, creamy, Roquefort-style cheese made from raw cow's milk that is regarded as one of the best in the world. Today, Ignacio (Ig) Vella, Thomas's son, continues to run the Sonoma creamery. In 2002, Ig chose Cary Bryant and David Gremmels to become the new owners of the Rogue Creamery. Cary and David have carried on the Vella tradition of hand-milled cheese, while at the same time adding award-winning cheeses to the lineup. The Rogue Creamery won the London World Cheese Award for best blue cheese (Rogue River Blue) in 2003, the first time an American cheese factory had ever won the high honor, and other varieties of its blue cheese have won high honors in subsequent years. The soup recipe below uses Oregonzola, Ig Vella's Gorgonzola-style cheese, to add a creamy texture (much like heavy cream or half-and-half in more traditional soup recipes) as well as a distinct salty/tart taste. Oregonzola is aged a minimum of 120 days in the creamery's caves, which results in a sharp, Old World Italian flavor and a velvet-like texture.

The Rogue Creamery

311 North Front Street

Central Point, OR 97502

(541) 665-1155

roguecreamery.com

Broccoli and Oregonzola Soup

SERVES 8   VARIETAL Syrah

2 tablespoons unsalted butter

¾ cup chopped white or yellow onion

1 cup peeled, chopped russet potato

1½ pounds trimmed broccoli, coarsely chopped (about 7½ cups)

2 cups vegetable stock plus 2 cups water, or 4 cups water

4 ounces Oregonzola blue cheese or other high-quality blue cheese, crumbled

Freshly grated nutmeg

Heat the butter in a large saucepan over medium heat. Add the onion and potato, cover, and cook, stirring occasionally, until the onion is slightly softened but not browned, 5 minutes. Add the broccoli and cook, stirring occasionally, for 5 minutes. Add the 2 cups of stock and 2 cups of water and bring to boil. Reduce the heat, cover, and simmer, stirring occasionally, until the vegetables are tender, 15 minutes.

Strain the vegetables, reserving the cooking liquid. Put the cooked vegetables in a food processor and moisten with a few tablespoons of the cooking liquid. Pulse until very smooth. With the motor running, gradually add the rest of the cooking liquid. Work in batches as needed.

Transfer the soup back to the saucepan. Reheat until almost boiling, then remove from the heat. Stir in the blue cheese. Add nutmeg, salt, and pepper to taste. Ladle the soup into 8 warm soup bowls and drizzle with the walnut oil.

Kosher salt

Freshly ground black pepper

Walnut oil, for drizzling

Cook's Hint: This soup is so creamy and satisfying that large bowls can easily serve as a main dish. If so, in keeping with the blue cheese theme, I like to pair it with a simple green or spinach salad topped with Creamy Blue Cheese Dressing, another recipe from the Rogue Creamery. The recipe makes use of the Creamery's award-winning Oregon Blue Vein. To make the dressing, whisk ½ cup of mayonnaise (low fat works well here) with ½ cup of sour cream or buttermilk. Whisk in 4 tablespoons crumbled Oregon Blue Vein or other good-quality blue cheese, a dash of Worcestershire sauce, a smidgen of garlic powder, and a dash of freshly squeezed lemon juice or dry sherry. Cover and refrigerate overnight to allow the flavors to meld. The recipe yields about 1⅓ cups of dressing.

A cheese plate displays some of the award-winning cheeses (Blue Vein, Oregonzola, Smokey Blue) produced at the Rogue Creamery, located in Central Point, Oregon.

The Quest for Tempranillo

Like Don Quixote and Sancho Panza tilting at windmills, the quest of Dr. Earl and Hilda Jones to find a proper vineyard site to grow their dream grape varietal—the noble Spanish grape Tempranillo—at first seemed impossible.

ut back in the early 1990s, with the help of Earl's son, an associate professor of geography at Southern Oregon University, the good doctor (a dermatologist in a past life) and his wife (a former medical technician) perused weather maps and geological surveys. The first question they had to answer: should they seek a Spanish-like soil or a Spanish-like climate?

They decided that climate was paramount, so the "Abacela Idea" was to search for an American region with a similar climate to that of the finest Tempranillo-growing areas—the legendary Ribero del Duero—in Spain. The optimal climate had to be just hot enough to ripen the fruit but not so hot, especially during ripening, as to overripen or "cook out" the essence of the grape. Dry summers and cool, but not cold, winters were also mandatory. The Joneses' quest ended on the western coast of the United States in southern Oregon's Umpqua Valley, near the small town of Roseburg. There, on a fault line and subduction zone near a geological vortex, the couple found winemaker nirvana.

Over the years, they have planted blocks of grapes in their "Fault Line Vineyards," vineyards with interesting names such as Cobblestone Hill, Chaotic Ridge, and Cox's Rock (named after John Cox, one of the first

homesteaders in the area, who settled on the modern-day Abacela acreage in 1849 and was awarded a Donation Land claim—DLC—in 1853).

The south-sloping hillsides are sunny and hot by day (summer temperatures sometimes soar upwards of 115°F) and cooled by Pacific breezes by

> "The Joneses' quest ended on the western coast of the United States in southern Oregon's Umpqua Valley, near the small town of Roseburg."

night (which helps preserve the grapes' fruitiness and acidity). The long growing season allows slow ripening of the fruit, which leads to excellent varietal flavors.

After purchasing their land in 1992, moving in in 1994, and bonding the winery in 1997, the Joneses' original "Abacela Idea" has grown into a 57-acre vineyard and 5,000-case-per-year winery. The three-level, gravity-flow structure is designed to facilitate production of small batches of their fine, handcrafted wines.

With a commitment to continuing research and development, the Joneses' original dream of growing Tempranillo has expanded, as the couple successfully grows and bottles varietals from Spain and

Portugal (Tempranillo, Grenache, and Albariño), Italy (Dolcetto), and France (Syrah, Merlot, Cabernet Franc, Malbec, and Viognier).

The Joneses have also experimented with other varietals, such as Bastardo, Nebbiolo, and Petit Verdot, which are used in blending. The Abacela terroir produces bold wines of deep color with intense varietal character, ample structure, and tannins for aging.

"Abacela" comes from an ancient Spanish word meaning "to plant a grapevine." The name signifies the Jones family's quest to plant the first commercial Tempranillo grapes in the Pacific Northwest.

Abacela Winery

12500 Lookingglass Road
Roseburg, OR 97470
(541) 679-6642
abacela.com

Dungeness crab is one of the iconic foods of the Northwest—creamy and sweet, with buttery-rich meat. Large of flake and firm in texture, it is more akin to lobster than other types of crab. Its delicate, yet distinctive, flavor pairs well with just about any dry white wine, such as dry Riesling, Chenin Blanc, Semillon, or Sauvignon Blanc (sometimes referred to as Fumé Blanc). Hilda Jones suggests less conventional pairings, such as Albariño (a Spanish varietal that Abacela produces in small quantities) or a dry rosé. The floral aromatics of Viognier also make a pleasing complement to the sweet white crabmeat and the spicy, creamy sauce with its brilliant green color. In keeping with the Spanish theme, fino sherry, a very dry, astringent wine with a distinctive nose, is also an appropriate match with Dungeness crab.

Abacela Winery
12500 Lookingglass Road
Roseburg, OR 97470
(541) 679-6642
abacela.com

Dungeness Crab with Ginger-Cilantro Mayonnaise

SERVES 4 to 6 as an appetizer   VARIETAL Dry rosé, Albariño, Viognier

1 large egg, plus 1 large egg yolk

2 tablespoons freshly squeezed lemon juice

½ teaspoon kosher salt

¼ teaspoon Dijon mustard

½ cup light olive oil

½ cup canola oil

1 bunch fresh cilantro, coarsely chopped (about 1 firmly packed cup)

1 tablespoon grated fresh ginger

2 to 3 precooked (2 to 2½ pounds) Dungeness crabs in the shell, chilled and cracked into pieces suitable for picking (see Techniques section, page 257)

At least several hours before you plan to serve, place the whole egg, egg yolk, lemon juice, salt, and mustard in the bowl of a food processor or a blender and pulse until the ingredients are well mixed, about 15 seconds. With the motor running, add the olive oil in a slow, steady stream, a few tablespoons at a time, incorporating well after each addition. Repeat with the canola oil until the sauce is thick and smooth. Add half the cilantro and all the ginger and pulse until incorporated, scraping down the sides of the work bowl once or twice. Taste and add the remaining cilantro if desired.

Transfer the mayonnaise to a clean nonreactive bowl, cover, and refrigerate for 6 hours or overnight to allow the flavors to meld (the flavors will become more pronounced the longer you refrigerate the sauce).

Transfer the mayonnaise to a small decorative bowl and place on a large platter. Surround with the cracked crab pieces and serve family style. Be sure to offer crab crackers or small mallets and lots of napkins for easy cleanup.

Cook's Hint: If you don't want to go to the trouble of picking your own crabmeat, simply buy fresh-picked crabmeat (about 1 pound for 6 people when served as an appetizer) and mix with enough Ginger-Cilantro Mayonnaise so the crab is lightly coated. Place in a decorative bowl, surround with crackers, and serve the crab as a dip. You can also spoon the dressed crab into endive leaves for a more formal presentation. The mayonnaise (without the crabmeat) makes a delicious substitute for tartar sauce with fried fish or remoulade sauce with seafood salads, as well as green goddess salad dressing (if thinned with a bit of milk or half-and-half).

Owners and founders of Abacela Winery, Hilda and Earl Jones, share a laugh.

The bucolic town of Eugene, Oregon, is home to the University of Oregon and Marché, which opened in August 1998. The 75-seat restaurant takes its name from the French word for "market," an appropriate moniker for two reasons. Marché is located in the bustling 5th Street Market, a funky destination shopping area rife with mom-and-pop-owned card and gift shops, boutiques, atmospheric cafés, and Eugene's beloved Metropol Bakery. And Marché's menu is based on the foods you find at your local farmers' market—fresh, seasonal, and regional produce—along with the bounty of local and regional ranchers, fishers, and foragers. Many of the products are organic, free range, and chemical free. Marché was founded by Executive Chef/General Manager Stephanie Pearl-Kimmel, a fixture in the Oregon wine country since 1972, when she opened the Excelsior Café in Eugene. The restaurant offered seasonal, regional menus and was also reportedly the first restaurant in Oregon to feature the wines of the young Oregon wine industry. Stephanie worked as culinary director at King Estate Winery (KEW) in Eugene, Oregon, (see page 170), wrote the *King Estate Pinot Gris Cookbook* and the *King Estate Pinot Noir Cookbook,* and hosted a 13-part PBS cooking series titled *New American Cuisine.* Today, Chef de Cuisine and son-in-law Rocky Maselli (the father of twin daughters Stella and Scarlett) carries on the family banner of market-driven regional cooking. The personable young chef, a transplant from the Bay area, appreciates life in Eugene because of the great young farmers, the sophisticated wine industry, the ready availability of ingredients, and the town's location just one hour from the coast. "Marché's fare is simple and all about the ingredients, plus it's super wine friendly," Rocky says. "It makes for wonderful pairings, since the food doesn't overpower the wine and the wine doesn't overpower the food." In this recipe, sorrel, a lemony perennial herb that appears in the garden in early spring, plays a starring role along with another Northwest favorite—spring salmon. Sorrel is known for its sour, acidic taste; when used in Rocky's sauce, it turns a lovely celadon color with a slightly sour lemon taste and a nice hint of white wine and shallot. A good-quality unoaked Chardonnay, with lots of citrus and pineapple and a lively/fresh mouthfeel, pairs perfectly.

Marché
296 East Fifth Avenue
Eugene, OR 97401
(541) 342-3612
marcherestaurant.com

Roasted Salmon with Sorrel Beurre Blanc

SERVES 4   VARIETAL Chardonnay (unoaked)

2 tablespoons minced shallots

½ cup dry white wine

1 cup heavy whipping cream

4 large fresh sorrel leaves

Preheat the oven to 425°F.

Combine the shallot and wine in a small nonreactive saucepan. Cook over medium-high heat until the liquid is reduced to about 1 teaspoon, 8 to 10 minutes. Add the cream and cook, stirring occasionally, until it is reduced

3 tablespoons cold unsalted butter, cut into ½-inch cubes

Kosher salt

Freshly ground white pepper

Four 6-ounce center-cut salmon fillets, rinsed, drained, and patted dry

Olive oil

Freshly ground black pepper

to the consistency of maple syrup and coats the back of a spoon, 8 to 10 minutes. While the cream is reducing, remove the ribs from the sorrel leaves and cut them into a chiffonade by stacking the leaves, rolling them like a cigar, and cutting crosswise into thin ribbons.

Stir the sorrel into the reduced cream, remove from the heat, and whisk in the butter piece by piece, incorporating the butter completely after each addition. Place a fine-meshed sieve over a mixing bowl, add the sauce, and strain, pressing out the solids with the back of a spoon to remove as much liquid as possible. (Alternatively, Chef Rocky suggests you can use a hand-held electric mixer, a blender, or a food processor for this step; the result will be a smoother sauce that will not have to be strained.) Season to taste with salt and the white pepper. Keep the sauce warm (a double boiler or a water bath—see Techniques section, page 258—works well for this) while you prepare the salmon.

Ten minutes before cooking, preheat the oven to 375°F. Line a baking sheet with parchment paper.

With a clean pastry brush, brush the salmon fillets lightly with olive oil, then sprinkle generously with salt and the black pepper. Place on the lined baking sheet and cook for 12 to 15 minutes, or until they reach the desired doneness.

Transfer the salmon fillets to 4 dinner plates and drizzle the sorrel sauce over the top.

Cook's Hint: Sorrel is available in limited supply year-round in the specialty herb section of produce departments or at your neighborhood farmers' market, although its peak season is in the spring. Look for bright-green, crisp leaves; store for up to three days in a plastic bag in the refrigerator. Chef Rocky suggests serving the dish with chive mashed potatoes or roasted new potatoes and spring vegetables such as asparagus, baby carrots, fava beans, or peas.

The Wisnovsky family, owners and operators of Valley View Winery, has been making wine in the Applegate Valley of southern Oregon for more than three decades. Their vineyard and winery, with its beautiful Pavilion Tasting Room, is located nine miles from historic Jacksonville, an atmospheric cowboy town. The winery is known for its reasonably priced yet premium-quality "weekday" wines bottled under the Valley View label. The more expensive and rare Anna Maria line ("weekend" wines) is reserved for wines of exceptional vintages. Varietals run the gamut from Chardonnay, Pinot Gris, and Viognier to Merlot, Syrah, Cabernet Franc and Sauvignon, and Tempranillo. There are also red blends (Claret and Meritage) and even a Late-Harvest Sauvignon Blanc.

This recipe, created by family friend Mary Chaplan, was part of a "Four Wineries, Four Chefs, One Ingredient" event sponsored by the Applegate Valley Wineries in the summer of 2005. Lavender was the key ingredient in this wine-and-gourmet series, during which Troon Vineyard served Lavender and Blueberry Cream Cake, Wooldridge Creek Winery offered Lavender-Grilled Salmon, and Bridgeview Vineyard served Lavender Pizza (!). Valley View's recipe is one of the most challenging, yet most satisfying, recipes in this book. Butter is infused with lavender before being brushed between paper-thin layers of phyllo. The goat-cheese filling is creamy and mildly flavored with onions. I enjoyed this both as a savory appetizer, garnished with fresh herbs, and as a dessert/cheese course, drizzled with good-quality honey, such as orange blossom. Thanks to the aromatic lavender, the strudel pairs nicely with the floral/musky aromas and flavors in a lush, mouth-filling Viognier.

Valley View Winery

1000 Upper Applegate Road

Jacksonville, OR 97530

(541) 844-8468

(800) 781-WINE

valleyviewwinery.com

Lavender–Goat Cheese Strudel

SERVES 6 to 8 as an appetizer or dessert/cheese course VARIETAL Viognier

12 tablespoons (1½ sticks) unsalted butter, plus 5 tablespoons unsalted butter at room temperature

½ cup dried culinary-grade lavender (see Cook's Hint, right)

½ cup diced shallots

¼ cup Anna Maria Viognier or other dry white wine

One 8-ounce package cream cheese, at room temperature, cut into small cubes

In a small saucepan, melt 8 tablespoons of the butter over low heat. Add the lavender, stir well, cover, remove from the heat, and let sit at room temperature for 20 minutes to steep. Place a fine-meshed sieve over a mixing bowl and add the lavender-butter mixture. Press the solids with a large spoon to remove as much of the liquid as possible. Discard the solids. Stir the 5 tablespoons room-temperature butter into the lavender-butter mixture until it forms a spreadable consistency.

Heat the remaining 4 tablespoons of butter in a small saucepan over medium-high heat and cook the shallots, stirring occasionally, until caramelized (medium golden in color but not browned), 18 to 20 minutes. Add the wine and stir well. Remove from the heat and set aside.

8 ounces fresh, soft goat's-milk cheese (chèvre)

½ teaspoon chopped fresh flat-leaf parsley, plus additional sprigs for garnish

½ teaspoon chopped fresh thyme leaves, plus additional leaves for garnish, or ¼ teaspoon dried thyme, crumbled

8 sheets phyllo dough

1 large egg, plus 1 tablespoon water, beaten

In a medium mixing bowl, mix the cream cheese, goat cheese, parsley, and thyme. Stir in the cooled shallots. Transfer the cream cheese mixture to a large piece of parchment paper, form it into a 16-inch log (using the parchment paper to manipulate it into shape), and reserve.

Lay the sheets of phyllo dough on a piece of parchment paper on a clean, dry work surface and cover with a clean, damp kitchen towel. Separate the first sheet of phyllo and place it on a piece of parchment paper large enough to hold it without crowding. With a clean pastry brush, brush the sheet lightly with the reserved lavender butter. Lay the second sheet on top of the first and brush lightly with the butter. Continue this process with the remaining 6 layers, until all 8 sheets are buttered.

Place the reserved cream cheese log along the bottom long edge of the phyllo. Starting with the bottom long edge, tightly roll the strudel jelly-roll fashion, using the parchment as an aid. Once rolled to within 1 inch of the edge, brush the inner exposed edge of dough with the egg wash, then finish rolling, pressing the edge into the roll to form a tight seam. Fold the dough at each end down and under, then press together to form a tight seal.

Ten minutes before cooking, preheat the oven to 375°F.

Using the parchment paper like a sling, transfer the strudel to a rimmed baking sheet and arrange the strudel seam side down. Score the top of the strudel with the tip of a small, sharp kitchen knife 6 or 8 times. With a clean pastry brush, lightly brush the top of the strudel with the egg wash. Bake for 25 to 30 minutes, or until the phyllo turns golden brown.

Place the baking sheet on a wire rack and cool the strudel for 5 to 10 minutes. With a sharp serrated knife, cut the strudel into 6 to 8 slices and divide among small plates. Garnish with the parsley sprigs and thyme leaves.

Cook's Hint: Culinary-grade lavender is available at spice shops, some better tea shops, and sometimes at health-food stores and upscale groceries. Or you can order it online at www.worldspice.com.

C elebrating its 15th anniversary in 2006, family-owned King Estate Winery (KEW) is situated on 1,033 certified-organic acres. More than 400 of the acres are planted with bucolic vineyards, orchards, and gardens. In 2005, Oregon Tilth recognized KEW as its "Producer of the Year." Located southwest of Eugene near the town of Lorane, KEW boasts a stunning French chateâu–like facility covering 110,000 square feet. It includes a 7,000-square-foot visitors' center with a commercial kitchen, a Finnish stove with two bread-baking ovens, a 28-seat tasting room, and an organic chef's garden. Just down the hill you'll find a brewery making Belgian-style beer, a distillery making fruit brandies, and a farmers' market selling organic fruits and vegetables and KEW-produced jams and jellies. KEW is renowned for its Pinot Noir and Pinot Gris, and it also produces limited amounts of Chardonnay. It's known as "a big winery with the boutique-winery mentality." This recipe comes from KEW's culinary department and makes use of one of the Northwest's great fish—Pacific troll-caught albacore tuna—which comes into plentiful supply during the summer months. The chunky, Mediterranean-leaning sauce that accompanies the fish, redolent with salty feta cheese, Roma tomatoes, kalamata olives, and fresh oregano, pairs nicely with the berry/earthy/spicy flavors characteristic of Oregon Pinot Noir.

King Estate Winery
80854 Territorial Road
Eugene, OR 97405
(541) 942-9874
kingestate.com

Seared Albacore Tuna with Feta, Olives, and Tomato

SERVES 4   VARIETAL Pinot Noir

4 tablespoons olive oil

Four 6- to 7-ounce albacore tuna steaks, rinsed, drained, and patted dry

Kosher salt

Freshly cracked black pepper

2 tablespoons chopped garlic

1 tablespoon minced shallots

½ pound fresh spinach leaves

1 tablespoon freshly squeezed lemon juice

8 plum tomatoes, cored and chopped

Preheat the oven to 400°F.

Heat 2 tablespoons of the olive oil in a large ovenproof skillet over medium-high heat. Sprinkle the tuna steaks lightly on both sides with salt and pepper. When the oil just begins to smoke, place the fish in the skillet without crowding and cook for 1 to 2 minutes on each side. Place the tuna in the oven and cook for 4 to 5 minutes (for medium rare), or to desired doneness.

Heat the remaining 2 tablespoons of olive oil in a large skillet over medium heat. When the oil is hot, add the garlic and shallots and cook, stirring often, until the shallots are translucent but not browned, 2 to 3 minutes. Add the spinach a handful or two at a time, turning with kitchen tongs and adding more spinach as it cooks down, until all the spinach is lightly wilted. Season to taste with salt, pepper, and the lemon juice.

Divide the spinach among 4 warmed dinner plates. Remove the fish from the oven and arrange 1 tuna steak over each bed of spinach.

1 cup (about 6 ounces) kalamata olives, pitted and halved lengthwise

¼ cup dry white wine

2 tablespoons chopped fresh oregano, or 2 teaspoons dried oregano, preferably Greek, crumbled

6 ounces feta cheese, crumbled

Working quickly, return the hot tuna skillet to the stove over medium-high heat and cook the plum tomatoes, stirring frequently, until they begin to break down, 1 to 2 minutes. Add the olives, white wine, and oregano and cook, stirring occasionally, until the wine is reduced by half, 1 to 2 minutes. Remove the pan from the heat and stir in the feta. Spoon the sauce around the tuna and serve immediately.

The flavor profile of Pinot Noir may include berries (strawberry and raspberry), cherries, earth, forest, mushrooms, truffles, vanilla, and violets, along with spicy notes such as cardamom, anise, and black pepper.

Idaho

G reg Koenig, co-owner with brother Andy of Koenig Distillery & Winery in Caldwell, Idaho, came to winemaking "after studying architecture—and food—in Italy." This recipe is his simplified version of a favorite pasta sauce he discovered in the kitchen of a small trattoria in Rome. Its peppery bite is mellowed by tomatoes, sour cream, and a boatload of Northwest shellfish. "I recommend the flinty, citrusy white wines from the Northwest with this dish, in particular our Semillon-Chardonnay blend, which I'm sure I created subconsciously to have something comparable to the great Friuli and Lazio whites I grew to love in Italy," Greg says. Try it with your favorite combinations of seafood, or with shrimp (or Alaskan spot prawns) alone, and accompany it with crusty bread and a simple green salad.

Koenig Distillery & Winery

20928 Grape Lane

Caldwell, ID 83607

(208) 455-8386

koenigvineyards.com

Creamy Tomato Seafood Linguine

SERVES 4 to 6   VARIETAL Semillon-Chardonnay

1 cup plus 1 tablespoon dry white wine

2 pounds Manila clams, shells scrubbed and rinsed

¼ cup olive oil

1 cup chopped white or yellow onion

4 teaspoons minced garlic

½ teaspoon crushed red pepper flakes

3 cups cored, chopped Roma tomatoes (5 or 6 tomatoes), or 3 cups canned chopped tomatoes, drained

½ cup fish stock, or ¼ cup clam broth plus ¼ cup water

½ cup sour cream

2 tablespoons chopped fresh basil or flat-leaf parsley, plus extra leaves for garnish

1 pound fresh or dried linguine

½ pound medium shrimp or Alaskan spot prawns, peeled and deveined

Place the 1 tablespoon of wine and the clams in a stockpot or large saucepan over medium-high heat. Cover the pan, and cook until the clams begin to open, shaking the pan occasionally to redistribute the shellfish and lowering the heat if needed, 5 minutes.

Uncover the pan and transfer any open clams to a large mixing bowl. Cover and continue to cook until the remaining clams open, about 2 minutes. Discard any clams that do not open. Pour the remaining clams and the pan juices into the mixing bowl. When cool enough to handle, remove the clam meat from the shells and discard the shells. Cover the bowl with aluminum foil and reserve.

In a Dutch oven or stockpot, heat the olive oil over medium heat. When the oil is hot, add the onion, garlic, and crushed red pepper flakes and cook, stirring occasionally, until the onion is softened but not browned, 5 to 7 minutes.

Add the tomatoes, the remaining 1 cup of wine, and the fish stock, and bring to a boil. Reduce the heat and simmer, stirring occasionally, until the tomatoes cook down and the sauce reduces to about 2 cups, 25 to 30 minutes. Remove from the heat and gently stir in the sour cream and basil. Cover and set aside.

While the sauce is cooking, bring a large pot of salted water to a boil. Add the linguine and cook until al dente.

Five minutes before serving, return the Dutch oven to the stove top and re-warm the tomato sauce over medium-low heat. Add the shrimp, stir well, and cook, stirring occasionally, until the shrimp just begin to turn pink and

½ pound cleaned squid tubes, rinsed, patted dry, and cut into ½-inch rings

Kosher salt

Freshly ground black pepper

2 to 4 tablespoons freshly grated Parmigiano-Reggiano cheese (optional)

the tails just begin to curl, 2 to 3 minutes. Add the squid and reserved clams and clam juice and stir gently so the shellfish is incorporated in the sauce. Cook until the calamari is just cooked through and the clams are warm, 1 to 2 minutes. Be careful not to overcook the seafood! Season to taste with salt and pepper.

Divide the linguine among 4 to 6 dinner plates. Divide the seafood and sauce over the pasta, sprinkle with the cheese, if desired, and garnish with basil leaves.

Greg Koenig, co-owner with brother Andy of Koenig Distillery & Winery, came to winemaking after studying architecture in Italy, a skill that came in handy when he and Andy designed and built the Tuscan-style winery in Caldwell, Idaho.

Dr. Ron and Mary Bitner are busy as bees as owners of Bitner Vineyards in Caldwell, Idaho. In his "day" job, Dr. Ron is a professional entomologist who travels the world helping farmers establish colonies of alfalfa leafcutting bees, which aid in the pollination of crops. Mary sticks closer to home, working as Administrative Assistant for the Alumni and Parent Relations Office at Albertson College of Idaho. Ron and Mary were the driving force behind the first "Taste of the Harvest" Festival, which started in 2000 and has since become an annual event at the college. Its gourmet foods, fine wines, and cultural music have brought renewed awareness of the Gem State's abundant harvest and bountiful foodways. This recipe, devised by Albertson College's former executive chef Maury Bennett, showcases Bitner Vineyards Reserve Chardonnay paired with Idaho's most famous fish—trout. Chardonnay is often described as "citrusy," and the lovely, light, lemon-flavored sauce that accompanies the fish definitely fits the bill for a match made in heaven.

Bitner Vineyards

16645 Plum Road

Caldwell, ID 83605

(208) 454-0086

bitnervineyards.com

Cedar-Planked Idaho Trout with Chardonnay-Lemon Beurre Blanc and Apple-Pecan Rice

SERVES 4   VARIETAL Chardonnay

Apple-Pecan Rice

2¼ cups water

1 cup long-grain white rice

2 teaspoons unsalted butter

2 medium (or 1 large) apples, preferably Gravenstein, Fuji, or Cameo, cored and diced

½ cup pecans, toasted (see Techniques section, page 258)

Kosher salt

Freshly ground black pepper

Chardonnay-Lemon Beurre Blanc

10 tablespoons (1¼ sticks) un-salted butter, cut into 1-tablespoon pieces

2 tablespoons all-purpose flour

¼ cup minced shallots

To make the Apple-Pecan Rice, bring the water to a boil in a medium saucepan. Stir in the rice and bring the water back to a boil. Reduce the heat to low, cover, and cook until all the water is absorbed and the rice is tender, 20 to 25 minutes. Remove from the heat, fluff with a fork, cover, and reserve.

While the rice is cooking, melt the butter in a medium nonstick skillet over medium-high heat. Add the apples and cook, stirring occasionally, until golden brown and tender, 5 to 7 minutes. Add the apples and pecans to the reserved rice. Season to taste with salt and pepper, cover, and keep warm until serving.

To make the Chardonnay-Lemon Beurre Blanc, make a roux by melting 2 tablespoons of the butter in a small skillet or saucepan over low heat. Whisk in the flour a little at a time and cook until the flour-butter mixture becomes smooth and turns pale ivory in color, stirring well after each addition and whisking constantly, 5 to 7 minutes. Remove from the heat, cover, and set aside.

Bring the shallots and wine to a boil in a large saucepan and cook until reduced by half, 2 to 3 minutes. Reduce the heat to low, add the cream and lemon zest, and stir well. Let the cream come just to a simmer (when the temperature reaches 120°F on an instant-read thermometer), then whisk in 2 tablespoons of the reserved roux, bit by bit, stirring well after each addition to avoid lumps. Cook, whisking constantly, until the sauce is smooth and slightly

½ cup Bitner Vineyards Reserve Chardonnay or other good-quality Chardonnay

1 cup heavy whipping cream

1 tablespoon freshly grated lemon zest

Kosher salt

Freshly ground white pepper

Two 12-ounce whole dressed trout, rinsed, patted dry, and halved lengthwise

2 teaspoons minced garlic

Kosher salt

Freshly ground black pepper

1 to 2 tablespoons olive oil

below left: Harvesting white-wine grapes at Bitner Vineyards in Idaho's Snake River Valley.

below right: While their parents are busy harvesting grapes for Koenig Distillery & Winery at Bitner Vineyards, two boys play a game of grape toss to help pass the time.

thickened, 1 to 2 minutes. Remove from the heat and whisk in the remaining 8 tablespoons of butter, piece by piece, incorporating well after each addition.

Place a fine-meshed sieve over a mixing bowl and strain the sauce, pressing the solids with the back of a spoon to remove as much sauce as possible. Discard the solids and return the sauce to the saucepan. Season to taste with salt and pepper, cover, and keep warm until serving.

To cook the trout, preheat an outdoor grill to medium heat or an indoor stove-top grill to medium-high heat. Lightly sprinkle the flesh side only of the trout with the garlic, salt, and pepper. If cooking on an outdoor grill, lightly oil the grill and place the trout fillets flesh side down on the grill without crowding. Cook until the trout just flakes, 3 to 4 minutes per side, turning once. Alternatively, if desired, brush an untreated cedar plank (or planks) lightly with the olive oil. Arrange the trout fillets skin side down on the plank(s) without crowding. Place the plank(s) on the grill and close the lid. Cook until the trout just flakes, 8 to 10 minutes. If cooking on an indoor stove-top grill, brush it lightly with the olive oil and place the trout fillets on the grill, flesh side down, without crowding. Cook until the trout just flakes, 3 to 4 minutes per side, turning once.

To serve, divide the rice among 4 dinner plates, angle the fish over the rice, and drizzle the fish and rice with the butter sauce.

Cook's Hint: For the most complex flavor in the trout, Chef Maury suggests cooking the fish on a cedar plank, a time-honored tradition of the Northwest First Nations people (see page xii). If cooking on a plank in the home oven, arrange the oven rack in the center of the oven, place the plank on the rack, and preheat the oven and the rack to 350°F for at least 15 minutes. Slide the oven rack and the plank partially out of the oven (to avoid moving a hot plank around the kitchen), arrange the trout halves on the plank, and cook for 10 to 12 minutes, or until it reaches the desired doneness.

Andy Koenig makes superlative fruit-flavored brandies in a distiller imported from Europe. With its copper vats and tubing and numerous dials and pressure gauges, it looks like something straight out of *Charlie and the Chocolate Factory* or *20,000 Leagues Under the Sea*. His award-winning plum brandy is put to excellent use in the fresh plum jam that accompanies the lamb medallions in this recipe. With a sweet-tart, zingy flavor and pale-pink, rosé-like color, it's reminiscent in texture of cooked rhubarb. Seasoned with plenty of fresh garlic, salt, and freshly cracked black pepper, the medallions form the perfect match for Cabernet Sauvignon (or a tannic Syrah), according to winemaker Greg Koenig, Andy's brother. The recipe, created by former executive chef Maury Bennett of Bon Appétit Catering, was served at the "Taste of the Harvest," an annual food-and-wine festival held at Albertson College of Idaho in Caldwell, Idaho.

Koenig Distillery & Winery

20928 Grape Lane

Caldwell, ID 83607

(208) 455-8386

koenigvineyards.com

Idaho Lamb Medallions with Plum Brandy Jam

SERVES 4   VARIETAL Cabernet Sauvignon

Plum Brandy Jam

One 375-ml bottle (1½ cups) Koenig Plum Brandy or other good-quality plum brandy

1 pound fresh red plums, peeled, pitted, and chopped (see Cook's Hint, below)

2 to 4 teaspoons sugar

Four 5-ounce lamb medallions (boneless loin), or 1½ to 2 pounds lamb chops

2 teaspoons minced garlic

1½ teaspoons kosher salt

½ teaspoon freshly ground black pepper

1 tablespoon canola oil

Fresh mint sprigs, for garnish

To make the Plum Brandy Jam, heat a small saucepan over medium-high heat. Add the brandy and cook until reduced by half to ¾ cup, 4 to 6 minutes. Stir in the plums and 2 teaspoons of the sugar. Reduce the heat and simmer gently, stirring occasionally, until the mixture is reduced to about 1 cup and forms a jam-like consistency, 12 to 15 minutes. Remove from the heat and, when slightly cooled, taste the jam and add an additional 1 to 2 teaspoons sugar, as desired. Serve warm or transfer to a covered container and chill until serving. Bring to room temperature or warm gently before serving.

Preheat the oven to 450°F.

Rub the lamb medallions with the garlic and sprinkle with the salt and pepper. Heat a large skillet over medium-high heat and add the oil. When the oil is hot, add the lamb. Brown for 2 minutes on each side, then reduce the heat to medium or medium low and cook to the desired doneness, turning occasionally, 8 to 10 minutes. If desired, the lamb can also be grilled.

Place a lamb medallion on each of 4 dinner plates, dollop with the jam, and garnish with the mint sprigs.

Cook's Hint: To peel plums, simmer plums in boiling water for 1 minute. Drain, cool, and remove the peels.

right: The distiller used to make fruit brandies at Koenig Distillery & Winery looks like something out of *20,000 Leagues Under the Sea* or *Charlie and the Chocolate Factory.*

below: The impressive lineup of fruit brandies produced by Andy Koenig at Koenig Distillery & Winery in Idaho.

S usan and Scott DeSeelhorst own Snake River Winery and Arena Valley Vineyard in Parma, Idaho. Arena Valley Vineyard, which they purchased in 1998, is a beautiful site and one of the "hottest" vineyards in the state, supplying the state's two largest wineries, Ste. Chapelle and Sawtooth, as well as Snake River. Scott, a trained chef and former restaurant owner, enjoys creating new dishes to pair with his wines, such as a dish he and Susan affectionately call Sticky Chicky. The Thai-style chicken dish is similar to satay, with a glossy, complex glaze reminiscent of a good-quality Chinese barbecue sauce. The key to successful Sticky Chicky is twofold: allow the meat sufficient time in the marinade, and pay attention while cooking the glaze so as not to overcook it (in which case, Scott warns, you'll end up with a saucepan full of hard candy due to the high sugar content!).

As far as wines go, Snake River Winery's Riesling is an excellent pairing with most foods, thanks to sufficient alcohol (12 percent) and well-balanced acids and sugar. The exception, Scott notes, is red meat and similar strong proteins. The chef/winemaker recommends Snake River Riesling as a match with Asian, Southwestern, and spicier foods; with dessert; or even as an after-dinner cordial.

Snake River Winery

24013 Arena Valley Road

Parma, ID 83660

(208) 722-5858

snakeriverwinery.com

Sticky Chicky (Coconut Chicken with Chili Glaze)

SERVES 4   VARIETAL Riesling

Chili Glaze

¾ cup unseasoned rice vinegar

½ cup sugar

3 tablespoons soy sauce

1 tablespoon minced fresh ginger

1 teaspoon crushed red pepper flakes

1½ cups regular or "light" (reduced-fat) coconut milk (shake the can before opening and stir well before measuring)

3 tablespoons minced fresh ginger

2 teaspoons freshly ground black pepper

At least three hours before you plan to cook, in order to allow the flavors to meld and the glaze to thicken, make the Chili Glaze. Place the rice vinegar, sugar, soy sauce, ginger, and red pepper flakes in a small saucepan and stir until the sugar is dissolved. Bring to a rolling boil over medium-high heat. Reduce the heat to medium and cook until the glaze reaches the consistency of maple syrup, 20 to 25 minutes. (It will thicken a bit more once it comes to room temperature or is refrigerated.) Be careful not to cook at too high a temperature or for too long, or the glaze will harden before you can drizzle it over the chicken. Set the glaze aside and re-warm it when ready to use.

Combine the coconut milk, ginger, black pepper, and red pepper flakes in a small bowl and stir well. Pour ½ cup of the marinade into a small glass mixing bowl, cover, and refrigerate until needed.

Pour the remaining marinade into a large, resealable plastic bag. Add the chicken and turn to coat on all sides. Refrigerate for at least 3 hours or, preferably, overnight, turning occasionally to redistribute the marinade over the chicken.

2 teaspoons crushed red pepper flakes

2 pounds boneless, skinless chicken thighs or boneless, skinless chicken breasts (see Cook's Hint, below)

2 cups cooked jasmine or long-grain white rice

2 tablespoons sliced green onions, for garnish

Ten minutes before cooking, preheat the broiler. Prepare a broiling pan with a rack and oil the rack lightly or spray with nonstick cooking spray.

Remove the reserved marinade from the refrigerator. Arrange the chicken pieces on the rack without crowding and cook for 3 minutes. Remove from the broiler, brush with the reserved marinade, return to the broiler, and cook for 3 minutes more. Remove from the broiler, turn the meat, brush with the reserved marinade, return to the broiler, and cook for 3 minutes more. Continue this process one or two more times, for a total of 12 to 15 minutes, or until the chicken is opaque throughout. Do not brush the chicken after it is out of the oven and completely cooked through, and discard any unused marinade.

Divide the rice among 6 dinner plates and arrange the cooked chicken on top of the rice. Drizzle with the re-warmed glaze or serve the glaze in separate small dipping bowls. Garnish the chicken with the green onions.

Cook's Hint: Susan and Scott DeSeelhorst prefer chicken thighs to breasts in this recipe because the dark meat retains its moistness and is more flavorful. The chicken can also be grilled on the stove top, although it tends to splatter and be a bit messier than cooking under the broiler. Be sure to oil the grill pan well before cooking the chicken to avoid tough cleanups. The Chili Glaze can be made up to two weeks ahead. Allow the glaze to cool completely at room temperature, transfer to a nonreactive container, and refrigerate until using.

Scott DeSeelhorst, winemaker and co-owner, with wife Susan, of Snake River Winery in Parma, Idaho, is a trained chef and former restaurant owner.

This recipe is reprinted from Chef Jonathan Mortimer's cookbook, *The Idaho Table: A Taste of the Intermountain West,* a superlative exploration of the Gem State's indigenous ingredients—fresh trout, venison, elk, and a wide assortment of wild mushrooms. The chef, who owns Mortimer's restaurant in the atmospheric Belgravia Building in downtown Boise, is a zealot for Idaho cuisine. He's cooked at the James Beard House, teaches at Boise State University's School of Culinary Arts, and hosts a weekly radio show I've had the pleasure of appearing on (*Radio Café*), and works as a television chef. He suggests serving the strudel slices with puréed red beets since the earthy tastes work well so well together. The mushroom flavors of this appetizer also pair perfectly with the musky richness of Pinot Noir or, on the wilder side, Mourvèdre. Mourvèdre is commonly associated with the wines of southern France, where it is used as a blending wine to improve color and structure thanks to its garnet color, characteristic spicy and peppery notes, inherent tannins, and hard texture.

Mortimer's

Belgravia Building

110 South Fifth Street

Boise, ID 83702

(208) 338-6550

mortimersidaho.com

Wild Mushroom Strudel

SERVES 20 as an appetizer   VARIETAL Pinot Noir or Mourvèdre

1 tablespoon virgin olive oil

1 tablespoon canola oil

½ cup minced red onion

1 pound assorted wild mushrooms, such as morel, chanterelle, or porcini, stems removed and discarded and remaining portion cleaned (see Cook's Hint, page 219)

1 cup dry red wine

1 tablespoon chopped fresh tarragon, or 1½ teaspoons dried tarragon, crumbled

Sea salt

Freshly ground black pepper

One 1-pound package phyllo dough

8 tablespoons (1 stick) unsalted butter, melted

1 large egg, whisked with 1 teaspoon water

Preheat the oven to 375°F. Line a rimmed baking sheet with parchment paper.

In a large skillet, heat the olive and canola oils over medium-high heat and cook the onion, stirring frequently, until softened but not browned, 2 minutes. Add the mushrooms and cook, stirring occasionally, 2 minutes more. Add the red wine and tarragon and stir well. Reduce the heat to medium and cook, stirring occasionally, until the liquid is reduced and the pan is almost dry, about 20 minutes. Season with salt and pepper and scoop the mushroom mixture onto a baking sheet to cool.

While the mushroom mixture is reducing, lay the phyllo dough on a clean, dry work surface and cut it in half lengthwise. Lay the two dough packets on individual pieces of parchment paper and cover with clean, damp kitchen towels. Separate the first sheet of phyllo from the first dough packet and, with a clean pastry brush, brush lightly with melted butter. Lay the next sheet on top and brush lightly with butter. Continue this process until all the sheets from the first packet are buttered. Re-cover the packet with the towel. Repeat with the phyllo sheets from the second packet.

Once the mushroom mixture has cooled completely, divide it evenly over the tops of the two phyllo packets, leaving about 1 inch uncovered around the entire length of one of the long edges and a little exposed dough along each short end so that you can form a tight seal. With a clean pastry brush,

brush the exposed long edge with the egg mixture. Using the parchment as an aid, tightly roll the strudel jelly-roll fashion, beginning with the long edge with the mushroom filling spread over it. Once rolled, press the exposed long edge into the roll tightly to affix the egg wash and form a tight seam. Press in the end pieces and seal tightly.

Use the parchment paper to transfer the strudels onto the prepared baking sheet. Place the strudels seam side down and bake for 25 to 30 minutes, or until the top of the phyllo turns golden.

Place the baking sheet on a wire rack and cool the strudels for 5 to 10 minutes. With a sharp serrated knife, cut each strudel into approximately 1-inch slices for 10 slices per strudel. Arrange the slices on a large platter and serve as a passed appetizer or on the buffet table, or place individual slices on small plates and serve as a first course.

Chef Jon Mortimer plating a dish at his eponymous restaurant in Boise, Idaho.

The Next Walla Walla: Idaho Winemakers

Most people would deduce that Idaho's combination of high altitudes, frigid winter weather, and low annual rainfall make wine-grape–growing a difficult proposition. But the state's growers insist that, from a purely geographical standpoint, southern Idaho offers the perfect conditions for wine.

A crop duster flies over a vineyard near Nampa, Idaho.

Cold winters force the vines to grow dormant, allowing them to conserve their energy and rest up for the coming season while heading off dreaded diseases and bugs. Summer's long, warm days keep the grapes' sugar levels high, while the cold nights bring up their acidity. The lack of rainfall drives away mold and rot and allows grape growers to control water levels through irrigation. Fast-draining volcanic-ash soils provide healthy growing conditions.

The presence of the Snake River, which travels over 1,000 miles from its headwaters in Yellowstone National Park to its junction with the Columbia River in Washington State, offers twofold protection. The flow of air over moving water draws off heat in the summer and spreads a moderating humidity in the winter. Running through the southwest corner of the state, the Snake is where the majority of Idaho's wineries are located.

And with 24 operating wineries, 60 growers, 1,400 acres planted with grapes, and wines characterized by a concentrated varietal character with high natural acidity and good overall balance, the Idaho wine industry is quickly making a name for itself in the Northwest and beyond.

Ste. Chapelle is considered the Idaho winery by many, since it is the oldest (established in 1976), the largest (with 160,000 cases produced per year, of which Riesling comprises more than 80,000 cases), and the most widely distributed (with key markets in New York, Pennsylvania, and Florida).

Winemaker Chuck Devlin, a self-described "hotshot red

"We produce 1,400 cases and eight varietals, and the two of us handpick and hand-sort everything…twenty-two tons of grapes pass through our fingertips each year."

winemaker from California who loves Alsatian-style wines," was brought on board shortly after Canandaigua Wine Company bought Ste. Chapelle in 2001. Although principally known for its Rieslings, Chardonnays, and ice wines before Devlin's hiring, the winery has since shown promise with its sparkling wines and reds, particularly Cabernet Sauvignon, Merlot, and Syrah.

While not nearly as behemoth as Ste. Chapelle, Sawtooth Winery in Nampa is large by Idaho standards; some years it produces upwards of 19,000 cases per year. "I convinced my Dad to turn a pasture into a vineyard in 1982, when I was still a college student," says winemaker Brad Pintler. "We planted Chenin

Blanc, Riesling, and Semillon. The next year we added Chardonnay and Cabernet Sauvignon." Brad started making wine in 1988, and, since then, the winery has grown from 15 acres to 300, expanded annual production from 3,000 cases to anywhere from 15,000 to 19,000 cases, and become part of the Corus Brands family.

Steve and Leslie Robertson, who own Hells Canyon Winery, planted Idaho's second oldest wine-grape vineyard in 1981 and have since been known as top-notch producers of Chardonnay, Merlot, and Cabernet Sauvignon. Their European-styled winery, which is surrounded by 40 acres of vineyards, includes the luxurious Bed & Breakfast at Hells Canyon Winery. "Where Washington was 25 years ago is where Idaho is today," Steve opines.

Brothers Greg and Andy Koenig brought together a singular vision of Old World craftsmanship when they started Koenig Distillery & Winery in 1995. Specimen stone fruit and pear trees chosen for their flavor, along with a small vineyard of Merlot, Semillon, and Chardonnay, were planted on an exquisite site in the Snake River Valley anchored by a sunny-yellow Tuscan villa. "We produce 1,400 cases and eight varietals, and the two of us handpick and hand-sort everything," Greg says. "Twenty-two tons of grapes pass through our fingertips each year."

Scott DeSeelhorst is a trained chef and former restaurateur who traded in whisk for wine thief in 1998 when he purchased Arena Valley Vineyard, one of the best grape-growing sites in the state. "I treat winemaking like cooking…the key to cooking and winemaking is using the best ingredients, and with wine, that means the grapes," Scott says. His Snake River Winery produces about 4,000 cases per year, with production of major varieties such as Riesling, Chardonnay, Merlot, and Cabernet Sauvignon, as well as a Bordeaux Blend composed of Merlot, Malbec, Cabernet Franc, and Cabernet Sauvignon. Scott also blends his estate-grown Syrah, Grenache, and Mourvèdre in a unique bottling, and works with lesser-known grapes such as Barbera, Tempranillo, and Blauer Zweigelt.

Retired American Airlines captain Dick Dickstein became enamored with wine in his early 20s and always dreamed of operating a winery. But not until 1998, when he and wife Shirley came to Idaho to attend a wedding reception at Ste. Chapelle, did he stumble across the perfect site. "We looked at this property on a Friday evening and bought it Saturday morning," he says as he reminisces about the nine-and-one-half-acre apple orchard overlooking the Boise River that has since become Parma Ridge Vineyards. "It was only the second property we saw."

"We're Walla Walla wannabes," admits Dr. Ron Bitner, a globetrotting entomologist by day who began growing grapes at Bitner Vineyards in 1981, with first production in 1985. In 1997, Bitner commissioned Greg Koenig to make reserve wines under the Bitner Vineyard label. Since that time, Bitner has become known for award-winning Chardonnay and Cabernet Sauvignon. In an interview for the *Idaho Press Tribune,* "Dr. Ron" stated, "Most people don't know we have a wine industry here. It's finally starting to grow. What we'd really like to get going here in the valley is [wine] tourism."

In March 2007, Dr. Ron and the other Idaho winemakers realized a long-held dream when the United States Alcohol and Tobacco Tax and Trade Bureau (TTB) designated the Snake River Valley as the state's first American Viticultural Area (AVA). This connotes the southern portion of Idaho as a unique grape-growing region capable of producing excellent wines.

"A combination of the area's microclimates, soil, and other growing conditions makes the Valley a premium grape-producing area," Dr. Ron says. "Those of us who produce wine here have known that for some time. Others are just now finding out."

Ste. Chapelle
19348 Lowell Road
Caldwell, ID 83605
(208) 459-7222
stechapelle.com

Sawtooth Winery
13750 Surrey Lane
Nampa, ID 83686
(208) 467-1200
sawtoothwinery.com

Hells Canyon Winery
18835 Symms Road
Caldwell, ID 83605
(208) 454-3300
hellscanyonwinery.org

Parma Ridge Vineyards
24509 Rudd Road
Parma, ID 83660
(208) 722-6885
parmaridge.com

A welcoming arch leads to the tasting room at Ste. Chapelle, Idaho's largest and oldest winery.

The barrel room at Domaine de Chaberton
in British Columbia's Fraser Valley.

Wine aficionados on both sides of the border have discovered Domaine de Chaberton (DdC), one of British Columbia's first estate wineries. Located south of Vancouver and near the U.S./Canada border in the picturesque town of Langley, DdC was founded by the husband-and-wife team of Claude and Inge Violet in 1991. Claude, who jokes that he was born in a wine barrel in the south of France, is a ninth-generation winemaker whose family began making wine in 1644. The winery's white grapes are Fraser Valley grown; the red grapes come from one of the Okanagan Valley's premier grape-growing areas—the Black Sage Bench, near Oliver. DdC produces a full line of white, red, and dessert wines, but is best known for producing two styles of Bacchus (dry and off dry). Bacchus, a cross of Silvaner, Müller-Thurgau, and Riesling, makes a good choice as an appetizer wine, but also pairs well with many foods, thanks to its peach/apricot, Muscat, and citrus flavors and sweet-spice notes. Eugene Kwan is the new Proprietor/Managing Director at DdC, where he is busy winning awards for his Canoe Cove line of wines. In 2006, Canoe Cove Shiraz won the Lieutenant Governor's Award of Excellence, one of only 11 wines so honored.

Part of the fun of visiting DdC is a meal at the appropriately named Bacchus Bistro. With its large outdoor seating area overlooking the vineyards and expertly prepared French bistro fare, the Bistro is so popular that reservations are always a good idea. You'll

Domaine de Chaberton Winery and Bacchus Bistro

1064-216th Street

Langley, BC V2Z 1R3

Canada

(604) 530-1736 (winery)

(604) 530-9694 (bistro)

(888) 332-9463

domainedechaberton.com

enjoy Chef Frederic Desbiens's Steamed Salt Spring Island Mussels *Marinière, Filet au Poivre,* daily-changing quiche and stuffed crêpes, and the recipe he shared with me, *Boeuf Bourguignon.* Burgundy's traditional beef stew is made special in Chef Frederic's version, thanks to the preparation of the garniture. The pearl onions, mushrooms, and bacon are sautéed separately from the stew so they retain their shapes and robust flavors. In combination with the meltingly tender meat and the well-balanced flavors from the slightly crunchy vegetables and smoky bacon, the stew forms the perfect pairing with the often leathery, peppery, smoked-bacon notes found in Syrah.

Boeuf Bourguignon

SERVES 6   VARIETAL Syrah

2½ pounds beef brisket, cut into 1½-inch cubes

2 teaspoons kosher salt, plus extra for seasoning

1 teaspoon freshly ground black pepper, plus extra for seasoning

2 to 3 tablespoons vegetable oil

2 cups diced white or yellow onions

Season the meat with the 2 teaspoons salt and the 1 teaspoon pepper. In a Dutch oven, heat 1 tablespoon of the vegetable oil over medium-high heat. Add half of the beef and cook, turning occasionally, until well browned on all sides, 5 to 7 minutes. Transfer to a large plate and repeat with the remaining beef and another tablespoon of oil, if needed.

Reduce the heat to medium. Add 1 tablespoon of oil to the Dutch oven, along with the onions, carrot, celery, and garlic. Cook, stirring occasionally, until the onion is translucent and softened, 5 to 7 minutes.

1 cup diced carrot

½ cup diced celery

2 tablespoons minced garlic

¼ cup all-purpose flour

3 cups dry red wine

½ cup sodium-reduced beef broth

1 tablespoon tomato paste

1 *bouquet garni* (see Techniques section, page 256)

4 cups fresh pearl onions

5 slices thick-cut bacon, cut cross-wise into ¼-inch slices

8 ounces white or cremini mush-rooms, quartered

¼ cup chopped fresh flat-leaf parsley

Return the meat and accumulated juices to the pan. Sprinkle the flour evenly over the meat and vegetables and stir well to avoid lumps. Add the red wine, broth, tomato paste, and *bouquet garni*. Stir well and bring to a boil. Cover, reduce the heat, and simmer gently, stirring occasionally, until the meat is tender, 2 hours. Season to taste with salt and pepper.

While the stew is cooking, bring a medium saucepan of water to a boil. Prepare an ice bath (see Techniques section, page 257) in a medium mixing bowl. Add the pearl onions to the boiling water and cook for 1 minute. Drain the onions in a colander and immediately plunge them into the ice bath. With a paring knife, trim the root ends and pull off the skins. Pat dry with a clean kitchen towel or paper towels and set aside.

Just before serving, heat a medium skillet over medium heat. Add the ba-con and cook, stirring occasionally, until crisp and brown, 5 to 7 minutes. Remove the bacon from the pan and drain on paper towels. Pour off all but 2 tablespoons of the bacon drippings. Return the skillet to the heat, add the reserved pearl onions, and cook, stirring occasionally, until the onions are tender-crisp, 3 to 5 minutes. Add the mushrooms and cook, stirring oc-casionally, until they just begin to give off their liquid and aroma, 5 minutes. Remove from the heat and season to taste with salt and pepper.

Remove and discard the *bouquet garni*. Divide the stew among 6 soup bowls. Garnish with the mushroom-and-onion mixture, bacon, and parsley.

above: The Bacchus Bistro at Domaine de Chaberton offers both an indoor and a large outdoor seating area, along with exquisite views of the vineyards and French bistro fare.

left: Domaine de Chaberton's vineyards near the U.S./Canada border display beautiful fall colors.

O pen 365 days a year, O'Doul's Restaurant & Bar is the kind of place where regulars from the neighborhood, as well as out-of-towners staying next door at the Listel Hotel, feel right at home. The restaurant and hotel are located right on Robson, downtown Vancouver's most vibrant, eclectic street for shopping and dining (good people watching, too!). The Listel positions itself as the place for "cultural tourists," is committed to "art, elegance, and comfort," and has been dubbed the city's "most art-full hotel." It's even published an anthology of short fiction titled *The Vancouver Stories* that is placed in each guest room. Featuring "West Coast eclectic cuisine," a *Wine Spectator* award-winning wine list, and 5,000-bottle cellar, not to mention jazz on tap seven nights a week, O'Doul's is a destination in and of itself.

The restaurant, which has been a tradition on the Vancouver dining scene for more than 30 years, is especially well known for its daily-changing preparation of wild British Columbia salmon (the management donates $1 per plate to the Pacific Salmon Foundation) and a wide variety of eggs Benedict dishes. After enjoying Champagne Brunch on Christmas day, I could hardly wait to ask Executive Chef Tim Muehlbauer and Executive Sous Chef Ken Joe to share their recipe for Eggs Haida, O'Doul's riff on the classic eggs Benedict. In the chef's recipe that follows, hot-smoked salmon substitutes for the more traditional ham or Canadian bacon, and the hollandaise is a snap to make. Assistant General Manager and Sommelier Calvin DesChene suggests pairing the dish with a King Estate Pinot Gris from Oregon or an Alsatian Pinot Gris from France. "The natural acidity of Pinot Gris will cut through the richness of all the butter, and the spicy fruitiness of the wine will go great with the smoked salmon. Both wines are rich enough to match the weight of the dish."

The Listel Hotel

O'Doul's Restaurant & Bar

1300 Robson Street

Vancouver, BC V6E 1C5

Canada

(604) 661-1400

odoulsrestaurant.com

Eggs Haida

SERVES 6   VARIETAL Pinot Gris

Quick 'n' Easy Hollandaise Sauce

3 large egg yolks

1½ tablespoons boiling water

½ cup very warm clarified butter (see Techniques section, page 256)

1 tablespoon freshly squeezed lemon juice

Kosher salt

Freshly ground white pepper

To make the Quick 'n' Easy Hollandaise Sauce, place the egg yolks in a blender and pulse briefly to break them. With the blender on, slowly add the water in a thin, steady stream. Slowly add the clarified butter in a thin, steady stream, blending until the sauce is thick and pale, 1 to 1½ minutes. Add the lemon juice and season to taste with salt and pepper. Serve immediately or keep warm until serving (a double boiler or water bath—see Techniques section, page 258—works well for this).

Heat the oil in a large nonstick skillet over medium heat. When the pan is hot, add the salmon and cook, turning gently so as not to break up the large flakes, until it is warmed through, 2 to 3 minutes. Remove from the heat, cover, and set aside.

One-of-a-kind, hand-painted plates adorn the tables at O'Doul's Restaurant & Bar overlooking trendy Robson Street in Vancouver, British Columbia.

1 teaspoon vegetable oil

¾ pound (12 ounces) hot-smoked salmon, coarsely chopped into large pieces (Note: Use hot-smoked salmon, as opposed to cold-smoked salmon, for this dish.)

3 tablespoons white vinegar

12 large eggs

6 English muffins, cut in half and toasted

Sweet paprika, for garnish

To poach the eggs, fill a large saucepan, stockpot, or Dutch oven with water and bring to a simmer. Add the vinegar. Crack an egg into a small ramekin, then gently pour the egg into the simmering water. Repeat with the remaining eggs, cooking in 2 or 3 batches to avoid overcrowding. Cook the eggs for 3 minutes for soft yolks, 5 minutes for firm yolks, or 8 minutes for hard yolks, depending on the desired doneness. With a slotted spoon, gently remove the eggs from the water and place on several thicknesses of paper towels or a clean kitchen towel to drain. If cooking in batches, transfer cooked eggs to a wide, shallow bowl of water warmed to 150°F and hold for up to 30 minutes.

Place 2 muffin halves on each plate. Arrange the smoked salmon over the muffins. Top each muffin half with a poached egg, then spoon the sauce over the eggs. Sprinkle lightly with paprika and serve immediately.

Throughout the summertime, and four times during the Christmas holiday season, the Rocky Mountaineer makes a spectacular two-day, 600-mile journey from Vancouver, British Columbia, to Banff, Alberta. So the passengers (an international crowd from places such as Brisbane, Australia; Napa, California; Long Island, New York; and Ontario, Canada) can take full advantage of the amazing scenery and appropriate photo opportunities, the Rocky Mountaineer travels at a leisurely pace and only during daylight hours, with an overnight stop in Kamloops, British Columbia. As you follow the historic train route constructed more than 100 years ago through Canada's West and the Canadian Rockies, lively commentary alerts you to the region's colorful history and its larger-than-life personalities. Bald eagles and hawks wheel overhead; osprey nests are a common sight. Of course, in addition to the scintillating scenery outside, the food and wine inside the train form one of the journey's main draws. Twice a day, it's down the spiral staircase and into the GoldLeaf dining room, where crisp white linens, gleaming silverware, fresh flowers, and delectable three-course meals await. Sumac Ridge Estate Winery (see page 250) Pinot Blanc and Cabernet Merlot are poured gratis; reasonably priced bottles from leading Okanagan producers are also available for purchase. The GoldLeaf Breakfast features lightly scrambled eggs wrapped in wild British Columbia smoked salmon, drizzled with dill crème fraîche, and topped with caviar. Serve it with hash-brown potatoes, fresh fruit salad, and a slightly sweet Pinot Gris or sparkling wine, and raise a glass to ridin' the rails.

Rocky Mountaineer Vacations

Pacific Central Station

100-1150 Station Street

Vancouver, BC V6A 2X7

Canada

(877) 460-3200 (USA/Canada)

(604) 606-7245 (international)

rockymountaineer.com

GoldLeaf Breakfast

SERVES 4   VARIETAL Pinot Gris or sparkling wine

1 cup heavy whipping cream

2 tablespoons buttermilk

2 tablespoons minced fresh dill, plus extra sprigs for garnish

½ pound thinly sliced cold-smoked salmon (Note: Use cold-smoked, as opposed to hot-smoked, salmon for this dish.)

12 large eggs

Pinch of kosher salt

Pinch of freshly ground black pepper

1 tablespoon unsalted butter

At least 1 day before you plan to serve, mix the cream with the buttermilk in a small, clean glass jar with a lid. Let stand at room temperature (about 70°F) without disturbing for 8 to 24 hours, or until the cream thickens. Stir well, cover, refrigerate, and use within 10 days. Ten minutes before serving, remove the crème fraîche from the refrigerator and stir in the minced dill.

Line the inside of 4 small ramekins or custard cups with plastic wrap. Line each bowl evenly with the smoked salmon, covering all areas completely, but being careful not to layer the salmon too thickly. Cover the ramekins loosely with plastic wrap and refrigerate for 30 minutes.

Whisk the eggs, salt, and pepper together in a large mixing bowl. Melt the butter in a large skillet over medium heat until it foams. Add the eggs and cook, stirring frequently to allow the eggs to cook, until medium-firm, 3 to 4 minutes. Remove from the heat. Immediately fill the salmon-lined ramekins with the scrambled eggs, pressing down firmly to mold the eggs.

1 ounce domestic (trout or paddlefish) caviar

To serve, place a dinner plate over each ramekin, hold the plate firmly over the ramekin, turn it over, and unmold, removing and discarding the plastic wrap. Drizzle each with ¼ cup of the crème fraîche and ¼ ounce of the caviar. Garnish with a sprig of dill and serve immediately.

Cook's Hint: If you do not want to make your own crème fraîche at home (although it is a fun "science project" that every curious cook should try at least once), simply substitute the store-bought variety.

Raspberries, indeed all sorts of berries and cherries, are iconic Northwest foods.

ob Feenie, the chef and owner of the ultra-elegant Lumière and the more casual Lumière Tasting Bar and Feenie's in Vancouver, is the young Turk among British Columbia chefs. With his puckish blond spiked hair, goatee, and piercing dark eyes, he's young, hip, and terribly telegenic. He appears on his own television show on Food Network Canada, and even beat out the always-daunting Chef Morimoto on *Iron Chef!* I first met Rob when I attended "A Dinner Without Borders." Sponsored by Lumière and Hastings House, a luxurious country inn on Salt Spring Island, the dinner promised nine courses, each course paired with two wines—one from Washington State and one from British Columbia. While the thought of nine courses prepared by two alternating chefs and paired with 18 wines seemed daunting, I knew that my fellow food-and-wine writers from Vancouver, a garrulous group known about town as "The Pack" for the power they wield, would keep me on track. They did, and I was overwhelmed by the generosity and virtuosity of the Canadian chefs and won over by Rob's first cookbook, *Lumière.* I was equally thrilled when I learned that Rob opened the Lumière Tasting Bar in 2002. The more casual, intimate sibling focuses on sophisticated cocktails paired with traditional bistro fare with a unique, modern twist. The Tasting Bar met with such great success that it spawned the chef's second cookbook, *Lumière Light,* from which this recipe is taken.

Feenie's (conveniently located right next door to Lumière and the Tasting Bar) opened in 2003. It's an airy, open, crimson-and-celadon-colored space with floor-to-ceiling windows that overlook lively West Broadway. Rob designed Feenie's for the locals—the kind of place they can drop in for Sunday brunch, Feenie's Weenies (his take on the traditional frankfurter), Braised Short Ribs, Alsatian Pizza, or White Chocolate Crème Brûlee. *Feenie's: Brunch—Lunch—Dinner,* Rob's third cookbook, came out in the spring of 2006. This salad is a cinch to make, yet beautiful to behold and a delight to eat. The caramelized asparagus, salty prosciutto, and sweet-tart balsamic vinaigrette work well with the lively texture and honeysuckle/pear/vanilla flavors typical of Pinot Gris.

Lumière
Feenie's
2551 and 2563 West Broadway
Vancouver, BC V6K 2E9
Canada
(604) 739-8185
lumiere.ca
feenies.com

Grilled Asparagus Salad with Prosciutto, Parmigiano-Reggiano, and Balsamic Vinaigrette

SERVES 4   VARIETAL Pinot Gris

2 tablespoons balsamic vinegar
2 tablespoons minced shallots
1 teaspoon honey
10 tablespoons extra virgin olive oil

In a small nonreactive bowl, whisk together the balsamic vinegar, shallots, and honey. Whisking constantly, add 6 tablespoons of the olive oil in a slow, steady stream, blending well after each addition, until the sauce becomes smooth and shiny, forming an emulsion. Season to taste with salt and pepper. Cover and refrigerate until ready to use.

1 to 2 tablespoons kosher salt, plus extra for seasoning

Freshly ground white pepper

2 pounds green asparagus, woody stems trimmed

8 slices prosciutto

4 cups mesclun or other salad greens

Parmigiano-Reggiano or good-quality Parmesan cheese (in block form), for garnish

Preheat a gas or stove-top grill to medium-high.

Bring a large pot of water to a boil and add enough of the salt so that it tastes like sea water. Prepare an ice bath (see Techniques section, page 257). Add the asparagus to the boiling water and cook for 1 minute, or until the asparagus turns bright green. Immediately transfer the blanched asparagus to the ice bath to stop the cooking process and preserve the color. When the asparagus has cooled in the water, transfer to a clean kitchen towel or several thicknesses of paper towels to drain. Pat dry.

In a large nonreactive bowl, toss the blanched asparagus with the remaining 4 tablespoons of olive oil to coat (to prevent the asparagus from sticking to the grill). Season to taste with salt and pepper. Grill evenly on all sides, turning occasionally, 2 to 3 minutes total.

Divide the asparagus among 4 warmed plates. Spoon the vinaigrette over and around the asparagus. Place 2 slices of prosciutto on top of each serving. Top with mesclun and drizzle with a little more vinaigrette. Use a vegetable peeler or sharp knife to slice the Parmigiano-Reggiano into thin curls, and place a few on top of each salad.

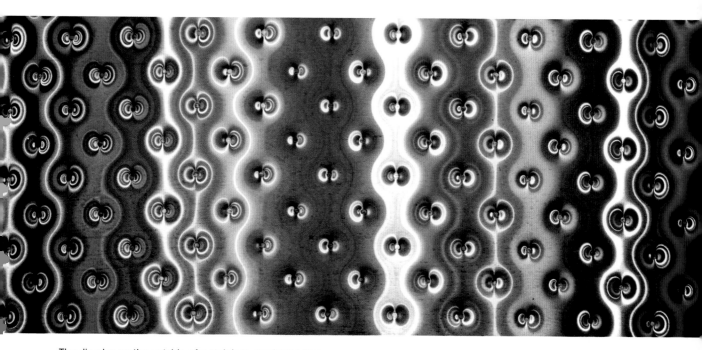

The dimples on the outside of a stainless-steel wine tank create an interesting pattern of darks and lights.

Whistler, British Columbia, is renowned for its world-class skiing and snowboarding, so much so that in early 2010, the luxury mountain resort will host the Olympics and Paralympic Winter Games. No doubt many of the athletes and visitors will seek the warm ambience, gourmet food, and stellar wines at Araxi, a culinary cornerstone located in the heart of the ever-lively Village Square. Since 1981, this multifaceted restaurant has become known for delivering the best of the Northwest, with ingredients sourced locally from land and sea. The expansive Chilled Seafood Bar offers a listing of Canadian-only oysters on the half shell ranging from Vancouver Island–grown Kusshis and Gorge Inlets to Prince Edward Island–produced Malpeques. Hamachi (Yellowtail) Sashimi, Albacore Tuna Tataki, Nova Scotian Lobster Salad, and multi-tiered seafood towers are also popular options here. In the dining room, Executive Chef James Walt is inspired by the abundance of fresh ingredients from local farms in the Pemberton Valley. He says his goal is "to handle food simply and creatively, enhancing its beautiful natural flavors." You'll find the proof is in the pudding in dishes such as Dungeness Crab Soufflé with Light Saffron Cream or Alaskan Scallops with Crisp Pork Belly, or this heart-warming recipe for Asian-inspired sablefish (black cod) swimming in a flavorful lemongrass broth along with Japanese buckwheat noodles. Don't miss a walk through Araxi's wine list, which includes

Araxi

4222 Village Square

Whistler, BC V0N 1B4

Canada

(604) 932-4540

araxi.com

800 different labels and 11,000 bottles, and has won a Best of Award of Excellence from *Wine Spectator* every year since 2000. With a connoisseur's collection of grappas, ports, and Cognacs also on the list, you're bound to find an appropriate after-dinner pairing with dessert, which ranges from Seckel Pear Napoleon to samples from the cheese cart, with offerings from such diverse places as Tasmania, Australia; Salt Spring Island, British Columbia; and Auvergne, France.

Miso-Crusted Sablefish with Soba Noodles and Lemongrass Broth

SERVES 4   VARIETAL Riesling

½ cup white miso

2 tablespoons sake

1½ tablespoons sugar

Four 4-ounce sablefish fillets, rinsed, drained, and patted dry

1 stalk fresh lemongrass, or 1 lemon, skin scrubbed and patted dry

4 cups water

To prepare the miso crust, in a large mixing bowl using a rubber spatula, stir the miso and sake until well combined. Add the sugar and stir until the sugar dissolves. Allow to rest at room temperature for 30 minutes to allow the flavors to meld. Add the sablefish to the marinade, turn several times to cover the fish completely with the marinade, then let rest at room temperature for 30 minutes with the fillets flesh side up (skin side down).

To make the broth, remove the tough outer leaves of the lemongrass, plus about 2 inches from the stem end and 6 inches from the top end. (You

¼ cup (about 2 ounces) peeled, chopped fresh ginger

One 1-inch piece dried kombu seaweed, or 1 heaping tablespoon dried, shaved kombu seaweed

1 cup firmly packed dried, shaved bonito flakes

2 tablespoons soy or shoyu sauce

1½ tablespoons unseasoned rice vinegar

About 4 ounces soba noodles

1 cup shiitake mushrooms, stems trimmed and caps sliced ¼ inch thick

3 green onions, root end and top 1 inch trimmed, remaining portions sliced ¼ inch thick

should have about 8 inches of lemongrass left.) Bruise the remaining portion by tapping quickly with the back of a large kitchen knife 10 to 12 times.

Cut the lemongrass stalk in half lengthwise. Lay the pieces cut side down and cut each piece in half lengthwise again. Gather the pieces together, line them up, then cut the stalks into ¼-inch slices. If using a lemon, with a clean vegetable peeler, remove the skin of the lemon. Stack several pieces of the skin and cut into fine slices. Repeat with the remaining lemon pieces until all the skin is sliced.

Place the water in a large saucepan and add the lemongrass, ginger, and seaweed. Bring to a simmer over medium heat. Add the bonito flakes, reduce the heat to low, stir well, and simmer for 3 minutes. Remove the pan from the heat, stir well, and allow to rest at room temperature, uncovered, for 30 minutes. Add the soy sauce and rice vinegar to the broth and stir well to combine. Place a large-meshed sieve over a large mixing bowl and strain the broth, pressing with the back of a spoon to remove as much liquid as possible. Discard the solids, pour the broth back into the saucepan, cover, and set aside. If not using within 30 minutes, cover and refrigerate.

To cook the fish, adjust the oven rack in the center of the oven and preheat the oven to 400° F. Prepare a rimmed baking sheet by lightly oiling it, spraying it with nonstick cooking spray, or lining it with parchment paper. Arrange the sablefish fillets on the sheet skin side down (flesh side up) without crowding. Cook until the fish flakes and turns light brown on the top and around the edges, about 15 minutes.

While the fish is cooking, bring a large pot of salted water to a boil. Add the soba noodles and cook, stirring occasionally, just until al dente, 5 to 7 minutes. Drain the noodles, rinse well, and set aside. A few minutes before serving, place the saucepan with the broth back on the stove over medium heat, add the mushrooms and soba noodles, and re-warm the soup.

To serve, remove the fish from the oven. If desired, slide a spatula under the bottom of the fillets to remove the skin and discard. Divide the soba noodles, mushrooms, and broth equally among 4 soup bowls. Arrange the sablefish fillets on top and sprinkle with green onions.

The cover of the menu at West restaurant, located in the South Granville neighborhood of Vancouver, British Columbia, is instructive. It proudly proclaims, "True to our region, true to the seasons. Inspired by British Columbia's finest organic, specialty, and heirloom suppliers." Under the direction of Executive Chef David Hawksworth, a native Vancouverite who worked abroad for over a decade with such culinary luminaries as Marco Pierre White and Raymond Blanc, West has won a boatload of awards for its seasonal and chef's tasting menus; small plates, first course, and main-course options; and wine list. The restaurant's contemporary design, with a fascinating mirrored sculpture that snakes through the restaurant suspended from the ceiling, has been featured in *Wallpaper* magazine. A temperature-controlled "wall of wine," complete with sliding library ladders, houses the wine selection, which has garnered several "Best of Awards of Excellence" from *Wine Spectator.*

When we dined at West, Chef David dusted his albacore tuna roll in fresh herbs, sliced the fish into rounds, and served it with an English cucumber–mango salsa. A glistening tower of bluefin tuna (on top) and baby greens (on the bottom) was sauced with spicy citrus. The sablefish entrée was served with Manila clams and pine mushrooms in an herb velouté, a velvety fish-fumet-based white sauce. While perhaps not the best wine pairing with my seafood selections (although it paired nicely with Spencer's beef tenderloin), we were still glad we ordered a bottle of Cedar Creek "Platinum Reserve" Pinot Noir. I had tried this wine at the winery on my first journey to the Okanagan back in 2000. I was so impressed that I brought home two bottles, which the winemaker had to specially label since the wine wasn't really ready for distribution at that time! Trying the Burgundian-style Pinot again, with its intriguing flavors of berries, leather, and earth, was like revisiting an old friend. In the recipe that follows, caramelized tomatoes and exotic spices form the core of a warm vinaigrette that makes an intriguing contrast to the oily goodness of Northwest sablefish. Pinot Gris, with its apple and citrus notes and lively mouthfeel, cleanses and refreshes the palate after the densely flavored dish.

West
2881 South Granville Street
Vancouver, BC V6H 3J4
Canada
(604) 738-8938
westrestaurant.com

Smoked Sablefish (Black Cod) with Spiced Cherry Tomato Vinaigrette

SERVES 4   VARIETAL Pinot Gris

5 tablespoons sake

5 tablespoons mirin

5 tablespoons soy sauce

At least 6 hours before you plan to serve, in a medium nonreactive bowl, stir together the sake, mirin, soy sauce, and lime juice. Add the fish and turn to coat both sides with the marinade. Cover and marinate in the refrigerator for up to 6 hours, turning occasionally.

3 tablespoons freshly squeezed lime juice

Four 5-ounce sablefish (black cod) fillets

3 tablespoons olive oil

1 cup diced onion

1 tablespoon grated fresh ginger

1 teaspoon minced garlic

1 tablespoon ground turmeric

1 teaspoon ground coriander

1 teaspoon ground fennel seed

1 teaspoon ground star anise

½ of a 3-inch cinnamon stick

1 pint cherry tomatoes, stems removed

1 tablespoon tomato paste

¼ cup extra virgin olive oil

Kosher or sea salt

2 to 3 ounces baby salad greens, for garnish

Ten minutes before you are ready to cook, preheat the oven to 350°F. Heat the olive oil in a medium ovenproof saucepan over medium heat. Add the onion, ginger, and garlic, and cook, stirring frequently, until the onion is softened but not browned, 4 to 6 minutes. Add the turmeric, coriander, fennel seed, star anise, and cinnamon stick, and cook, stirring frequently, for about 3 minutes.

Add the cherry tomatoes and tomato paste, stir well, and transfer the saucepan to the oven. Cook for 20 to 25 minutes, or until the tomatoes are very soft and slightly browned (caramelized).

Place a fine-meshed sieve over a mixing bowl and add the tomato mixture. Press the solids with the back of a spoon to extract as much of the juice as possible, and discard the solids. Return the tomato mixture to the saucepan, cover, and keep warm over very low heat.

Preheat the broiler. Lightly oil a rimmed baking sheet. Pat the sablefish fillets dry and arrange on the sheet without crowding. Cook for 10 to 12 minutes, or until just cooked through (still slightly translucent in the middle), for medium rare.

Just before serving, make the vinaigrette by removing the saucepan from the heat and whisking in the extra virgin olive oil. Add a few drops at a time and whisk well after each addition until the sauce is smooth, glossy, and thickened. Season to taste with salt.

Place the sablefish fillets on 4 plates, garnish with the baby greens, and drizzle with the vinaigrette.

C restaurant, located on the False Creek waterfront in downtown Vancouver, modestly bills itself as "a contemporary fish restaurant," but I think it is simply one of the best restaurants in the world. Executive Chef Robert Clark, a great champion of sustainability of our seas, offers tantalizing tasting menus as well as *à la carte* choices in a neutral-toned, two-story, glass-walled setting. With nonstop views of Vancouver's historic bridges, Granville Island Public Market, and romantic sunsets in the evening, the setting lives up to the food and extensive wine list overseen by restaurant owner Harry Kambolis. Each time I've been there, I've opted for the tasting menu along with wine pairings, as it is pure joy to see what this über-chef creates. Among the "star" courses of my meals at C have been a single local Kusshi oyster (a petite oyster reminiscent of Washington State's own native Olympia) topped with Mignonette Fizz and paired with one of my favorite Northwest sparkling wines—Sumac Ridge Steller's Jay Brut (see page 250). This preparation was the essence of oyster. Seared Skeena River Wild Salmon with Yellowfoot Chanterelle Purée and "Nordic Spirit" 200-Mile Sablefish with Double-Smoked Bacon Consommé were also standouts. We also enjoyed one of Chef Rob's signature dishes. Octopus-Bacon-Wrapped Kagan Bay Scallop was served with a foie gras croquette, sautéed spinach, and a Cognac-and-dark-veal reduction. I was entranced by the way the chef effortlessly merged earth (chanterelles, bacon, berries) with ocean. Every dish spoke to Chef Clark's understanding of, appreciation for, and finesse with the local provender. Rob's recipe for a succulent salmon salad is a clever riff on the traditional Swedish gravlax, which is often served as an appetizer with dark bread and a sweet mustard-dill sauce. I like pairing the salad with a Northwest sparkling wine, which cleanses the palate of the rich salmon while taking full advantage of its earthy, minerally, thyme-tinged taste.

C restaurant

#2 1600 Howe Street

Vancouver, BC V6Z 2L9

Canada

(604) 681-1164

crestaurant.com

Wild Salmon Gravlax Salad

SERVES 6   VARIETAL Sparkling wine

1½ pounds wild salmon fillet, skin on, pin bones removed (see Cook's Hint, right)

¼ cup sugar

¼ cup plus 2 tablespoons quince or apple jelly

¼ cup kosher salt, plus extra for seasoning

Line a baking dish that is large enough to allow the salmon to lie flat without crowding with plastic wrap. Use two long pieces of plastic wrap, placing one horizontally and one vertically in the pan, with enough left over on each side so the salmon can be easily wrapped. Rinse the salmon fillet, pat dry with paper towels, and set aside.

In a small bowl, combine the sugar, the ¼ cup of the jelly, the ¼ cup of the salt, the peppercorns, and thyme leaves. Spread one-quarter of the sugar-salt mixture (the cure) evenly over the bottom of the prepared baking dish and lay the fish over the cure skin side down (flesh side up). Spread the

1 tablespoon white peppercorns, placed in a small resealable plastic bag and coarsely cracked with the back of a heavy skillet or meat mallet

1 tablespoon fresh thyme leaves

3 tablespoons extra virgin olive oil

1 tablespoon freshly squeezed lemon juice

1 teaspoon Dijon or country-style mustard

1 pound mesclun salad mix

Freshly ground black pepper

remaining cure evenly over the flesh of the fish. Fold the long ends of the plastic wrap neatly over the fish so it is impermeable to the air. Place a slightly smaller baking dish on top of the fish. Put several large cans or clean bricks on the smaller baking dish to evenly weigh down the salmon. Refrigerate the salmon for 16 to 24 hours if using pink or sockeye salmon; 24 to 48 hours if using king (Chinook) salmon, turning the fish every 6 to 8 hours. You will notice that a clear liquid leeches from the salmon; this is normal and expected.

When the salmon feels firm to the touch, but not hard around the edges, remove from the plastic wrap, gently rinse under cold running water to remove all the cure, and pat dry with a clean kitchen towel or paper towels. Using a very sharp knife and starting at the tail end of the fish, slice the salmon (moving toward the tail end) thinly, and set aside.

In a large bowl, whisk the remaining 2 tablespoons of the jelly, the olive oil, lemon juice, and mustard until combined. Add the fish slices and gently toss them with the vinaigrette.

Divide the salad greens among 6 salad plates. Arrange some of the gravlax salad in the center of each plate. Season to taste with the salt and pepper.

Cook's Hint: Gravlax or *gravlaks* is a traditional Swedish specialty made from two whole raw salmon fillets cured in salt, sugar, and dill. Modern chefs have taken the liberty of substituting albacore tuna, halibut, and other types of hearty fish for the salmon, and experimenting with all manner of herbs (fresh basil, fennel, and tarragon), spices (caraway, allspice, and juniper berries), and heat (crushed red pepper flakes, chipotle chiles, and even barbecue sauce). Spirits, such as aquavit (see Cook's Hint page 69) or Scotch, are also sometimes added to vary the flavor. Chef Rob originally devised this recipe to use pink (also known as humpback, humpy, or humpie) salmon from Prince Rupert in British Columbia. The fish are small (4 to 6 pounds), with thin bodies, a low fat content, and a delicate fish flavor. The most abundant species of salmon in the North Pacific, most are canned or frozen. If they are unavailable, substitute sockeye fillets or the larger, thicker king (Chinook) fillets, adjusting marination time as described above.

Coriander-Crusted Albacore Tuna with Spicy
Buckwheat Noodle Salad is an enticing dish
from the award-winning Sooke Harbour House.

Twenty years ago, long before "local, seasonal, sustainable" became the mantra of every young chef in town, Frederique and Sinclair Philip were quietly going about their business creating a "new" cuisine on Vancouver Island at Sooke Harbour House. The Philips and other Vancouver-area chefs (such as Harry Kambolis at Raincity Grill and Michael Noble at Diva at the Met) combined the best local provender from farm, field, and sea with culinary concepts from Canada, Europe, and Asia. Indeed, Frederique and Sinclair made the sometimes difficult commitment to use only the best ingredients from the southwestern coast of Vancouver Island on their daily-changing menus. The resulting "West Coast cuisine," as it has been called, distinguished British Columbia's style of cooking from other parts of Canada, as well as from the Pacific coast states of America. In 2003, Frederique self-published a tome that blurs the lines between cookbook and art book. *The Art of Sooke Harbour House,* from which this recipe is taken, captures the unique ambience of Sooke—the self-styled "Hotel, Restaurant, Gallery, and Spa"—with four-color photos of the sculptures, woven baskets, paintings, and glass art that you'll discover throughout the inn. Interspersed with the photos and narrative are Executive Chef Edward Tuson's recipes, which Frederique describes as "art on a plate."

With its bold flavors from albacore tuna (one of the Northwest's great summertime catches!), buckwheat noodles, and grated fresh vegetables, this recipe makes a lovely appetizer or luncheon dish. It demonstrates the merging of Asian ingredients with Western cuisine that is such a calling card of Pacific Northwest cuisine. The perfect wine pairing, according to Sinclair, is a minerally, spicy-style Gewürztraminer, such as one from Hainle Vineyards Estate Winery in the Okanagan Valley. Winery owner Walter Hainle is known as the father of the Okanagan ice wine industry, having made a batch of true ice wine (frozen on the vine, not in a freezer!) way back in 1973, with commercial production beginning in 1978.

Sooke Harbour House

1528 Whiffen Spit Road

Sooke, BC V0S 1N0

Canada

(800) 889-9688

(250) 642-3421

sookeharbourhouse.com

Coriander-Crusted Albacore Tuna with Spicy Buckwheat Noodle Salad

SERVES 6 as an appetizer; 4 as a main course   VARIETAL Gewürztraminer

Spicy Buckwheat Noodle Salad

⅓ **cup grated carrot**

⅓ **cup grated celery**

⅓ **cup grated turnip or daikon radish**

At least an hour before you plan to serve, prepare the Spicy Buckwheat Noodle Salad. Place the carrot, celery, turnip, onion, mayonnaise, sour cream, ginger, garlic, green onions, soy sauce, and jalapeño in a medium bowl and mix well. Add the noodles and gently mix until well coated with the sauce and the vegetables are distributed throughout. Cover and refrigerate for at least 1 hour or up to 1 day.

¼ cup minced red onion

¼ cup homemade or store-bought mayonnaise (Best Foods or Hellmann's brand recommended)

¼ cup sour cream

1 tablespoon minced fresh ginger

2 teaspoons minced garlic

2 tablespoons minced green onions (white and light green parts only)

2 tablespoons soy sauce

2 tablespoons minced jalapeño pepper, seeds and membranes removed

4 ounces cooked Japanese soba noodles (see Cook's Hint, right)

2 tablespoons ground coriander

1 tablespoon kosher salt

1 tablespoon coarsely ground black pepper

12 to 14 ounces albacore tuna loin, chilled

¼ cup safflower oil

Edible flowers, such as calendulas, nasturtiums, or begonia petals, for garnish (optional)

To prepare the tuna, place the coriander, salt, and pepper in a small bowl and mix well. Slice the chilled tuna in half lengthwise to form two cylinders of tuna. Rub the spice mixture onto the round portion (not the ends) of the tuna pieces, being sure to spread it evenly on all sides.

Heat the oil in a large skillet over medium-high heat. When the oil just begins to smoke, carefully add the tuna pieces and sear for 2 minutes on each side. The tuna should be opaque on the outside, but still raw on the inside; lower the heat if the tuna starts to brown too quickly. Transfer the tuna to a plate, cover, and refrigerate for a minimum of 30 minutes and up to 1 day.

When ready to serve, decoratively mound some of the noodle salad on each of 4 or 6 serving plates. Cut the chilled tuna into ½-inch-thick slices and arrange on top of the noodles. If desired, garnish with edible flowers.

Cook's Hint: Japanese soba noodles are made from buckwheat and wheat flour, and are dark brownish-gray in color. They are available in Asian markets and some grocery stores. To cook them, bring a large pot of salted water to a boil. Add the noodles and cook for 5 to 7 minutes, or until al dente, stirring occasionally. Rinse them in cool water and drain well before using. If not using immediately, spray with nonstick olive-oil spray and toss gently, or toss with a teaspoon or two of canola oil, to keep the noodles from sticking together. If soba noodles are unavailable, the seared tuna also works well when served on a bed of steamed rice, couscous, or salad greens. Or try cutting leftover tuna into small cubes and using it as a soup garnish or mixing it with pickled beets, walnuts, and feta cheese for a main-dish salad.

above: The herb garden at Sooke Harbour House often inspires the daily-changing menu of dishes made of local, seasonal, and regional ingredients.

left: Northwest artwork is proudly displayed (and for sale) at Sooke Harbour House on Vancouver Island.

top: The breathtaking sunset views of Finlayson Arm, the fjords, and the Olympic Mountains from a guest room at the Aerie Resort in Malahat, British Columbia.

right: Brother Michael, a Benedictine monk from the Sole Dao Monastery in the Cowichan Valley, supplies local restaurants with mushrooms and leads seasonal mushroom hunts.

One cool, overcast Saturday in October, eleven intrepid souls and I went mushroom hunting in the Malahat with Brother Michael, a Benedictine monk from the Sole Dao Monastery. The Great Fall Mushroom Hunt, as it was called, began at the Aerie Resort, a luxurious Relais & Châteaux property in Canada's Cowichan Valley. Along for the hunt was Christophe Letard, the resort's boyish executive chef. Christophe seems to have a sixth sense for spotting the fragile fungi, which is all the better since he and his staff are charged with creating a two-hour, three-course lunch back at the resort after the weekly hunts. "Chef" is dedicated to using the local products of the Valley in his famous daily-changing tasting menus that revolve around the best ingredients from the region's farms, fields, forests, and oceans. It's a joy to attend his daily menu discussion and review of the tasting menus, which he conducts every afternoon at 4:30. You'll enjoy his recipe for light, herb-flecked gnocchi paired with butter-basted forest mushrooms and a brilliant emerald-green coulis. Serve this with a glass of cool, bracing Pinot Gris, the apple and citrus notes of which will cut through the richness of the dish.

The Aerie
600 Ebedora Lane
Malahat, BC V0R 2L0
Canada
(250) 743-7115
aerie.bc.ca

Garbanzo Bean Gnocchi with Forest Mushrooms and Garlic-Chive Coulis

SERVES 4 as a main course; 6 as a side dish   VARIETAL Pinot Gris

1 pound russet potatoes, well scrubbed

½ cup garbanzo bean flour or all-purpose flour

¼ to ½ cup all-purpose flour

¼ cup chopped fresh flat-leaf parsley

¼ cup chopped fresh thyme, sage, or basil

1 teaspoon kosher salt

½ teaspoon freshly ground black pepper

2 large egg yolks

2 tablespoons plus 1 teaspoon unsalted butter

Preheat the oven to 400°F and arrange the oven rack in the center of the oven.

With a fork, prick the potatoes in several places. Place directly on the oven rack and bake for 1 hour, or until easily pierced with a fork. While still warm, cut the potatoes into quarters, cut the skin from the pulp, and push the pulp through a ricer (see Cook's Hint, next page). You should have about 2½ cups of riced potato (lightly spooned into a cup, without packing).

Add the potato pulp, garbanzo bean flour, ¼ cup of the all-purpose flour, the parsley, thyme, ½ teaspoon of the salt, and ¼ teaspoon of the pepper to a large mixing bowl. Mix gently to blend the ingredients. Add the egg yolks one at a time, stirring after each addition. Stir in enough of the remaining ¼ cup of all-purpose flour to make a soft, but still slightly tacky, dough.

Turn the dough out onto a lightly floured work surface. With lightly floured hands, form the dough into a ball and knead very briefly, just a couple of turns, to make a smooth dough. Divide the dough into three pieces and roll the pieces into ropes about ¾ inch in diameter. Cut the ropes into 1-inch

1½ pounds wild mushrooms, such as chanterelle, morel, porcini, boletus, or oyster, stems trimmed, remaining portions cleaned, and cut in half if needed (see Cook's Hint, page 219)

1 medium red onion, cut in half and thinly sliced

½ teaspoon minced garlic

3 tablespoons minced fresh herbs, such as chives, parsley, tarragon, or a combination

Sliced fresh chives, for garnish

pieces. For traditionally shaped gnocchi (with ridges and a lengthwise indentation along one side), hold a piece with your thumb parallel to its length. Roll it down the tines of a floured fork, to make small ridges and an indentation. Gnocchi can be placed on a baking sheet lined with parchment paper, sprinkled with flour, and refrigerated for up to 12 hours before cooking.

Bring a large pot of water to a boil.

Melt 1 tablespoon of the butter in a large skillet over medium-high heat. Add the mushrooms and cook, stirring occasionally, for 2 to 3 minutes. Add the red onion and garlic and cook, stirring occasionally, until the mushrooms give off their liquid and aroma and the onions become translucent and soften, 4 to 5 minutes. Stir in the minced herbs, 1 teaspoon of the butter, the remaining ½ teaspoon of salt, and the remaining ¼ teaspoon of pepper. Remove from the heat, cover, and keep warm.

Drop about one-third of the gnocchi into the boiling water and simmer until they float to the top of the water and are cooked through, 4 to 5 minutes. The gnocchi should hold their shape, yet still be a bit chewy. With a slotted spoon or skimmer, transfer the cooked gnocchi to a large bowl. Toss with the remaining 1 tablespoon of the butter, and cover to keep warm. Repeat the procedure with the remaining gnocchi.

Gently toss the gnocchi with the mushroom mixture, sprinkle with the chives, and serve.

Cook's Hint: If a ricer is unavailable, substitute a medium- to wide-meshed sieve. Place the sieve over a mixing bowl and press the potato pulp through the sieve with the back of a large spoon.

far left and left: Brother Michael points out a chanterelle mushroom during the Great Fall Mushroom Hunt.

The Aerie Resort's executive chef, Christophe Letard, keeps his eyes to the ground as he hunts for mushrooms during the Great Fall Mushroom Hunt.

The number-one, "mother" barrel of balsamic vinegar—the first barrel Giordano Venturi ever produced—rests among hundreds of others at the Venturi-Schulze Vineyards' vinegary on Vancouver Island.

The Vinegary on Vancouver Island

For the Venturi-Schulze family—grape growers, winemakers, and balsamic vinegar producers in the Cowichan Valley on Vancouver Island—seven-day workweeks April through October are the norm.

"Most of the time, I don't know what day of the week it is," admits Giordano Venturi, *pater familias* and latter-day Renaissance man.

Giordano, a distinguished silver-haired gentleman with dark, serious eyes, was born and raised in Modena, Italy. But because his family was of modest means, it wasn't until he immigrated to Canada in 1967 that he tasted his native region's best-known product—Traditional balsamic vinegar. By 1970, he was fascinated with the prospect of making balsamic vinegar in the traditional way, based on a strict *solera* system of casks in decreasing capacities, similar to the barrel process used to make Spanish sherry.

"It's like going into a cathedral; you have to genuflect when you go into a vinegary in Italy," he explains. "But nowadays, here at Venturi-Schulze we are probably more traditional than they are."

Traditional balsamic vinegar–making is an "anxious process," according to Giordano, because of the many variables and steps that can go wrong along the way. Vinegar is a corrosive liquid, and barrels can leak. Because the barrels are open to the air, invasive molds can migrate from barrel to barrel, destroying years' worth of work.

At Venturi-Schulze Vineyards (VSV), "traditional" balsamic vinegar–making begins when Madeleine Sylvaner grapes grown on the property are picked and gently pressed. The juice is then boiled over an open wood fire until it becomes concentrated. After cooling, the boiled-down juice is transferred to large barrels, where it will spend at least four years, during which the initial natural microbial and enzymatic reactions occur.

Additional aging takes place in barriques and smaller, custom-made barrels constructed of chestnut, cherry, acacia, ash, and oak wood. The wood from each barrel imparts a different "footprint" to the vinegar, but the real skill is in the blending of the barrels to form the final vinegar. The vinegar that evaporates each year from the oldest and smallest barrel is replaced by the vinegar from the next barrel, a year younger and a little larger. That is topped up by the next, and the process continues through the entire sequence of barrels. As it picks up the characteristics of each barrel over the years, the vinegar becomes sweeter, denser, and more complex. Over 12 to 15 years, the volume can decrease from 1,000 gallons of juice to just 30 of balsamic vinegar.

While VSV's balsamic is composed mainly of barrels ranging from 8 to 17 years in age, a little comes from the "mother barrel" produced in 1970. At $49 CDN/$43 US, an eight-ounce bottle of VSV balsamic vinegar is truly a gustatory bargain—the color of rich, dark raisins, with nutty, winey, toasty flavors and a dense texture.

In addition to balsamic vinegar, Venturi-Schulze Vineyards produces an impressive array of pesticide- and herbicide-free

"The winery and vinegary sit on 30 acres, with 18 acres planted with grapes and the remaining 12 left to forest, creek, pond, and wildflowers."

wines, ranging from Pinot Gris, Pinot Noir, and Auxerrois to Madeleine Sylvaner, Ortega, and Kerner. The winery and vinegary sit on 30 acres, with 18 acres planted with grapes and the remaining 12 left to forest, creek, pond, and wildflowers. Giordano, wife Marilyn Schulze-Venturi, Marilyn's daughter Michelle Willcock Schulze, and Cobbles the cat (named for the rural town of Cobble Hill, where the winery is located) live in a restored farmhouse dating back to 1893.

VSV wines are limited in production and high in demand and are best sourced at leading restaurants on the Island and in

Vancouver. They are known for their beautiful labels and imaginative names, such as Fear of Flying (a rich, red, fruit-driven dry sparkling wine made from the Blue Gamay grape), Brandenburg No. 3 (a sweet amber wine made by concentrating the juice over an open fire, the same way as the balsamic vinegar), and Micky's Dream (a Pinot Noir rosé dreamed up by Michelle—Micky—Willcock Schulze).

This winery has always been a bit unconventional. Since 1996, all VSV wines in 750-milliliter bottles have been sealed by crown caps instead of corks, a trend (along with Stelvin, or screw cap, closures) that is just now catching on in wineries in the Northwest and around the world. "After so much effort in the vineyard and winery, we are not willing to compromise on quality by putting an unpredictable piece of bark in the neck of the bottle," the Venturi-Schulze family reasons.

Venturi-Schulze Vineyards

4235 Trans Canada Highway
Cobble Hill, BC V0R 1L0
Canada
(250) 743-5630
venturischulze.com

A perfectly balanced balsamic vinegar is produced at Venturi-Schulze Vineyards on Vancouver Island.

Devised by Giordano Venturi and based on a recipe he enjoyed in the Valais region of Switzerland, this heady mushroom and balsamic cream sauce is best served over fresh tagliatelle (homemade or store bought). Minus the pasta, it also serves as an alluring side dish or sauce with meat entrées such as grilled chicken, pork, or beef. The dish is very versatile as far as wine pairing goes. Giordano advises that a full-bodied Pinot Gris, such as those produced by King Estate Winery (see page 170) in Oregon, or a Gewürztraminer work nicely in addition to an unoaked Chardonnay.

Venturi-Schulze Vineyards

4235 Trans Canada Highway

Cobble Hill, BC V0R 1L0

Canada

(250) 743-5630

venturischulze.com

Tagliatelle with Balsamic Cream

SERVES 4 as a main dish; 6 to 8 as an appetizer   VARIETAL Chardonnay (unoaked), Pinot Gris, or Gewürztraminer

1 pound homemade or store-bought fresh or dried tagliatelle (if you opt for the dried, increase the amount of mushrooms to 1½ pounds)

Extra virgin olive oil

4 tablespoons (½ stick) unsalted butter

1 pound small, whole cultivated mushrooms (such as white or cremini) or small, whole wild mushrooms (such as chanterelle or morel; see Cook's Hint, below)

½ cup dry white wine

Pinch of sea salt

Pinch of freshly ground black pepper

1 tablespoon all-purpose flour

½ cup heavy whipping cream

2 tablespoons Venturi-Schulze balsamic vinegar or other high-quality balsamic vinegar

3 tablespoons freshly grated Parmigiano-Reggiano cheese

Cook the homemade pasta until al dente, 2 to 3 minutes, or cook the store-bought pasta according to the package instructions until al dente. Drain well. Sprinkle lightly with extra virgin olive oil, toss to coat well, and keep warm until serving.

Melt 2 tablespoons of the butter in a heavy skillet over medium-high heat. When it begins to foam, add the mushrooms and cook, stirring occasionally, until they begin to release their juices and aroma, 5 to 7 minutes. Lower the heat if the mushrooms begin to brown. Add the wine, salt, and pepper and simmer over medium heat, stirring occasionally, until most of the liquid has evaporated, 3 to 4 minutes.

Sprinkle the flour over the mushrooms and stir quickly and evenly to prevent lumps. Cook, stirring constantly, until the flour is fully incorporated and loses its raw aroma, 1 to 2 minutes. Slowly add the cream, stirring well after each addition to avoid lumps, and cook, stirring constantly, for 2 to 3 minutes. Turn off the heat. Cut the remaining 2 tablespoons of butter into small pieces and add it a few pieces at a time, stirring well after each addition. Remove the pan from the heat and stir in the balsamic vinegar.

Pour the mushroom-cream sauce over the pasta and toss to coat. Divide the pasta among soup dishes or pasta bowls. Sprinkle with the cheese, and serve immediately.

Cook's Hint: There is much debate over the best way to clean mushrooms. For cultivated mushrooms that are smooth and relatively clean (such as white or cremini), I find that a quick rinse in cold water, then thorough drying with a clean kitchen towel or paper towels, works best. For wild mushrooms (such as chanterelles) that may contain deep furrows, pine needles, and other debris, a mushroom brush and a gentle wipe with a damp cloth does the trick. Badly bruised or spongy spots, and signs of insects, should always be removed before cooking. Morels are another story, because their honeycomb surface can contain a lot of grit. To clean morels, if they are large enough, tap them gently (stem side down on a hard surface) to remove as much grit as possible. Then fill a large mixing bowl with cool water and add 1 tablespoon of table salt, stirring well to dissolve the salt. Add the morels and swish them through the water to remove as much grit (and insects, which are repelled by the salt) as possible. Drain the water and replace with clean cool water. Repeat the cleaning process two to three times, or until the water runs clear. After draining the last time, squeeze out as much water as possible from the morels, then pat them dry with a clean kitchen towel or on paper towels. Cut out any discolorations or spoiled spots and discard any mushrooms that are spongy (which means they are old). Slice large mushrooms in half; leave small and medium mushrooms whole.

A whimsical wood carving adorns the walls at Venturi-Schulze Vineyards.

Venturi-Schulze Vineyards' winemaker and patriarch, Giordano Venturi, explains the lengthy process required to make balsamic vinegar using the traditional *solera* system.

Ofri and Ofer Barmor, owners of Carmelis Goat Cheese Artisan, emigrated from Israel to a quiet residential neighborhood outside of Kelowna, British Columbia, to offer their daughters, Lior and Carmel, a safer way of life. But in August 2003, just four days after the family's herd of 80 goats and two billies had been delivered, tragedy struck. An early-morning lightning storm ignited dry leaves and underbrush in Okanagan Mountain Park. The Barmor family and their goats were evacuated; the family home, constructed of logs, was damaged; and the farm, including both barns and the milking parlor, the cheese dairy, the aging cellar, and the visitors' center, was almost completely reduced to ashes. Nonetheless, within three weeks of the evacuation, the family was back home, rebuilding and recovering from their financial and psychic losses. By early 2004, the family was making cheese again. Today, the Barmors haven't lost their original philosophy of producing homemade cheeses to complement the fine wines of the Okanagan. "What doesn't kill you makes you stronger," Ofri explains in her gentle accent. "We didn't lose our spirit."

Carmelis makes a wide variety of cheeses, including Vintage (soaked in red wine and Foch grape skins from nearby St. Hubertus Winery), Lior (reminiscent of Parmigiano-Reggiano cheese), and Goatgonzola. Blue Velvet is a fairly ripe, Camembert-style cheese with a blue-gray rind and a rich mushroom aroma and flavor. If you can't find Carmelis cheese rounds, substitute your favorite Camembert or Brie. Once you try this salad, you'll discover an intriguing melding of flavors and textures: the earthy taste and pleasant crunch of the baby greens, the salty flavor and creamy texture of the cheese, and the sweet/sour blend of aged balsamic vinegar and Pinot Noir in the lush berry syrup. Freshly grated orange zest forms the final high note, all of which pairs perfectly with Pinot Noir in this easy-to-make yet elegant appetizer, main-course salad, or cheese/dessert course.

Carmelis Goat Cheese Artisan, Inc.
170 Timberline Road
Kelowna, BC V1W 4J6
Canada
(250) 764-9033
carmelisgoatcheese.com

Blue Velvet Salad with Raspberry-Balsamic Syrup

SERVES 6 as an appetizer; 2 as a main course   VARIETAL Pinot Noir

Raspberry-Balsamic Syrup

2 cups Pinot Noir

3 tablespoons good-quality raspberry jam

3 tablespoons good-quality aged balsamic vinegar

To make the Raspberry-Balsamic Syrup, place the Pinot Noir, jam, balsamic vinegar, and berries in a medium saucepan and bring to a simmer over medium heat. Cook, stirring occasionally, until the mixture becomes syrupy and about ¾ cup remains, 25 to 30 minutes. Watch carefully toward the end of the cooking process so the syrup doesn't burn. Cool the syrup to room temperature, and use as described below or cover and refrigerate for up to 2 weeks.

½ cup fresh raspberries, blueberries, cranberries, or sliced strawberries

1 large egg

1 to 1½ cups fresh bread crumbs (see Techniques section, page 256)

1 to 2 tablespoons extra virgin olive oil

2 Carmelis Blue Velvet cheeses or two 6- to 8-ounce rounds of Camembert or Brie cheese

1 pound mesclun salad mix

1 to 2 tablespoons freshly grated orange zest

Whisk the egg in a large bowl. Place the bread crumbs on a large plate. Line a plate large enough to hold both cheeses without crowding with several layers of clean, dry paper towels.

In a large skillet, heat the oil over medium heat. While the oil is heating, dip one of the cheeses into the egg, then into the bread crumbs, lightly coating the cheese all over with the crumbs. When the oil is hot, place the cheese in the skillet. Repeat this process with the remaining cheese. Cook, turning once, until the cheeses are golden brown on each side yet still slightly soft in the center, 2 minutes per side. Transfer to the paper towels to absorb any excess oil.

Divide the baby greens among salad plates and divide the cheese over the greens. If serving as an appetizer, carefully cut the cheeses into individual wedges before transferring to the greens. Drizzle the cheese with the Raspberry-Balsamic Syrup, sprinkle with orange zest, and serve immediately.

Ofri Barmor prepares samples of goat cheese in the Carmelis Goat Cheese Artisan tasting room in Kelowna.

Education is the watchword at Tinhorn Creek Vineyards, located in the sunny south Okanagan Valley (the self-styled "Wine Capital of Canada"), along the "Golden Mile" near Oliver. Winemaker Sandra Oldfield, a native of Sonoma, California, and husband Kenn, from Ontario, Canada, met in an educational environment, when both attended the highly respected viticulture program at the University of California at Davis. Because the couple went to UC Davis, education is very important to them, Kenn confided. The Oldfields "hope to demystify the process of wine." Kenn and Sandy help illuminate the grape-growing process for visitors with a demonstration vineyard just outside the tasting room. Its 15 stations cover topics such as climate, disease and pests, soil profiles, and varietals. Another element of education at Tinhorn Creek is the self-guided tours. (Good news: If you can't visit the winery in person, you can take a virtual wine tour on the Web site.) Of course, just tasting through Sandy's award-winning, 100 percent estate-grown wines is a pleasant way to become "educated." Her lineup includes Chardonnay, Gewürztraminer, Pinot Gris, Pinot Noir, Merlot, Cabernet Franc, Kerner Ice Wine, and late-harvest wine.

Sandy and Kenn's healthy pancakes become decadent thanks to the additions of cardamom-scented mascarpone (Italian cream cheese) "lightened" with whipped cream and peaches flavored with Okanagan-produced ice wine. Pair the pancakes with the leftover ice wine or a slightly sweet Champagne or sparkling wine for a truly unforgettable Sunday brunch treat.

**Tinhorn Creek
Vineyards, Ltd.**
32830 Tinhorn Creek Road
Oliver, BC V0H 1T0
Canada
(250) 498-3743
(888) 4 TINHORN
tinhorn.com

Buckwheat-Honey Pancakes with Mascarpone Cream and Ice-Wine Peaches

SERVES 4   VARIETAL Dessert wines or sparkling wines

Ice-Wine Peaches

3 to 4 ripe peaches, peeled and sliced into bite-sized pieces, or 3 to 4 cups frozen peach slices, defrosted

1 cup Tinhorn Creek Ice Wine or other good-quality ice wine

Mascarpone Cream

1 cup mascarpone cheese

2 tablespoons sugar

1 teaspoon pure vanilla extract

At least 2 hours before you plan to serve, make the Ice-Wine Peaches. Place the peaches in a medium nonreactive bowl with a lid, pour the wine over the fruit, and stir gently. Cover and let stand for 2 hours at room temperature or overnight in the refrigerator.

To make the Mascarpone Cream, in a medium bowl using a whisk, whip the mascarpone until smooth and lightened. Add the sugar, vanilla, and cardamom, and whisk until well blended. With a spatula, fold in the whipped cream. Use immediately or cover and refrigerate.

Preheat the oven to 200°F. Line a rimmed baking sheet with parchment paper.

In a large bowl, sift together the flours, baking powder, baking soda, and salt. In a separate bowl, whisk the eggs, 1 cup of the soy milk, the melted butter,

½ teaspoon ground cardamom

½ cup heavy whipping cream,
whipped to stiff peaks

¾ cup all-purpose flour

¾ cup buckwheat flour

1 tablespoon baking powder

1 teaspoon baking soda

½ teaspoon table salt

2 large eggs

1 to 1½ cups plain soy milk or
whole milk

2 tablespoons melted butter or
canola oil

1 tablespoon honey

1 to 2 tablespoons vegetable oil

and honey. Make a well in the center of the dry ingredients and add the liquid ingredients, whisking until almost smooth (only a few lumps should remain). If needed, add additional soy milk until the mixture reaches the proper consistency.

Heat 1 tablespoon of the oil in a large skillet or griddle (nonstick works well for this) over medium-high heat. When the oil is hot but not smoking, spoon the pancake batter into the skillet in the desired amount. Cook until bubbles appear on the surface of the pancakes, 2 to 3 minutes. Turn and cook until the pancakes turn light brown on the underside, 1 to 2 minutes more. Repeat with the remaining batter, adding more oil as necessary. Transfer the cooked pancakes to the prepared baking sheet and keep them warm in the oven until serving.

Divide the pancakes among 4 plates, divide the Mascarpone Cream over the pancakes, and top with the peaches.

Cook's Hint: The peaches are good on other things besides pancakes. For a simple and elegant summer dessert, serve them over good-quality vanilla ice cream or frozen yogurt and pound or angel-food cake. Make an extra batch of peaches during the summer, freeze, and defrost for a taste of summer during the long, cold winter!

A dramatic view through the arbor at Tinhorn Creek Vineyards in Oliver, British Columbia.

Callebaut Chocolate Rolls and other breads for sale at Okanagan Grocery Artisan Breads in Kelowna, British Columbia.

Okanagan Grocery Artisan Breads is a pioneer in the Okanagan Valley—the first company devoted to making quality artisan breads in the traditional and time-honored manner. The bakery is based out of Peachland, where the breads are made on a small scale from organic flour, proofed with natural starter, and hand shaped. Although you can sample Okanagan Grocery Artisan Breads products at many of the leading restaurants up and down the Okanagan Valley, it's most fun to buy them at the retail outlet in Guisachan Village. This tiny slice of a space is located next door to Codfather's Seafood Market, another "must-see" site for foodies visiting the Okanagan. Reading the list of Okanagan Grocery breads is risky business, as it's sure to make you hungry. Loaves available every day include the Baguette/Batard, Okanagan Grocery Loaf, Village Loaf, and Rosemary Focaccia. On varying days you'll find Cheese, Olive, & Artichoke Focaccia; Asiago & Black Pepper; Fig & Anise; Apple & Currant Rye; and Raisin Brioche. Luckily, Callebaut Chocolate Rolls are available every day. The concept for this customer favorite originally came from a bakery in Montreal. Over the years, Rhys Pender and Alishan Driediger, the bakery's founders, adapted the recipe to fit in more and more chocolate and gooey fudge. The couple sold the bakery in early 2007 to Monika Walker, an enthusiastic baker with strong German bread traditions who had worked closely with Alishan, and her husband and business partner, Bill Walker. Rhys, a well-known wine writer and wine educator, continues his successful wine-consulting business, while Alishan has retired her rolling pin to stay home with their two small children. Of course, you can eat the chocolate rolls for breakfast accompanied by a good caffe latté and your favorite morning newspaper. Or, the rolls also make a sumptuous dessert. Serve them warm with fresh summer berries simmered in port (with a glass of port for sipping on the side, of course!) or with ripe seasonal fruit (such as pears or apricots) and a scoop of top-quality vanilla ice cream.

**Okanagan Grocery
Artisan Breads**

2355 Gordon Drive

(Guisachan Village)

Kelowna, BC V1W 3C2

Canada

(250) 862-2811

okanagangrocery.com

Callebaut Chocolate Rolls

MAKES 36 rolls   VARIETAL Dessert wines

Chocolate Fudge

6 tablespoons unsalted butter

1⅓ cups firmly packed brown sugar

1¾ cups high-quality Dutch-processed cocoa powder

4 cups warm water (105° to 115°F)

1½ tablespoons active dry yeast

To make the Chocolate Fudge, melt the butter in a large saucepan on low heat. Combine the brown sugar and cocoa in a bowl and mix well. Remove the pan from the heat and stir in the brown sugar and cocoa using a wooden spoon or heatproof rubber spatula. Beat until well mixed. Cover with plastic wrap and reserve.

Pour the water into a large mixing bowl. Stir in the yeast until it dissolves. Add about half the flour, plus all the cocoa, sugar, and salt, and stir well. Gradually add the remaining flour and mix until the dough comes together and forms a rough ball.

9 cups all-purpose flour

1 cup minus 2 tablespoons high-quality Dutch-processed cocoa powder

3 tablespoons granulated sugar

4 teaspoons sea salt

7 ounces Callebaut milk chocolate, coarsely chopped

7 ounces Callebaut dark chocolate, coarsely chopped

Transfer the dough to a clean, cool work surface and knead for 15 to 20 minutes, or until the dough is smooth, silky, and pliable, adding more flour as necessary. (If using an electric mixer with the dough hook, knead on low speed for 8 to 10 minutes.)

Lightly oil a large mixing bowl with canola oil or nonstick cooking spray. Form the dough into a ball and transfer to the bowl. Turn once to coat the dough with oil, and cover completely, but loosely, with plastic wrap. Let rise for 1 to 1½ hours, or until doubled in size.

Once doubled in size, deflate the dough by gently punching it in the middle. Turn the dough out onto a lightly floured work surface, cover with a clean kitchen towel, and let rest for 10 minutes. (This makes it easier to handle.)

Lightly oil 3 muffin tins (or enough tins to hold 36 standard-sized muffins) with vegetable oil or spray with nonstick cooking spray. (If desired, use extra-large muffin pans, which hold only 24 muffins.) On a clean, cool work surface, roll the dough into a large rectangle, approximately 3½ to 4 feet long and about 1 foot wide. Crumble the reserved Chocolate Fudge evenly over the dough, then sprinkle evenly with the chopped chocolate.

Roll the dough up from the long side, jelly-roll style. Pinch to form a tightly sealed seam. Cut into 36 equal pieces and arrange, cut side up, in the prepared muffin tins. Allow the rolls to rise for another 45 minutes to 1 hour, or until doubled in size.

Ten minutes before you are ready to cook, preheat the oven to 375°F.

When the oven is hot, bake the rolls for 18 to 20 minutes; when done, they will sound hollow when tapped lightly with your fingertips and the chocolate will be melted and gooey. Transfer the muffin tins to wire racks and cool for 10 minutes. Remove the rolls from the tins and serve warm, or transfer to wire racks and allow to cool completely.

Cook's Hint: The secret to making Callebaut Chocolate Rolls is to use good chocolate. The bakers at Okanagan Grocery Artisan Breads prefer the Callebaut brand, as its flavor and texture are superior to less expensive chocolates. The bakery uses a 50-50 mixture of dark and milk, but for a more intense chocolate flavor, you can use just dark. Valhrona or any other good-quality chocolate can be substituted.

opposite: Okanagan Grocery Artisan Breads, the Okanagan Valley's first artisan bread company, is located in Guisachan Village next door to Codfather's Seafood Market, another "must-see" site for food-and-wine lovers.

oie, an ever-evolving winery on the Naramata Bench, is owned by the husband-and-wife team of Heidi Noble and Michael Dinn. In 2002, this dynamic chef and sommelier duo chucked life in Vancouver, British Columbia, along with their high-profile positions at restaurants such as C (see page 204), Cin Cin, and Il Giardino. With his extensive wine background, Michael dreamed of offering wine education to guests and opening a winery. Heidi wanted to teach people not only how to cook during her legendary cooking classes, but also how food gets from field to table. Heidi has since gone on to write *Menus from an Orchard Table,* a collection of menus, recipes, and photos from four seasons of Joie's renowned outdoor orchard dinners and cooking-school menus. Michael produces multiple-award-winning wines under the Joie label, including "A Noble Blend," Pinot Noir rosé, unoaked Chardonnay, and, most recently, a purportedly mouthwatering Riesling.

Joie Wines
2825 Naramata Road
Site 5 Comp 4
Naramata, BC V0H 1N0
Canada
(866) 422-5643
joie.ca

Heidi created this biscuit, a.k.a. "cookie" to Americans, for her friend and neighbor Pati Mathias of Claybank Farm Lavender. With their golden color (flecked with specks of orange zest and lavender) and lovely orange-lavender scent and taste, these sablé-style (butter) cookies are a beautiful way to end a meal when paired with seasonal fruit, lemon curd, or homemade ice cream or sorbet. Or, wine-pairing guru Michael suggests simply serving them with Elephant Island's Apricot Dessert Wine from the Naramata Bench. *Joie* to the world!

Claybank Farm Lavender Biscuits

MAKES 36 cookies   VARIETAL Dessert wines

2 cups all-purpose flour

½ teaspoon baking powder

½ teaspoon salt

¾ cup (1½ sticks) unsalted butter, softened, cut into pieces

1 cup granulated sugar

1 large egg

½ teaspoon pure vanilla extract

4 teaspoons freshly grated orange zest

1½ teaspoons freshly grated lemon zest

Whisk together the flour, baking powder, and salt in a mixing bowl.

Beat together the butter and granulated sugar in a large bowl with an electric mixer on medium-high speed for about 3 minutes, or until pale and fluffy, scraping down the sides of the bowl as needed. Beat in the egg and vanilla, and then the orange and lemon zests and lavender. Reduce the speed to low and add the flour mixture, mixing until just combined, being careful not to overwork the dough. (The dough will look crumbly at first, but will eventually come together.)

Turn the dough out onto a large piece of plastic wrap or parchment paper and form it into a 12-inch log (2 inches in diameter). Roll up the dough in the plastic wrap, and chill in the refrigerator for at least 4 hours, or until firm.

Ten minutes before baking, preheat the oven to 375°F. Line two baking sheets with parchment paper.

1 teaspoon dried culinary lavender, crumbled (Pink lavender or Blue Rosea variety recommended; see Cook's Hint page 169)

½ cup turbinado sugar (see Cook's Hints, below)

Spread the turbinado sugar on a third baking sheet, unwrap the dough log, and roll the cold log in the sugar until the outside is coated. If the sugar doesn't stick easily, pat it on and press it in evenly. Discard any remaining sugar. With a heavy kitchen knife, cut the log into ¼-inch-thick slices. Arrange the slices 1 inch apart on the prepared baking sheets.

Bake the cookies for 10 to 14 minutes, or until they turn slightly golden around the edges. Place the baking sheets on wire racks for 2 to 3 minutes, then transfer the cookies to the wire racks and cool completely before serving.

Cook's Hints: (1) Heidi warns that it is very important not to use too much lavender, or your cookies will taste like a bar of soap! Less is more when cooking with lavender, she stresses. (2) Turbinado sugar is a blond-colored raw sugar with a delicate molasses flavor. It's available in the baking aisle of upscale grocery stores or at health-food stores.

Louise Acoulon collects freshly harvested lavender for drying at Claybank Farm Lavender in Naramata, British Columbia.

One of the more northerly wineries in the Okanagan, Gray Monk Estate Winery is located on the 50th parallel, the same as the Rhine region in Germany and the Champagne region in France. The moderate climate of the gorgeous lakeside setting, about half an hour's drive from downtown Kelowna, encourages a range of cool-climate grape varieties to flourish in the 50-acre vineyard, including Pinot Gris, Pinot Blanc, Chardonnay, Gewürztraminer, Kerner, Ehrenfelser, and Pinot Auxerrois. Gray Monk was established in 1982 by Trudy and George Heiss, although the couple had been growing grapes on the land since the early 1970s. Originally from Europe, they came to the Okanagan from Edmonton, Ontario. You feel the Old World charm throughout the Gray Monk property, and sense the pride of generations in Trudy and George's gentle accents.

The Grapevine Restaurant, under the direction of beloved Okanagan chef Willi Franz (who was named "Chef of the Year" in 2005 by the Okanagan Chefs Association, the same year the Grapevine Restaurant was chosen "Best Winery Restaurant" by the readers of *Okanagan Life Magazine*), serves simple fare, with organic greens and vegetables taking center stage, and each entrée paired with a suggested wine. As you sip your wine and sample an appetizer of Camembert Croquettes with Blackberry Dressing or Grilled Okanagan Goat Cheese and Apple Salad or Hot Chicken Salad with Mushrooms and Bacon, keep your eyes peeled as you gaze out over the lake. Gray Monk is an official Lake Country siting station for Okopogo, the Loch Ness–styled sea creature who (legend has it) charts its depths. Chef Willi's halibut recipe is a classic preparation, with a delicious dose of heavy cream, Dijon mustard, parsley, and Pinot Gris. It's the same varietal the chef suggests drinking with the dish, as well as the signature varietal at Gray Monk.

Gray Monk Estate Winery

1055 Camp Road

Okanagan Centre, BC V4V 2H4

Canada

(250) 766-3168

(800) 663-4205

graymonk.com

Grilled Halibut with White Wine–Mustard Sauce

SERVES 4   VARIETAL Pinot Gris

Four 6-ounce halibut fillets, rinsed and patted dry

1 to 2 tablespoons olive oil

4 tablespoons (½ stick) unsalted butter

¼ cup diced white or yellow onion

½ cup Pinot Gris

1 cup heavy whipping cream

1 Roma tomato, cored, seeded, and chopped

Preheat an outdoor gas grill or an indoor grill pan over medium heat.

With a clean pastry brush, lightly brush the halibut fillets on both sides with olive oil, place flesh side down on the grill, and cook for 4 minutes. Turn and cook until still slightly translucent in the center (for medium rare), 4 minutes, or to the desired doneness.

While the halibut is cooking, melt the butter in a medium saucepan over medium-high heat. Add the onion and cook, stirring frequently, until softened, 3 to 5 minutes, adjusting the heat as necessary so the onion does not burn. Add the Pinot Gris and cook, stirring occasionally, until reduced by half, 4 to 5 minutes.

1½ tablespoons Dijon mustard

1 tablespoon chopped fresh flat-leaf parsley

Kosher salt

Freshly ground black pepper

Add the cream and cook, stirring occasionally, until reduced by half, 5 to 7 minutes. Add the tomato, mustard, and parsley and cook, stirring occasionally, until heated through, 1 to 2 minutes. Season to taste with salt and pepper.

Divide the sauce among 4 dinner plates. Place the halibut in the center of the sauce and serve immediately.

right: George and Trudy Heiss are founders and proprietors of Gray Monk Estate Winery in the Okanagan Valley.

below: In Austria and Hungary, Pinot Gris, the signature wine at Gray Monk Estate Winery in the Okanagan Valley, is called *Grauar Mönch,* which translates to "Gray Monk" or "Gray Friar."

Native Indian Crisp Bread with Snake Bite Dip is the signature appetizer at Nk'Mip Cellars in the Okanagan Valley.

Located in the southernmost tip of the Okanagan Valley, Nk'Mip (pronounced IN-ka-meep) Cellars is North America's first aboriginal-owned and -operated winery. The 18,000-square-foot, state-of-the-art winemaking facility, built in contemporary "desert-heritage" design, produces 18,000 cases of wine per year. Current varietals include Riesling, Pinot Blanc, Chardonnay, Pinot Noir, Merlot, Meritage, and Riesling ice wine. The Qwam Qwmt line of wines (pronounced kw-EM kw-EMPT and nicknamed "Q2") represents Nk'Mip's top-tier efforts in winemaking.

The Osoyoos Indian Band, which runs the winery, the Desert & Heritage Center, the Spirit Ridge Vineyard Resort & Spa, and the Sonora Dunes golf course, is made up of about 400 members and is part of the Okanagan First Nations. Their reserve inhabits some of the last large tracts of desert land left in Canada. In this "place where the creek joins the lake," stark landscapes punctuated by sage grasslands, ponderosa pines, and bleeding-heart sunsets set the stage for a lake-view dining experience never to be forgotten. The meal begins with a wooden platter heaped with irregular pieces of Native Indian Crisp Bread. The boldly colored bread is accompanied by Snake Bite Dip, a spicy-hot chickpea purée. A variety of skewers—chicken with sweet chili sauce, bison with berries, wild-game sausage flavored with juniper, and roasted vegetables—are arranged over saffron-scented rice. On special-occasion evenings, salmon barbecues harken back to the tribe's ancient, time-honored traditions, the noble fish threaded between alder planks and cooked over a bed of glowing embers in the fire pit.

Simple ingredients formed the dough in the traditional Indian bread, which was thinly rolled to produce a crisp, cracker-like bread that was baked over a fire. In the modern-day version here, former Nk'Mip chef, Jeff Miller, adds cayenne and black pepper (symbolizing the heat of the desert) to complement the heat of the dip. Hot spices—cayenne, crushed red pepper flakes, black pepper—add to the slow building of warmth on the palate, which is perfectly quenched by the aromatic and mineral notes of a good-quality Northwest Riesling. The large, unbroken crackers—the terra-cotta color of a desert landscape—are dramatic to serve; simply break them into smaller pieces to scoop the dip.

Nk'Mip Cellars
1400 Rancher Creek Road
Osoyoos, BC V0H 1V0
Canada
(250) 495-2985
nkmipcellars.com

Native Indian Crisp Bread with Snake Bite Dip

SERVES 6 as an appetizer   VARIETAL Riesling

4 cups all-purpose flour

1 tablespoon ground sweet paprika

2 teaspoons baking powder

2 teaspoons table salt

Preheat the oven to 400°F. Line two large rimmed baking sheets with parchment paper or lightly coat with nonstick cooking spray.

Sift the flour, paprika, baking powder, salt, garlic powder, cayenne pepper, and black pepper together in a large bowl. Cut the lard into the flour mixture

2 teaspoons garlic powder

1 teaspoon cayenne pepper

1 teaspoon freshly ground black pepper

¼ cup lard or vegetable shortening, cut into pieces

1 cup very cold water

Snake Bite Dip (recipe follows)

using a pastry blender or two dull knives (cutting in crisscross motions) until the pieces of lard are about ⅛ inch and evenly distributed.

Make a well in the center of the mixture. With a wooden spoon, slowly mix in the cold water until the dough comes together to form a ball. On a clean work surface, knead the dough for 5 minutes, or until it becomes smooth, silky, and pliable. Divide the dough into four equal pieces and form each piece into a ball. Wrap the balls in plastic wrap and let rest for 10 minutes.

On a large, lightly floured work surface, roll out each piece of the dough to a thin (about 9 x 15-inch) rectangle. (Don't worry if the rectangles are somewhat unevenly shaped.)

To bake the first two rectangles, place one on each prepared baking sheet. With the tines of a fork, prick the surface of the dough repeatedly at about ½-inch intervals. Bake for 20 to 25 minutes, or until the bread is golden brown and crisp, switching the positions of the sheets in the oven after 10 minutes for even browning. Cool the baked crisp bread on a wire rack. Repeat the baking with the remaining two rectangles.

Arrange whole or broken crackers on a platter and serve with the dip, breaking the crackers into smaller pieces to scoop the dip.

Cook's Hint: For the faint of palate, the crisp bread can be cooked without the addition of the spices. Unspiced crisp bread also produces the perfect palate-cleansing cracker for wine tasting. Store leftover crisp bread in a large, resealable plastic bag for up to 2 weeks. If needed, place on a baking sheet in a 325°F oven for 10 minutes to re-crisp and refresh. Serve warm or allow to cool before serving.

An unusual traffic sign warns drivers at Nk'Mip Cellars in Osoyoos, British Columbia.

The vineyards at Nk'Mip Cellars in the Okanagan Valley.

Snake Bite Dip

MAKES about 1¾ cups

One 15- to 16-ounce can garbanzo beans, drained and liquid reserved

1 teaspoon coarsely chopped garlic, or more to taste

½ cup diced red onion or thinly sliced green onions

2 tablespoons olive oil

4 teaspoons freshly squeezed lemon juice

½ teaspoon freshly grated lemon zest

½ teaspoon sea salt

½ teaspoon freshly cracked black pepper

¼ teaspoon crushed red pepper flakes

1 tablespoon FRANK'S RedHot Original Cayenne Pepper Sauce or Tabasco sauce

1 tablespoon finely chopped fresh flat-leaf parsley

In a blender or food processor, pulse the garbanzo beans, garlic, and 7 tablespoons of the reserved garbanzo bean liquid until almost smooth; little chunks should remain. Discard the rest of the bean liquid.

Transfer to a nonreactive bowl and add the onion, olive oil, lemon juice, and lemon zest. Stir well with a wooden spoon or rubber spatula. Add the salt and pepper, crushed red pepper flakes, and hot sauce, and stir well. Taste and add additional seasonings as needed. Transfer to a small, nonreactive serving bowl and serve within 1 hour, or cover and refrigerate for up to 2 days. Remove from the refrigerator 30 minutes before serving and sprinkle with the parsley.

Native American–inspired artwork is featured at Nk'Mip Cellars, which is co-owned by the Osoyoos Indian Band.

ocated on Sunset Drive in the heart of Kelowna's cultural district—with neighbors such as the cozy French bistro Bouchons and the sophisticated white-tablecloth restaurant Fresco—Waterfront Wines, Spirits & Ales offers wine, spirits, and food enthusiasts the best of all worlds; a sophisticated bar and bistro on one side and an inviting wine and liquor store on the other. The concept here is simple—try it before you buy it. You might "try and buy" a wine you like at a complimentary wine tasting at the store. Or you might discover a wine you'd like to purchase at the undulating stone bar in the bar/bistro, a narrow space with pale lime walls and a truly urban feel. The bar/bistro offers about a dozen wines by the glass and 75 by the bottle, heavily weighted toward mostly recent vintages from leading Okanagan wineries, such as Blasted Church, Burrowing Owl (see page 247), Poplar Grove, and Pentage, divided into creative categories such as "Blondes" (white wines), "Airheads" (sparkling), "Redheads" (reds), or "Goes Both Ways" (rosé). If you're wined out, I recommend the Lemon Ice cocktail, an Okanagan favorite made of ice wine, Citron vodka, and lemon juice. Bracing! Chef and Sommelier Mark Filatow's food complements the liquid refreshment, with "Nibblies," "Bigger" plates, the "Substantial" platter, and a three-course prix-fixe menu that changes every five days. Our springtime sampler featured Steamed Smoked Black Cod with Lobster Riesling Emulsion—sweet and salty and playfully highlighted with a tiny dice of carrots and peas. Roasted duck breast swam happily with truffled potato ravioli in an inspired rhubarb *jus*. Tiramisù with the crunchy contrast of hazelnut brittle rounded out our meal on a sweet note, although I was equally tempted by the long list of "Liquid Desserts." These included Okanagan ice wines (Jackson-Triggs), dessert wines (Elephant Island), port (Sumac Ridge Pipe), and two-ounce "Dessert Martinis."

Waterfront Wines, Spirits & Ales

103 & 104-1180 Sunset Drive

Kelowna, BC V1Y 9W6

Canada

(250) 979-1222

(866) 979-1222

waterfrontwines.com

Chef Mark cooks with the seasons, and he suggests making the following dish in late July or early August—when the first cherries of the season arrive and fresh garden peas are at their peak. (Good news: You can substitute frozen cherries and peas in order to prepare the dish year round.) You'll enjoy the contrast of the peppery thyme crust on the steak, the comforting warmth of the peas, and the mellow cherry-balsamic flavors in the sauce that pair so well with the berry and black pepper notes in a good-quality Syrah.

Peppercorn-Marinated Beef Flatiron Steak with Okanagan Cherries and English Peas

SERVES 4   VARIETAL Syrah

2 tablespoons black peppercorns, toasted (see Techniques section, page 258)

2 tablespoons chopped fresh thyme

Four 6- to 8-ounce flatiron, top sirloin, or other steaks (see Cook's Hint, below)

1 teaspoon sea salt, plus extra for seasoning

1 tablespoon vegetable oil

2 cups fresh English peas or best-quality frozen petite peas

½ cup chicken or vegetable stock or broth

2 tablespoons unsalted butter

40 fresh, sweet red cherries, pitted and cut in half, or individually-quick-frozen (IQF) unsweetened pitted cherries, partially defrosted and cut in half

1 tablespoon balsamic vinegar

The day before cooking the steak, place the toasted peppercorns in a 1-gallon, heavy-duty, resealable plastic bag and crack with the back of a heavy skillet or a meat mallet (or crack the peppercorns in a mortar and pestle). Mix the pepper with the thyme and rub it into the steaks. Place the steaks in the bag, seal, and refrigerate for up to 24 hours.

Thirty minutes before cooking, remove the steaks from the refrigerator and allow to sit at room temperature. Heat a large cast-iron or other heavy-duty skillet over medium-high heat. Sprinkle the steaks on both sides with the 1 teaspoon sea salt.

Swirl the vegetable oil in the hot skillet. Transfer the steaks to the pan and cook until browned, 1 minute per side. Reduce the heat to medium if needed, and continue to cook the steak, turning once or twice, an additional 4 to 5 minutes for medium rare, or until the desired doneness is reached.

Transfer the steaks to a warm plate and tent loosely with aluminum foil to keep warm. Remove the skillet from the heat and set aside.

Heat a small saucepan over medium-high heat and add the peas, stock, butter, and a pinch of sea salt. Stir well and bring to a boil. Cook the peas, stirring occasionally, until the liquid reduces significantly and the butter and stock become smooth and glisten (emulsified), 7 to 10 minutes. When the liquid has almost evaporated, remove the pan from the heat and set aside.

While the peas are cooking, place the cherries, cut side down, in the reserved skillet. Add any juices from the resting steak to the skillet, along with the balsamic vinegar. Swirl the pan to mix the liquids. Return the skillet to the stove top over medium heat and simmer to warm the cherries for 30 seconds to 1 minute. Take the pan off the heat.

To serve, cut each steak across the grain into slices. Spoon the peas into the centers of 4 dinner plates. Arrange the steak slices over the peas. Scatter the cherries around the plates and drizzle everything with the sauce.

Cook's Hint: Beef flatiron steak is a previously underutilized, and newly trendy, cut of meat among Northwest chefs that's filtering down to home cooks as well. The cut is economical (when compared to pricier tenderloin) and flavorful—rather like a more tender and refined version of flank steak. If you can't find the flatiron cut, substitute one of the loin cuts—tender, top, or sirloin—or New York steak.

The monolithic, 12-story bell tower at Mission Hill Family Estate houses a collection of bells forged by seventh-generation bell masters to commemorate the family members of winery founder and owner Anthony von Mandl.

A Sanctuary to the World of Wine

In the midst of a quiet residential neighborhood near Kelowna, British Columbia, on a panoramic hilltop surrounded by commanding views of Okanagan Lake, towering mountains, and demonstration vineyards, sits the Northwest's most beauteous winery—Mission Hill Family Estate.

Visitors pass through an imposing archway and descend into an inner courtyard with a 12-story bell tower as its focal point. The Terrace (an al fresco dining area), a Roman-inspired amphitheater, and an airy loggia are painted in gentle tones of burnt ochre and resemble a Tuscan estate. An imposing 17th-century Renaissance fountain and landscape plantings of close to 4,000 trees and shrubs add to the air of permanence here. In the barrel room, visitors are invited to peer inside the Vault, home to priceless collections of library wines and ancient wine vessels.

With its world-class collections, monolithic bell tower, and signature courtyard, Mission Hill is at once part art museum, part monastery, and part university campus.

But the mission at Mission Hill is not the study of art or books. The key figures are not professors or monks, but winery founder and owner Anthony von Mandl and longtime winemaker John Simes.

The story of Mission Hill Family Estate began in Vancouver, British Columbia, when Anthony was born to European parents, who later took him to live in Europe during his formative years. After earning a degree in economics from the University of British Columbia and apprenticing in the wine trade in Europe, the young man returned to the Okanagan Valley in 1981 to put down roots.

Although others scoffed, Anthony was convinced that his beloved Valley would, one day, produce sophisticated wines for an international audience. It didn't happen overnight. To finance his dream, the entrepreneur made millions in the wine trade, the hard-cider business, and by creating Mike's Hard Lemonade. He built the winery, reputed to have cost $30 million, to satiate his wine-making dream and as a tribute to his family and its European heritage.

Anthony, along with Seattle-based architect Tom Kundig, left nothing to chance in his vision to create a timeless monument. Every detail, from the 7,500-pound hand-chiseled keystone in the winery's curved entryway (emblazoned with the pelican, part of the von Mandl family crest) to the four bells in the 12-story bell tower that were forged by seventh-generation bell masters (each commemorating a member of the von Mandl family) to the 800-barrel underground cellars (that were blasted out of volcanic rock), reinforces Anthony's vision that this winery will still stand, monument-like, 200 to 300 years from now.

For many of the 110,000 annual visitors to Mission Hill, a trip to the cellars is akin to a religious experience. As a hush falls over the group, the barrels

"For many of the 110,000 annual visitors to Mission Hill, a trip to the cellars is akin to a religious experience."

of red wine that are aged there seem to march in precise formation. The only source of natural light into the cellar comes from an oculus that sits above ground. "Oculus," the Latin word for "eye," is also the name of Mission Hill's premium Bordeaux blend. The sumptuous wine is made from specially selected grapes sourced from estate-owned vineyards in the southern part of the Valley.

Of course, a winery is more than a physical plant alone. As part of his vision, Anthony recruited John Simes, an award-winning winemaker from New Zealand, back in 1992. The apocryphal story took place in 1994, when Mission

Hill's 1992 Grand Reserve Barrel Select Chardonnay was entered in London's prestigious International Wine & Spirit Competition (IWSC). John's Chardonnay took home first place, but when the judges discovered the wine's origin, they demanded a re-tasting. The results held in the second tasting, bringing the Okanagan Valley to the attention of the international wine world for the first time.

In a rather fitting irony, Anthony von Mandl assumed the presidency of the IWSC in 2006 and passed along that appointment to Gina Gallo for 2007. He joins the ranks of past presidents Robert Mondavi, the Baroness Philippine de Rothschild, and the Marchese Piero Antinori; it's another outstanding accolade for a visionary Canadian who dreamed of growing world-class grapes in the Okanagan Valley.

Mission Hill Family Estate
1730 Mission Hill Road
Westbank, BC V4T 2E4
Canada
(250) 768-6448
missionhillwinery.com

Visitors enjoy views of Lake Okanagan along with their meals at the Terrace restaurant at Mission Hill Family Estate.

Winery Chef Michael Allemeier, who oversees the Terrace restaurant, is well known for his inspired food-and-wine pairings. He came to Mission Hill in the summer of 2003, after starting out in the restaurant business at the age of 15 working in a country-club kitchen in Winnipeg, Manitoba. Since then, the young chef has lived at 22 different addresses on three continents and enjoyed chef stints in Montreal, Vancouver, Whistler, and Calgary. For two years, he and his wife even followed the crush (grape harvest), travels that led them to the wine regions of California, Ontario, Germany, Italy, and South Africa.

You'll enjoy the many kinds of seafood in his cioppino recipe—everything from clams and mussels to spot prawns and octopus (!). Unlike many fishermen's stews that are thick and tomato based, this one relies on fish stock (or clam broth) and just a hint of tomato, plus the unmistakable flavors of fennel and crushed red pepper flakes, to create a gently perfumed, aromatic broth with a bit of a kick. Seared halibut fillets perch atop the cioppino, for the final crowning touch. Pinot Gris is Chef Michael's favored wine pairing here; it is generally a good choice with seafood, thanks to its lively texture and refreshing flavors of green apple and citrus.

Mission Hill Family Estate

1730 Mission Hill Road

Westbank, BC V4T 2E4

Canada

(250) 768-6448

missionhillwinery.com

Roasted Halibut with Shellfish Cioppino

SERVES 6   VARIETAL Pinot Gris

2 tablespoons canola oil

Six 5-ounce halibut fillets

1 teaspoon olive oil

1 teaspoon fennel seed

Pinch of crushed red pepper flakes

1 small red onion, halved and sliced ⅛ inch thick

1 small red bell pepper, cored, seeds and membranes removed, and sliced ⅛ inch thick

1 Roma tomato, cored, seeded, and diced

1 cup homemade or store-bought fish stock, or ½ cup clam broth mixed with ½ cup water

½ cup Mission Hill Family Estate Reserve Pinot Gris or other good-quality Pinot Gris

Heat a large nonstick skillet over medium heat and add the canola oil. Arrange the halibut fillets flesh side down without crowding, and cook until the fillets turn a soft golden brown and caramelize, 3 to 4 minutes. Turn and cook until medium rare (still a bit translucent in the center), 2 to 4 minutes more, being careful not to overcook. If desired, remove the skin. Cover to keep warm, and set aside.

Heat a Dutch oven or stockpot over medium heat and add the olive oil. When the oil is hot, add the fennel seeds and red pepper flakes and cook, stirring constantly, for 30 seconds. Add the onion and red bell pepper and cook, stirring constantly, for 1 minute. Add the tomato, fish stock, and wine, stir well, and cook for 1 minute.

1 pound Manila clams, shells scrubbed and rinsed

1 pound mussels, shells scrubbed and rinsed and mussels debearded just before cooking

4 ounces cooked octopus, very thinly sliced

4 ounces Alaskan spot prawns or medium-sized shrimp, peeled, deveined, and cut in half lengthwise

⅓ cup chopped fresh flat-leaf parsley

Kosher salt

Freshly ground black pepper

Add the clams, cover, and cook for 2 minutes. Add the mussels, cover, and cook for 4 minutes. When most of the clams and mussels have opened, add the octopus and prawns, cover, and cook until the prawns just turn pink and their tails curl slightly, 1 to 2 minutes. Remove from the heat and discard any clams or mussels that have not opened. Gently stir in the parsley, and season to taste with salt and pepper.

Divide the cioppino among 6 soup or pasta bowls. Arrange one halibut fillet in the center of each bowl and serve at once.

The 12-story bell tower at Mission Hill Family Estate as seen through the entry archway.

L ike many wineries in the Okanagan Valley, Burrowing Owl started life growing grapes for other winemakers. That was back in 1993. When those same winemakers started winning medals, owner Jim Wyse decided to forge ahead with his own winery, which he built on 28 acres in the middle of Burrowing Owl Vineyards. The winery produced its first vintage in 1997 with four varieties—Pinot Gris, Chardonnay, Merlot, and Cabernet Sauvignon—and captured cult status from the get-go. Its wines remain highly sought after, with production of about 25,000 cases annually made up of two whites (Pinot Gris and Chardonnay) and five reds (Merlot, Cabernet Sauvignon, Cabernet Franc, Pinot Noir, and Syrah).

From the maple-wood floors to the soaring ceilings, Burrowing Owl's light-filled Sonora Room is one of the Okanagan Valley's most beautiful winery restaurants. You can eat inside or opt for outside on the wraparound patio. The latter overlooks 300 acres of vineyards in the Black Sage Bench. Either way, you are in for a treat, with dishes prepared by Executive Chef Ray A. Durk and his culinary team such as Black Truffle-Scented Duck Breast with Brandied Cherries (paired with Burrowing Owl Merlot) or Flame-Grilled Bison (paired with Syrah) or Citrus-Marinated Fillet of Arctic Char (paired with Pinot Gris).

The recipe that follows features one of my favorite foods—duck breast—with my favorite sauce in this book, a dense, complex mix of shallots, balsamic vinegar, and Cabernet Sauvignon mellowed by the nutty richness of caramelized sugar. Dried figs plumped by port and more Cab Sauv form the crowning touch on this decadent duck dish, which was given to me by Burrowing Owl's former executive chef Dominique Couton. Dominique is now the chef/partner at Bouchons, a traditional French bistro in Kelowna's lively cultural district. Neighboring restaurants include Fresco and Waterfront Wines, Spirits & Ales (see page 240).

Burrowing Owl Estate Winery
100 Burrowing Owl Place
Oliver, BC V0H 1T0
Canada
(250) 498-6202
(877) 498-0620
burrowingowlwine.ca

Bouchons
#105–1180 Sunset Drive
Kelowna, BC V1Y 9W6
Canada
(250) 763-6595
bouchonsbistro.com

Skillet-Roasted Magrets de Canard with Caramel-Cabernet Sauce and Glazed Mission Figs

SERVES 4   VARIETAL Cabernet Sauvignon

Glazed Mission Figs

12 dried Mission figs

1¼ cups Cabernet Sauvignon

½ cup port

To prepare the Glazed Mission Figs, place the figs, Cabernet Sauvignon, and port in a medium nonreactive saucepan over medium-high heat and bring to a boil. Reduce the heat to low and cook, stirring occasionally, until the wine becomes syrupy and glazes the figs, 55 to 60 minutes. Cover and reserve, keeping the figs warm until ready to serve.

Caramel-Cabernet Sauce

2 tablespoons sugar

2 tablespoons water

6 tablespoons balsamic vinegar

4 tablespoons (½ stick) unsalted butter, plus 1 teaspoon unsalted butter, cut in half

¾ cup chopped shallots

1¼ cups Cabernet Sauvignon

2 whole boneless duck breasts, split and trimmed of excess fat and nerve tissue

Kosher salt

Freshly ground black pepper

1 teaspoon ground allspice

To make the Caramel-Cabernet Sauce, in a small heavy-bottomed saucepan, mix the sugar with the water until dissolved. Bring to a boil over medium heat. Cook, without stirring, until the caramel turns medium brown, 6 to 8 minutes. Remove from the heat and let rest for 2 minutes.

Return the pan to medium heat and add the vinegar to deglaze the pan. Stir well with a wooden spoon (you will need to work hard to scrape the hardened caramel off the bottom of the pan, but keep working it!). Bring to a simmer and cook, stirring frequently, until the liquid is reduced to 3 tablespoons, 6 to 8 minutes. Remove from the heat and set aside.

Melt the 4 tablespoons of butter in a medium skillet over medium heat. Add the shallots and cook, stirring occasionally, until light golden but not browned, 7 to 10 minutes, adjusting the heat as necessary so the shallots do not burn. Add the Cabernet Sauvignon and stir well. Bring to a boil and cook until the liquid is reduced to about ½ cup, 8 to 10 minutes.

Add the reserved caramel reduction to the skillet and simmer for 2 minutes. Remove from the heat and whisk in the 1 teaspoon of butter piece by piece, whisking well after each addition, or until the sauce is smooth and shiny. Strain the sauce through a fine-meshed sieve, if desired, for a more elegant presentation. Keep warm until ready to serve.

Ten to 15 minutes before you want to cook the duck, preheat the oven to 375°F.

With the tip of a very sharp knife, score a crisscross pattern across the skin side of the duck breasts. (Do not cut all the way through into the meat.) Season the duck breasts on the flesh side only with salt and pepper. Sprinkle ¼ teaspoon of allspice over the flesh side only of each breast.

Heat a large ovenproof skillet over medium heat. When the skillet is very hot, arrange the breasts skin side down without crowding. (Don't add any extra fat; the fat rendered will be enough to cook the breasts.) Cook, draining the melted fat every 2 minutes, or until about ⅔ of the original fat covering the breast melts away and the fat is browned and crispy, a total of 5 minutes.

Turn the breasts, transfer the skillet to the oven, and cook until pale pink in the middle (for medium rare), 5 to 6 minutes. Remove from the oven and transfer (skin side up) to several thicknesses of paper towels to absorb any extra oil. Let rest for 5 minutes before slicing each breast on the diagonal into 7 pieces.

To serve, arrange the sliced duck breasts in the center of 4 dinner plates. Spoon one-quarter of the Caramel-Cabernet Sauce around the duck and garnish each plate with 3 glazed figs.

Cook's Hint: Chef Dominique prefers true *magrets de canard*—large, beef-like breasts from the force-fed ducks raised to produce foie gras—for this recipe. The breasts are very thick, and often weigh upwards of one pound apiece. However, because true *magrets* can be difficult to find, ordinary duck breasts can easily substitute. Whichever type of duck breast you choose, it should be cooked to no more than medium to appreciate all the flavors his dish has to offer. He suggests serving the duck with your favorite vegetables, or you might consider mashed parsnips and dollar-sized corn griddle cakes. Position the griddle cakes under the sliced duck breast, where they will soak up the juices and become moist and flavorful.

Visitors to Burrowing Owl Estate Winery, which is named for a small, endangered native owl that makes its home in burrows abandoned by gophers and badgers, enjoy inspired food-and-wine pairings at the Sonora Room restaurant.

Pioneer of the Okanagan Wine Industry

A love of home winemaking and his proven skill as a salesman led young Harry McWatters to trade a secure corporate position with United Van Lines for the uncertain future of the Okanagan wine industry. Only after he moved to the small town of Summerland in 1968 to take a sales job with Casabello Winery did the young man realize this new "opportunity" paid only half as much as his former job.

But by 1979, after a change in provincial laws that made it easier to establish small wineries, Harry began to dream of opening British Columbia's first estate winery. He and viticulturist Lloyd Schmidt paid $475,000 for a golf club with a nine-hole course and a clubhouse. Vines were planted along the fairways; greens fees supplied much-needed cash flow for the money-strapped partners; the clubhouse became the first winery restaurant in the Okanagan.

Sumac Ridge Estate Winery produced its first vintage in 1980, and throughout its history has been an industry innovator. Harry was one of the first people to plant vinifera grapes (as opposed to hybrid grapes, which were more popular at the time) in the Okanagan. The winery's 1983 Chardonnay was one of the first Chardonnay wines made in the Okanagan from British Columbia–grown grapes. Sumac Ridge was western Canada's first producer of sparkling wines made in the classic *méthode champenoise*.

Even during the late 1980s, when the free trade agreement with the United States stripped away many of the advantages enjoyed by small wineries, Harry, ever optimistic, purchased the

Black Sage Vineyard. Today, the sun-drenched, sandy-soil site in the southern Okanagan is considered one of the premier vineyards in the region.

Sumac Ridge was the first winery outside of the United States licensed to use the term

> "Harry was one of the first people to plant vinifera grapes (as opposed to hybrid grapes, which were more popular at the time) in the Okanagan."

"Meritage." Meritage refers to white- or red-wine blends made of Bordeaux varietals on non-French soil. Adopting the Meritage label gave Sumac Ridge a leg up, as consumer interest has lately shifted from wines made from one grape variety (such as Chardonnay, Merlot, or Cabernet Sauvignon) to blended wines.

In 1995, Sumac Ridge purchased LeComte Estate Winery for $3.2 million and renamed it Hawthorne Mountain Vineyards. The hefty purchase price speaks volumes about the newfound confidence in the once-maligned Okanagan wine industry. In 2000, Sumac Ridge joined Ontario-based

Vincor International, Inc.'s global collection of wineries; in 2003, Sumac Ridge won the Winery of the Year award from *Wine Press Northwest;* and in 2006, the winery celebrated its 25th anniversary.

"Those of us who were pioneering Okanagan-grown wines in the early 1980s needed thick skin and endless resilience. I lost count of the ways people could turn down a glass of BC wine," Harry reminisces. "While we knew we had something special to offer, it took those outside of the Okanagan Valley a little longer to jump on board."

Sumac Ridge Estate Winery
P.O. Box 307, Highway 97
Summerland, BC V0H 1X0
Canada
(250) 494-0451
sumacridge.com

Warm Babas with Ice-Wine Syrup and Rhubarb Compote is the culinary creation of Chef Neil Schroeter of the Cellar Door Bistro at Sumac Ridge Estate Winery.

Warm babas (small yeast cakes traditionally soaked in a rum or kirsch syrup) make an elegant finale to a meal. It's said that the cakes were invented by a Polish king in the 1600s. He soaked his stale *kugelhopf* in rum and named the dessert after Ali Baba, hero of children's storybook fame. You'll enjoy Chef Neil Schroeter's version, in which the classic is given a modern (and Northwestern) twist by substituting Okanagan ice wine for the rum and accompanying the babas with a sweet-tart rhubarb compote. It's served at the Cellar Door Bistro, the casual-in-atmosphere, yet serious-in-culinary-execution, dining spot overlooking the vineyards and golf course at Sumac Ridge. Although well worth the time and effort, babas are a bit of a challenge to make. For a simple but still elegant dessert, pour the beautifully light and fragrant Ice-Wine Syrup over goblets of fresh berries, and serve with a dollop of whipped cream or crème fraîche and crisp butter cookies or shortbread.

Sumac Ridge Estate Winery

P.O. Box 307, Highway 97

Summerland, BC V0H 1X0

Canada

(250) 494-0451

sumacridge.com

Warm Babas with Ice-Wine Syrup and Rhubarb Compote

SERVES 10   VARIETAL Dessert wine

Ice-Wine Syrup

1 cup sugar

½ cup water

⅔ cup Sumac Ridge Estate Winery Gewürztraminer Ice Wine or other good-quality ice wine

¼ cup Grand Marnier or triple sec or other good-quality orange-flavored liqueur

¼ teaspoon pure vanilla extract

Rhubarb Compote

4 cups coarsely chopped fresh rhubarb

1½ cups sugar

To prepare the Ice-Wine Syrup, in a small saucepan, stir together the sugar and water and bring to a boil. Remove from heat and add the ice wine, Grand Marnier, and vanilla. Stir well and use immediately (while the syrup is still warm), or cover, refrigerate, and reheat before using.

To make the Rhubarb Compote, place the rhubarb, sugar, lemon juice, and lemon zest in a medium nonreactive saucepan over medium-high heat, and cook, stirring constantly, until the sugar dissolves, 2 to 3 minutes. Bring to a simmer, reduce the heat to medium, cover, and cook, stirring occasionally, until the rhubarb is tender, 5 to 7 minutes. Remove from the heat, uncover, and cool to room temperature. Transfer to a nonreactive bowl and refrigerate until ready to serve.

Lightly oil or coat with nonstick cooking spray ten 3-ounce ramekins or custard cups or 10 standard (2½-inch) muffin pan cups. In a small bowl, stir together 1 cup of the all-purpose flour, the cake flour, sugar, and salt and set aside.

Place the milk in a medium saucepan over low heat. When the milk is warm (105° to 115°F), stir the yeast into the milk, remove from the heat, and let stand for 5 minutes to dissolve the yeast.

Place the eggs, vanilla, and the yeast mixture in the bowl of an electric mixer. Mix on low speed to blend. Gradually add the reserved dry ingredients and

6 tablespoons freshly squeezed lemon juice

6 teaspoons freshly grated lemon zest

1½ to 1¾ cups all-purpose flour

¾ cup cake flour (not self rising)

2 teaspoons sugar

Pinch of salt

¼ cup whole milk

1 teaspoon active dry yeast

3 large eggs

½ teaspoon pure vanilla extract

4 tablespoons (½ stick) unsalted butter, at room temperature, cut into 1-teaspoon pieces

Confectioners' sugar, for garnish

beat for 1 to 2 minutes, or until the dough comes together but is still quite wet and sticky. Switch to the dough hook attachment and continue mixing at low speed for 6 minutes, sprinkling in the additional ½ to ¾ cup all-purpose flour, until a soft dough that clings to the hook and no longer sticks to the sides of the bowl forms. (Or stir in the remaining flour with a wooden spoon and then transfer to a lightly floured surface and knead by hand.) Add the butter 1 piece at a time, incorporating well after each addition. Continue to knead for a minute or two, until the dough is soft and pliable.

With lightly oiled hands, divide the dough into 10 equal pieces. Place the dough into the prepared ramekins. Cover loosely with oiled plastic wrap and let rise for 30 minutes to 1 hour, or until the dough doubles in volume.

Fifteen minutes before you are ready to bake (when the dough is almost doubled in size), preheat the oven to 375°F.

Place the ramekins on a baking sheet and transfer the baking sheet to the oven. Bake for 25 minutes, or until the babas are golden brown and a toothpick inserted in the middle comes out clean. Cool the babas in the ramekins on a wire rack.

Leaving the cooled babas in the ramekins on the baking sheet (or in the muffin pan), gently spoon about 2½ tablespoons warm Ice-Wine Syrup over each baba. Spoon any syrup that pools in the bottom of the pan back over the babas to saturate. Place one baba (still in the ramekin) on one side of each dessert plate. (Or remove babas from muffin cups to dessert plates and drizzle with any syrup remaining in the cups.) Spoon some of the compote next to the ramekins. Sprinkle the babas and compote with the confectioners' sugar and serve immediately.

Ever the showman, Harry McWatters, founder of Sumac Ridge Estate Winery in the Okanagan Valley, has mastered the French technique of "sabering," or slicing off the neck of a Champagne or sparkling wine bottle in one quick motion with a long saber or knife.

Summerhill Pyramid Winery, situated on the flank of Lake Okanagan, may be the only place in the world where each bottle of wine is aged from one month to one year in a pyramid cellar.

Techniques

I take it for granted that readers already have an understanding of the fundamentals of cooking, or have a good basic cookbook in which to look up answers to questions that might arise. However, I have included the following descriptions of a few unusual techniques mentioned within these pages that might be unfamiliar or difficult to find elsewhere.

ACIDULATED WATER: Use a blend of 1 quart of cold water to 1 tablespoon of lemon juice or white vinegar to help slow browning on the cut surface of certain fruits and vegetables, such as apples, peaches, pears, artichokes, and parsnips.

BOUQUET GARNI: To make a *bouquet garni,* cut an 8 by 8-inch square of clean cheesecloth and fill with fresh herbs of your choice; the classic combination is thyme, parsley, and bay leaf. Pull up the ends of the cheesecloth and tie with kitchen string. Use the bag to flavor stews or soups, removing and discarding the *bouquet garni* before serving the dish.

BREAD CRUMBS AND CUBES: To make unseasoned soft (fresh) bread crumbs, tear slices of white or whole-wheat bread into chunks and place them in a food processor. Process until crumbs of the desired size form. Fresh bread crumbs can be stored in the refrigerator for up to 1 week; in the freezer, tightly wrapped, they keep for about 6 months.

To make unseasoned dry bread crumbs, place a single layer of white or whole-wheat bread slices on a baking sheet and bake at 300°F for about 10 minutes, or until the bread turns light brown and dries completely, turning once. Allow the bread to cool, then place it in a food processor or blender and process until the crumbs reach the desired texture. Unseasoned dry bread crumbs can be kept in the refrigerator for several months; in the freezer, tightly wrapped, they keep for up to 1 year.

To make unseasoned dry bread cubes, remove crusts from slices of white or whole-wheat bread. Cut slices into ¼-inch cubes. Place a single layer of bread cubes on a baking sheet and bake at 300°F until the cubes turn light brown and dry completely, about 10 to 15 minutes, tossing occasionally during cooking. Allow the cubes to cool and use immediately; refrigerate for up to 1 week; or freeze, tightly wrapped, for up to 6 months.

CHIFFONADE: Pull leaves, such as basil, sorrel, mint, etc., from their stems, stack neatly one on top of another, and roll tightly like a cigar. Using a very sharp knife, cut the leaves into thin slivers. Unroll the slivers, fluff, and measure.

CITRUS ZEST: Although the "peel, "rind," and "zest" of citrus fruits are sometimes thought to be the same thing, they are not. The zest is the vibrantly colored, thin outer layer of the peel. It has a bright, clean, sometimes perfume-y taste and isn't bitter. The remainder of the peel, the white portion called the albedo, is often quite bitter in taste and pithy in texture, and doesn't have the same aromatic flavor of the zest. Handy tools for removing the zest of citrus fruits include a citrus zester, a sharp vegetable peeler, or a Microplane grater.

CLARIFIED BUTTER: Melt small pieces of unsalted butter in a small saucepan or skillet over low heat (about 1¼ pounds of unsalted butter yields 1 pound of clarified butter). Do not stir and do not allow the butter to sizzle.

Simmer for 10 to 15 minutes, then strain the mixture through several layers of cheesecloth. The clarified butter is the heavy yellow liquid that remains after straining. Cool the clarified butter before covering, then refrigerate for up to 4 weeks. Re-melt before using, as the butter can become grainy when chilled. Use only in cooking, not as a spread.

CROSTINI: To make crostini ("little toasts" in Italian), preheat the broiler. Cut 1 narrow loaf of French or Italian bread into ¼-inch slices. Arrange the bread slices on a baking sheet and place 3 to 4 inches from the heat source. Broil 1 to 2 minutes on each side, or until golden brown and crispy. Remove from the oven and serve warm or at room temperature.

DUNGENESS CRAB PREPARATION: To prepare a whole, cooked Dungeness crab for picking, hold the crab with one hand from underneath and, with the other hand, pry off the large top shell. Scoop out and save the cream-colored "crab butter," if desired. Run your thumb along the sides of the body cavity to scrape away the feathery gills. Rinse under cold water to remove any remaining viscera.

Grasp the crab in both hands and break the body in half lengthwise, forming two sections with the legs attached. Remove the legs by breaking off at the joints closest to the body. Separate the claw portion from the leg at the first joint. Bend back and remove the smaller claw pincer, along with the attached claw cartilage. Crack the claw with an aluminum crab cracker, the back of a heavy kitchen knife, or a mallet, being careful not to crush the meat. Repeat with the second claw.

With kitchen shears, cut along each side of the leg shells, or simply crack carefully to open. With the palm of your hand, press the top of the crab body until you feel the interior shells give slightly. Do not press so hard that you smash the top and bottom shells together.

You are now ready to eat your crab. Remove the meat from the legs, claws, and body of the crab using your fingers, a crab pick, a seafood fork, or a crab "toe" (the tip of a crab claw)—anything is legal when eating Dungeness crab.

ICE BATH: Ice baths are called for when blanching vegetables or fruits; the cold water immediately stops the cooking process so that the produce doesn't become overcooked. To make an ice bath, simply fill a large mixing bowl with ice cubes and add cold water to cover the cubes.

PLUMPING DRIED FRUITS: Add the fruits to a small saucepan and cover with water, stock, or liqueur. Bring to a boil, cover, and remove the pan from the heat. Allow to stand for 10 to 20 minutes, or until the fruit is plumped. To speed the plumping process, put ½ cup of water into a microwave-safe glass dish. Add the fruit and microwave on HIGH for 30 seconds. Stir and repeat. When the fruit begins to plump, remove from the microwave and cover. Let rest for 5 minutes, drain water, and use the fruit as directed.

ROASTING BELL OR CHILE PEPPERS: Roast peppers in one of these three ways. Roast over a gas burner on high heat, turning frequently with kitchen tongs, until well charred on all sides; broil under a hot broiler several inches from the heat, turning frequently, until brownish-black blisters form; or roast in a preheated 400°F oven for 10 to 15 minutes, turning frequently, until brownish-black blisters form. Put the roasted peppers in a paper or plastic bag, close the top, and let stand for 10 minutes. Remove the peppers from the bag and scrape off the skin; cut away the seeds and ribs. Wipe away any remaining black particles with a damp cloth, then slice or chop as needed. If desired, use thin plastic or rubber gloves to protect your hands while preparing chile peppers.

ROASTING GARLIC: Preheat the oven to 375°F. Slice ½ inch off the top of the garlic bulb, wrap in aluminum foil, and bake for 35 minutes, or until the garlic is very tender and easily squeezed from the garlic cloves. If roasting individual cloves, remove as much skin as possible, place the whole cloves in a small baking dish, cover with aluminum foil, and bake as described above.

TOASTING NUTS, SEEDS, AND PEPPERCORNS: To toast hazelnuts, arrange them on a cookie sheet in a single layer and toast in a 375°F oven for 10 minutes. Remove from the oven and allow to cool slightly. Place the nuts between two rough terry-cloth towels and rub off as much of the nuts' brown skins as you can, or rub a handful of nuts between your palms, or a single difficult-to-skin nut between forefinger and thumb. Alternately (particularly for small quantities of nuts), use the toasting method described below.

To toast a small amount (1 cup or less) of nuts, seeds (sesame, mustard, coriander, pumpkin, or cumin), or peppercorns, heat them in a small, dry skillet over medium heat for 3 to 5 minutes, or until they begin to turn light brown and/or give off their aroma (mustard seeds begin to pop), shaking the pan back and forth often so the ingredients do not burn. Remove from heat, cool, and proceed as directed.

TOMATO PEELING AND SEEDING: To peel a tomato, cut a shallow "X" in the bottom end and drop it into boiling water for 1 minute. Remove and transfer the tomato to an ice bath (see page 257). After 15 to 20 seconds, remove the tomato, pat dry, and slip off the skin with a sharp knife. To seed, cut the tomato in half horizontally and gently squeeze the halves over a bowl to force out the seeds. Fingers or a small spoon work well to remove any remaining seeds.

WATER BATH: A water bath (*bain marie* in French) is used in the making of baked custards, flans, savory mousses, sauces, and cheesecakes to surround the food with gentle heat, which helps keep the egg mixture around the edges of the baking dish from cooking before the interior has had a chance to cook. To make a water bath, bring a kettle of water to a boil. Arrange the custard cups or springform pan without crowding in a metal baking pan and place on the center rack of a preheated oven. Pour the hot water carefully into the baking pan, until it comes about halfway up the sides of the cups or springform pan.

Northwest Wine and Food Festivals

One of the joys of moving to a new city and region is discovering the unusual local customs of the place. When my husband and I moved from Dallas, Texas, to Seattle in early 1990, we were struck by the large number of festivals that occur every weekend.

We discovered festivals devoted to everything from kite-flying to specific ethnic groups (Thai, Laotian, African), music (bluegrass and folk dance) to literature (Shakespeare and cowboy poetry). Foods such as garlic, strawberries, vegetables, and crayfish were regularly featured. Even quilts and quilt-making were honored with a festival.

Once, while traveling the Oregon coast, we happened upon the tiny, atmospheric town of Yachats (pronounced YAH-hots), and enjoyed several hours at a festival devoted entirely to miniature steamboat racing!

Of course, our favorite festivals revolve around food and wine. The list below represents a select month-by-month grouping of festivals that will be of interest to food-and-wine aficionados. Events in Washington State are listed first, followed by those in Oregon, Idaho, and British Columbia.

I must confess that I haven't personally experienced the majority of these festivals (that would and could have been another book!), so I have relied on information provided on the festivals' respective Web sites for the descriptions.

January

Icewine Festival

Sun Peaks Resort, Sun Peaks,
British Columbia
thewinefestivals.com
Spectacular wines and Sun Peaks Resort, an award-winning alpine getaway as the setting, create an unbelievable weekend of education and recreation. From winemakers' dinners to educational seminars to a unique progressive tasting, this is a memorable weekend in the making.

February

Red Wine and Chocolate

Yakima Valley, Washington
wineyakimavalley.org/events
Visit the more than 50 wineries in the Yakima Valley wine country during this Presidents' Day weekend celebration of fine chocolate and fine wine. Each winery pairs sumptuous chocolate desserts with its very own remarkable red wines.

Seafood and Wine Festival

Portland, Oregon
seafoodandwine.com
This winter event is a celebration of all things Oregon, but most specifically Oregon seafood and wines. Scheduled in the quiet of winter, and in the middle of the Dungeness crab season, the festival is a popular event in Portland, gateway to the Oregon coast and the Oregon wine country.

Newport Seafood & Wine Festival

Newport, Oregon
newportchamber.org/swf/
This annual winter event features dozens of wineries and restaurants from Oregon and Washington, and includes both a commercial wine competition and an amateur wine competition.

Vancouver Playhouse International Wine Festival

Vancouver, British Columbia
playhousewinefest.com
The Web site says it all: 1,550 wines, 180 wineries, 17 countries, 58 events, 21,000 people, seven days.

March

McMinnville Wine & Food Classic

McMinnville, Oregon
macwfc.org
The Classic features an annual wine competition, wine tasting, guest-chef appearances, food vendors, and artwork displays.

April

Taste Washington

Seattle and Spokane, Washington
tastewashington.org
In Seattle, Taste Washington is a two-day event designed to create a rich and rewarding experience for wine lovers. It kicks off with a full day of wine-education seminars, a keynote luncheon, and wine tasting with the Masters (of Wine and Sommeliers), and culminates in the "Ultimate Wine Experience" grand tasting, which claims to be the country's largest single-region consumer wine tasting. In 2007, Taste Washington celebrated its tenth year. Also held in Spokane, Taste Washington is a one-day event in that city.

Passport to Woodinville

Woodinville, Washington
woodinvillewinecountry.com
During this weekend event, participants receive a Woodinville wine country glass along with a label-filled "passport" and enjoy tastings and food pairings at many of the area's exclusive boutique wineries.

Astoria-Warrenton Crab & Seafood Festival

Astoria, Oregon
oldoregon.com/Pages/crabfestandevents.htm
The Astoria-Warrenton Crab & Seafood Festival claims to be the Oregon coast's largest, with more than 200 vendors bringing together the flavor of the Northwest in food, arts, crafts, and wines.

Celebration of Syrah

Troutdale, Oregon
celebrationofsyrah.com
McMenamins Edgefield hosts the annual Celebration of Syrah, an extravagant two-day revelry of wine and food in which winemakers and distributors from the Pacific Northwest, California, Australia, and France showcase their best Syrah throughout the weekend.

EAT! Vancouver, The Everything Food + Cooking Festival

Vancouver, British Columbia
eat-vancouver.com
The three-day event features celebrity-chef cooking demos, *Iron Chef*-style cooking competitions, more than 200 food-and-wine-related vendors, food-and-wine-pairing demonstrations, and a barbecue competition.

May

Seattle Cheese Festival

Seattle, Washington

seattlecheesefestival.com

Three full days are devoted to the many splendors of cheese and include cheese samplings, educational seminars, a wine garden, and cooking demonstrations.

Memorial Weekend in Wine Country

Willamette Valley, Oregon

willamettewines.com/events.shtml

More than 100 of the wineries in the Willamette Valley open their doors for tasting of new releases and older vintages, barrel tastings, sales of limited-quantity wines, and specialty-food sampling during this annual event. Winemakers and owners are on hand to personally greet their guests.

America's Wild Rivers Coast Art, Seafood, and Wine Festival

Gold Beach, Oregon

goldbeachchamber.com/Wine-FestivalIndex.htm

This two-day event in Gold Beach celebrates wine, the arts, and fine dining in a bistro-festival atmosphere.

Oregon Coast Gourmet Fest

North Bend, Oregon

(no Web site)

(541) 756-0433

This wine-tasting event features 15 southern Oregon wineries, local cheese makers, musicians, and artists. Attendees can sample, then purchase, wines from award-winning wineries such as Henry Estate, Girardet, Hillcrest, Spangler, and others.

Okanagan Spring Wine Festival

Okanagan Valley, British Columbia

thewinefestivals.com

The Okanagan Spring Wine Festival is a perfect marriage of wine and culinary tourism during which guests can choose among an incredible 100-plus events throughout Okanagan wine country during the sunny springtime.

July

International Pinot Noir Celebration (IPNC)

McMinnville, Oregon

ipnc.org

IPNC is the annual "love fest" for Pinot Noir aficionados. It features seminars, tastings, tours, and gourmet meals, with 60 Pinot Noir producers from across the globe. It's held at Linfield College, in the heart of the Willamette Valley.

August

Prosser Wine & Food Fair

Prosser, Washington

prosserchamber.org

Nearly 3,500 wine enthusiasts gather for an afternoon of fine wine, local food specialties, and music from two live jazz bands.

Auction of Washington Wines

Woodinville, Washington

wwauction.org

The three-day extravaganza raises money for uncompensated care at Children's Hospital & Regional Medical Center and the

Washington Wine Education Foundation. Held on the luxurious grounds at Chateau Ste. Michelle winery in Woodinville, the wine industry's annual gift to its community includes PICNIC and winemakers' dinners, and culminates in a black-tie gala auction.

Okanagan Summer Wine Festival

Star Mountain Resort,
Vernon, British Columbia
thewinefestivals.com
The summer wine festival offers unique wine seminars, great evening entertainment, a foot-stomping musical outdoor wine tasting, and wonderful presentations by local artists. Enjoy gourmet meals, wine-education seminars, a unique consumer wine tasting, and a wide variety of on-mountain activities.

September

Festival of the Grape

Oliver, British Columbia
oliverchamber.bc.ca/to_do/c_events/
grapefest/grapefest.htm
Oliver's Festival of the Grape opens with a special ceremonial "blessing of the harvest" and continues with wine tasting, face painting, live entertainment, food vendors, a trade show, games, and even a grape stomp.

September/October

Okanagan Fall Wine Festival

Okanagan Valley, British Columbia
thewinefestivals.com
For ten days in late September/early October, enjoy over 165 events—such as vineyard tours, lunches, and dinners— along with the fall wine harvest in one of North America's most spectacular settings, the Okanagan Valley.

Cowichan Wine and Culinary Festival

Vancouver Island, British Columbia
wines.cowichan.net
Held in late September/early October, this festival celebrates Vancouver Island wines, culinary excellence, and original art and music. During the three-day extravaganza, the wineries and farms of the Cowichan Valley invite wine and culinary aficionados to their doorsteps to experience the best of the region firsthand with educational seminars, winemakers' dinners, and a grape stomp.

October

OysterFest

Shelton, Washington
oysterfest.com
OysterFest celebrates the Northwest's favorite bivalve, with speed and half-shell oyster-shucking contests, a seafood cook-off, a wine tasting, microbreweries, seafood delicacies, exhibits, and entertainment.

Wine by the River

Bend, Oregon
winebytheriver.com
Wine masters share secrets from the vineyard, teaching the ways they keep the traditions alive. Savor chocolate in the warmth of an Indian-summer afternoon, indulge, and enjoy.

November

Thanksgiving in the Wine Country

Yakima Valley, Washington

wineyakimavalley.org/events

More than 45 wineries open their doors following Thanksgiving to celebrate the season with their finest wines and carefully selected culinary pairings.

Wine Country Thanksgiving

Willamette Valley, Oregon

willamettewines.com

During this annual county-wide extravaganza, more than 100 of the wineries of the Willamette open their doors for tastings and special events to welcome the holiday season. Festivities include tasting of new releases and older vintages, barrel tastings, sales of limited-quantity wines, and specialty-food sampling.

Tri-Cities Wine Festival

Pasco, Washington

tricitieswinefestival.com/about.asp

Started in 1978, the festival features a professional wine tasting, as well as a consumer tasting that offers upwards of 200 wines. There is also a gourmet dinner, with wines from around the world paired with creations by Tri-Cities chefs.

¡Salud! Oregon's Pinot Noir Auction

Portland, Oregon

saludauction.org

The ¡Salud! auction focuses on Pinot Noirs created exclusively for the event by each of 39 premium Oregon wineries and benefits healthcare outreach services for the wine industry's seasonal workers and their families.

Cornucopia: Whistler's Wine and Food Festival

Whistler, British Columbia

whistlercornucopia.com

This stylish festival features out-of-the box educational seminars, one-of-a-kind chef and winemakers' luncheons and dinners, and signature events such as Crush! A Gala Grand Tasting, featuring 400 local and international wines and food samples from more than a dozen Whistler restaurants.

December

Walla Walla Valley Holiday Barrel Tasting Weekend

Walla Walla Valley, Washington

wallawallawine.com/events.html

On the first full weekend of December, 50 Walla Walla Valley wineries open their doors during this annual tasting. Visitors are encouraged to sample future releases straight from the barrel and be the first to enjoy the wines of a new vintage. Each winery participates in its own special way, offering food, music, art exhibits, wine dinners, cooking demonstrations, and poetry readings, all within the festive atmosphere of the season.

Note: Excellent resources for the latest information on Pacific Northwest wine and food festivals, and the inspiration for many of the entries in this listing, can be viewed at the following Web sites:

localwineevents.com

winepressnw.com

wineevents-calendar.com

winesnw.com/calendarmain.htm

foodreference.com

bellaonline.com

Index

Page numbers in *italics*
indicate illustrations